DISCOURSE AND CONTEXT

An Interdisciplinary Study
of
John Henry Newman

Edited by
Gerard Magill

Southern Illinois University Press
Carbondale and Edwardsville

Library of Congress Cataloging-in-Publication Data

Discourse and context : an interdisciplinary study of John Henry
Newman / edited by Gerard Magill.
    p. cm.
  Includes bibliographical references and index.
  1. Newman, John Henry, 1801–1890. I. Magill, Gerard, 1951– .
BX4705.N5D487   1993
282'.092—dc20   92-17309
ISBN 0-8093-1836-9   CIP

Frontispiece: *Cardinal Newman*, by Theodore T. Wood, 1990, after the
painting *John Henry Newman* by W. W. Ouless. Used by permission.

To Dad, in memory of Mum,
for learning and love

CONTENTS

Part 4. Commitment

Part 5. Interpretation

ACKNOWLEDGMENTS

I am most grateful to Saint Louis University for enabling me to organize the Newman Centenary Conference in fall 1990, from which I have selected the essays in this collection. All of these essays were written originally for that conference.

To Professor Edward E. Kelly and Professor Lawrence Barmann, I extend my heartfelt gratitude for working with me so closely in organizing the conference and advising me on the collection. In particular, I am grateful to Professor Barmann for his assistance in the preparation of the index. The successful preparation of this volume is due to the generous help of many in the Department of Theological Studies. Especially, I thank Janice A. Harbaugh, our departmental graduate secretary, for invaluable assistance with word processing; Colleen Heyns, our departmental secretary's assistant, for long hours of typing; and my graduate assistants Guido Stucco, Michael Testa, and Peter A. Huff for patiently carrying out so many requests during the project. I thank Peter especially for his attentive reading of the entire manuscript and his astute observations about textual changes for the graduate reader. Also, I thank Dr. Kathleen Warden, University of Tennessee, for advice on selecting an appropriate title for this collection.

Two essays have appeared elsewhere. Edward Jeremy Miller's "Newman's *Idea of a University*: Is It Viable Today?" was published in *Current Issues in Catholic Higher Education* 12, no. 1 (1991): pp. 4–11. A shorter draft of the essay "The Living Mind: Newman on Assent and Dissent" by Gerard Magill appeared as "Newman and 'The Ecclesial Vocation of the Theologian'" in *Current Issues in Catholic Higher Education* 12, no. 1 (1991): pp. 17–23.

ABBREVIATIONS OF NEWMAN'S WORKS

The standard abbreviations of the works of John Henry Newman are adopted in this collection.

Apo.	*Apologia Pro Vita Sua: Being a History of His Religious Opinions*
Ari.	*The Arians of the Fourth Century*
AW	*John Henry Newman: Autobiographical Writings*, ed. Henry Tristram
Call.	*Callista, A Sketch of the Third Century.* In the later editions of 1889, 1890: *Callista, a Tale of the Third Century*
Cons.	*On Consulting the Faithful in Matters of Doctrine*, ed. John Coulson
Dev.	*An Essay on the Development of Christian Doctrine*
Diff. I, II	*Certain Difficulties Felt by Anglicans in Catholic Teaching.* 2 vols.
Ess. I, II	*Essays Critical and Historical.* 2 vols.
GA	*An Essay in Aid of a Grammar of Assent*
HS. I, II, III	*Historical Sketches.* 3 vols.
Idea	*The Idea of a University Defined and Illustrated*
LD	*The Letters and Diaries of John Henry Newman*, ed. Charles Stephen Dessain et al.
Phil.N. I, II	*The Philosophical Notebook of John Henry Newman*, ed. Edward Sillem. 2 vols.
PS. I–VIII	*Parochial and Plain Sermons.* 8 vols.
Proof	*The Argument from Conscience to the Existence of God, according to J. H. Newman*, ed. Adrian J. Boekraad and Henry Tristram
SD	*Sermons Bearing on Subjects of the Day*

TP. I	*The Theological Papers of John Henry Newman on Faith and Certainty*, ed. Hugo M. de Achaval and J. Derek Holmes
US	*Fifteen Sermons Preached before the University of Oxford 1826–43*
VM. I, II	*The Via Media of the Anglican Church.* 2 vols.

Introduction: The Intellectual Ethos of John Henry Newman

GERARD MAGILL

As a university scholar and a religious minister in nineteenth-century Britain, John Henry Newman (1801–90) had a remarkable influence upon his age. His intellectual ethos pervaded the interdisciplinary interests of his writings and elicited widespread recognition in secular and religious circles alike. The intellectual achievement and the broad spectrum of his works are evident from the considerable number that have become classics: the *Oxford University Sermons* (1826–43) in theology;[1] the Dublin university discourses (1852) in his *Idea of a University* (1873) in education;[2] the *Apologia Pro Vita Sua* (1864), his spiritual autobiography, in literature;[3] and the *Grammar of Assent* (1870) in philosophy.[4] Appointed a Fellow at Oriel College, Oxford, in 1822, Newman quickly established himself as a creative and an original writer. As an Anglican, his influence was extensive, especially in his charismatic leadership of the Oxford Movement in the 1830s, which produced the Tracts that generated a diversity of religious inquiries in Victorian England. After his conversion to Catholicism in 1845, his reputation became widespread, especially by his opposing rationalism in his philosophy of liberal education as rector of the new university in Dublin (1854–58) and by his upholding the legitimacy of faith as a reasonable and a nuanced commitment in his epistemology of belief (1870).

Today scholars in many disciplines continue a critical dialogue with Newman's thought. The present collection arises from papers presented during the three-day Newman Centenary Conference at Saint Louis University in fall 1990. This selection of essays examines the contribution of Newman's writings from an interdisciplinary perspective. The specialties of literature and history, theory of rhetoric and education, and philosophy and theology provide diverse horizons for engaging Newman's insights with contemporary scholarship. An amazing array of intellectual giants

1

throughout history are called upon to understand Newman and to offer a scholarly appraisal of his creativity and genius. As a result, the cluster of issues discussed portrays the enduring prominence of Newman today. The following essays have been selected to reflect the impressive and increasing variety of literature on Newman studies, constructively expanding the boundaries of interdisciplinary scholarship.

This collection, then, should attract a broad range of readers who are interested in Newman's intellectual ethos. The title of this book, *Discourse and Context*, is intended to depict the interplay between discourse and context that pervades his writings. Newman consciously impressed upon his readers the relevance of historical context for appreciating the supple and malleable nature of persuasive discourse (logical, rhetorical, and prudential). In this reflective, introductory essay, I explain the organizing divisions that I use to elucidate the relation between discourse and context in Newman's works: *individuality*, *understanding*, *education*, *commitment*, and *interpretation*. First, Newman's *individuality*, portraying the personal context of his thought, had a significant impact upon his vision. Second, his approach to *understanding* was determined by a keen sense of the historical nature of practical reason for meaningful discourse. Third, his view of *education*, celebrating freedom of inquiry toward progress in knowledge, was sensitive to the role of culture. Fourth, *commitment* was important for his epistemology to apprehend historical reality as a basic condition for religious perception. Fifth, the *interpretation* of his thought today flourishes by means of the study of later historical contexts (for example, modernism) to illumine his discourse.

Newman was an *individualist* and a controversialist. Edward E. Kelly ("Identity and Discourse: A Study in Newman's Individualism") shows how Newman emphasized individuality. This emphasis was a drive to self-realization both in his way of thinking and of living. That natural characteristic was nourished by an inclination in his youth toward Calvinistic Evangelicalism, with its tendency to isolate self from reality. His self-will was accompanied by an anxiety that fueled his fear of shame and failure as a university student at Trinity College, Oxford. That characteristic also spawned a self-protective personality, evident in his selective account of his tutorial quarrel with Edward Hawkins, provost of Oriel college, Oxford, and in his self-vindication in the *Apologia*.

Nonetheless, self-assurance prevailed in Newman's temperament. His confidence was allied closely to the controversial state of mind that thrived on conflict, paradox, and challenging disjunction as rhetorical instruments. They were evident especially in his *Letters and Diaries* during his years at

Oxford.[5] He delighted in taking opponents to the brink in argument, sporting with dull adversaries and thriving on more substantial polemic in religion: against Catholicism as an Anglican and, much later, against Anglicanism as a Catholic.

It is no surprise, then, to find in Newman a commitment to individualistic and controversial theology. Unfortunately, this commitment was encumbered with personal bias, witnessed most especially in his study against Arianism (1833)[6], and in his remarks against Luther on the question of justification (1838).[7] Still, Newman's approach also yielded a rich harvest in theological discourse: his theory on doctrinal development as an Anglican and his interpretation of infallibility as a Catholic. Because of his individual, controversial spirit, he sidestepped the systematic theologies of Catholic scholasticism and of the Anglican Caroline divines.

However, Newman's individualistic use of those seventeenth-century Anglican theologians, whom we know as the Caroline divines, reveals the weaker side of his scholarship. Kenneth L. Parker ("Newman's Individualistic Use of the Caroline Divines in the *Via Media*") suggests that Newman's use of the Caroline divines appears superficial and selective. This occurs despite Newman's professed interest in synthesizing Anglican doctrine. Newman appealed to those scholars when writing his *Lectures on the Prophetical Office of the Church* and also in *The Via Media* (1836)[8] in which he hypothesized a *via media* between the apparent excesses of Roman Catholicism and of popular Protestantism. The Caroline divines, he claimed, were one of the cornerstones of his argument. But Newman's unreflective quotations suggest that he used those theologians not in a scholarly way. Rather, he used them to support his own vision of a renewed Anglican tradition and to win polemical battles. There is little evidence that Newman seriously studied those thinkers. Rather, his casual and unsystematic interest can be attributed to his fascination for another tradition, the early Church.

In the 1830s Newman became closely acquainted with the patristic writings of the early Church. Previously, however, he had been schooled in the more ancient works of Greek philosophy, especially in what can be called the *phronesis* tradition of Aristotle. Mary Katherine Tillman ("Economies of Reason: Newman and the *Phronesis* Tradition") explains that the mode of reasoning in the *phronesis* tradition primarily shaped Newman's outlook on *understanding*. Three different contexts facilitate a grasp of the subtle understanding that engenders the variety of discourse in Newman's texts: the ancient thought of Aristotle and the modern thought of Heidegger and Ricoeur.

The *phronesis* tradition, from Parmenides, Socrates, Plato, and Aristotle, provided the context for Newman's economies of reason. In the *phronesis* tradition, practical reason cannot be isolated from the discursive community in which it arises. Insightfully, that tradition recognized the indeterminate, time-bound nature of human discourse while seeking progress in understanding. Likewise, by coining the term *illative sense* Newman introduced into his own epistemology the economizing activity of practical reason as the regulating principle for all reasoning. That is, the practical reason of the illative sense adjusts (economizes) to its subject matter with deliberation moving back and forth dialectically. The illative sense adjusts in relation to the whole person within the community of discourse as the context within which thought develops progressively. There are many examples of Newman's economies of reason: his different appeals to organic growth to mediate his hypothesis of doctrinal development, to biology to unfold his theology of the Church, to mathematics to interpret the processes of reasoning, and, above all, to music to accommodate the energy and subtle intricacies of thought. For Newman the disclosure of every economy was the fruit of *phronesis*, the means for inquiry to break through to insight.

Aristotle adopted ethical deliberation (*phronesis*) by using rhetoric as an intellectual function oriented to the contingent, to the indeterminate, and to praxis. To interpret the meaning of contingent matters, he explained, requires a dynamic framework of values, beliefs, laws, and practices. Within the context of that framework, Aristotle's rhetoric was the communication of good reasons for inquiry, argument, and judgment. In an extension of that intellectual stance, Newman and Heidegger share this common ground, which Walter Jost ("Philosophic Rhetoric: Newman and Heidegger") calls philosophic rhetoric. The function of philosophic rhetoric, in part, is to argue and deliberate persuasively on contingent matters. Heidegger's indirect appeal to rhetoric is located in his use of horizons, forestructures, and, more obliquely, poetic language. According to Heidegger, we know through historically specific horizons of understanding. Because the horizons are necessarily topical (mediated in human experience of language and time) and ethical-political (constituted by established traditions, beliefs), they depend, in part, upon persuasive interpretation, not rational demonstration. Horizons of understanding are structured by prior orientations toward the world, called forestructures of understanding. These forestructures of understanding grasp the past and present as a meaningful whole; moreover, they open us to the future, to what is new. Together, the horizons and the forestructures of understanding are circumscribed by the insight and language of poetry, requiring the imaginative use of analogy, metaphor, and the "naming" word.

Heidegger's analysis illumines the extent to which the poetic imagination pervades Newman's epistemology of belief. For Newman the primacy of the real over the notional required an interpretative apprehension. As for Heidegger's horizons, for Newman the concrete or real was mediated by personal experience (through values, beliefs, traditions) as a persuasive interpretation (philosophic rhetoric). This approach contrasted with the rationalist and romantic approaches in the nineteenth century. Akin to Heidegger's forestructures of understanding, Newman used dynamic and situational concepts in his rhetorical language to argue for a persuasive interpretation of reality. Newman's use of "antecedent probabilities" drawn from past experience and culture, his "openness" to what is new, and his confidence in holding a "view" to organize and interpret are interdependent dimensions of his philosophic rhetoric. However, Newman's philosophic rhetoric as mental understanding did not abandon conceptual speech because all language, as explained later by Ricoeur, is multilayered.

Ricoeur's theory of discourse focuses upon the interpretation of texts and of action in the world considered as text. Alan J. Crowley ("Theory of Discourse: Newman and Ricoeur") shows that Ricoeur's literary theory, like Heidegger's philosophy, encourages an interdisciplinary integration of Newman's thought today. This approach portrays Newman's rhetoric not as style but as a mode of intellectual understanding that controls his theoretical discourse. Ricoeur illumines Newman by tracing the relation between respecting the text (as a structured entity that has a message) and reconceiving the text (through reading and rewriting). This relation requires a critical consciousness of language, personal commitment, and appropriation of meaning. Ricoeur's explanation of the language of discourse (the reading and interpretation of text) clarifies Newman's method as one of rhetorical performance. For Ricoeur the efficacy of discourse depends upon a provisional position of value (believed, received, or intuited) in understanding. As a result, there can be a process of interpretation that seeks new meaning in the original text. For Newman the efficacy of discourse depends upon the personal commitment of assent to propositions as meaningful. Thus, we can interpret the text and live out its interpretation. By applying Newman's view of rhetorical understanding, we can attempt to resolve the tension of tradition and value *versus* pluralism in liberal education today. Newman's methodology suggests that the teacher makes a personal commitment in moral assent: there is established a structure of values that can be examined and reformed. This development will occur when others reconstruct meaning and enact new values. Hence, Newman's rhetoric establishes a balance between structure and interpretative critique. As a consequence, liberal education encourages the preservation of pluralistic discourse.

The essays in the third division of this collection examine Newman's approach to liberal *education* in *The Idea of a University*. The essays discuss the relation of Christianity to culture and evaluate the viability of Newman's argument today. James C. Livingston ("Christianity and Culture in New-man's *Idea of a University*") claims that Newman anticipated the continuing discussion in the twentieth century on the relation of Christianity to culture. This relation arises from the fundamental question in Newman's *Idea* about the interplay between religious and secular knowledge. Different resolutions to the question are offered: on the one hand, by the quest for resonance among diverse traditions in correlationist theology (Paul Tillich, Karl Rahner, Bernard Lonergan, David Tracy); on the other hand, by the opposition to Enlightenment modernity in postliberal theology (Karl Barth, Hans Frei, George Lindbeck). The question can be posed by com-paring Matthew Arnold and John Henry Newman. Arnold proposed a correlational and dialectical understanding of the relation between Chris-tianity and culture. Newman developed a metaphor of the circle of knowl-edge to explain the intellectual function of theology (adopting a dialectical approach) and the moral function of theology (adopting an authoritative approach) in university education.

In a similar vein, Edward Jeremy Miller ("Newman's *Idea of a University*: Is It Viable Today?") shows that the viability of Newman's *Idea* can be addressed in terms of his dialectics where free inquiry and regulation come together. These are sustained by a creative tension that enables a civility of discourse. Newman's philosophy of liberal education emphasizes the active, formative power of knowledge as the source of intellectual order and meaning. They belong to the personal process of learning in the quest for truth. Today Newman's vision is consonant with upholding university autonomy, academic freedom, and the role of critical theology within the liberal arts tradition. His emphasis upon the centrality of personal commitment in the process of learning remains an important question for the philosophy of education. Knowledge is a capacity to discriminate and to discern relations between facts and ideas and then to judge and to act upon them.

The importance of *commitment* also is at the basis of Newman's religious epistemology and theological method. M. Jamie Ferreira ("The Grammar of the Heart: Newman on Faith and Imagination") explains that Newman's religious epistemology deals with the legitimacy of religious conversion. This approach entails an appeal to the imagination as a personal commitment to informal inference and assent. Newman's appeal is described as "the grammar of the heart" in the sense of expanding upon the motto on his coat of arms as a cardinal of the Catholic Church: "Heart speaks to heart." Newman avoided the dangers of deception in using the imagination by emphasizing that it is integral to the process of informal reasoning. It is this rational process that leads to assent and certitude. The imagination, Newman argued, rationally achieves religious certitude by recognizing what Ferreira calls a critical threshold. This threshold entails the qualitative transition (conversion) from evidence and inference to certitude. In the transition the conclusion (certitude) is continuous with, though different from, what preceded (evidence and inference) in the way that the point of boiling is a critical threshold for water turning to steam. Certitude, therefore, has two characteristics as a function of the imagination. First, certitude entails a personal recognition of a truth: it is not merely the passive acceptance of a conclusion that is proven demonstratively. Second, certitude occurs all at once: it does not admit of degrees, even though continuous with preceding evidence, just as the boiling point of water (continuous with the preceding temperature increase) is a critical threshold for a qualitative transition to steam.

By ascertaining a critical threshold, the imagination yields a reorienting vision. That is, certitude legitimately perceives the preceding inferences from a different perspective. In a united act of reasoning and judgment, the imagination interprets a coalescence of evidence (inference) to generate certitude (assent) as a new seeing, a re-visioning. This imaginative shift to a new vision through a critical threshold requires clustering the evidence into a proof (inference) and affirming the conclusion with certitude (assent). In this way Newman justified the qualitative transition (conversion) to religious faith. Conversion, then, like certitude, entails a personal commitment that answers to the imagination.

The role of personal commitment in informal inference and assent constitutes Newman's appeal to the imagination (as the grammar of the heart). Also, his appeal to the imagination is crucial in his theological method (as the dynamism of the living mind). Just as commitment can lead the heart to assent, commitment also can impel the mind to dissent legitimately from ecclesial authority and doctrine. Gerard Magill ("The Living Mind: Newman on Assent and Dissent") offers a systematic account of the relation between assent and dissent in Newman's writings. The analysis is based upon Newman's commitment to inference and assent in his theological method. The apparent chasm between assent and dissent can be bridged metaphorically by three interlocking spans: conscience, theology, and authority. By implementing the theory of assent in his understanding of conscience, Newman illumines his method in theology. In turn, his theological method elucidates the parameters of ecclesial authority and, therefore, the possibility of legitimate dissent. Newman realized, however, that when the living mind (committed to inference and assent) gains insight to warrant opposing a received tradition, intellectual subtlety and personal courage are needed to articulate dissent.

Newman's development of thought led him to private dissent as an Anglican in writing Tract 90 (1841) on the Thirty-Nine Articles. He also dissented privately, but less dramatically, as a Catholic in his essay "On Consulting the Faithful in Matters of Doctrine" (1859). Further, he found himself expressing public dissent in converting to Catholicism in 1845. Those experiences illustrate in a practical way his theoretical stance: theological method demands an interpretation that can warrant dissent as a form of legitimate assent. The driving force of his theological method as interpretative reasoning was his commitment to informal inference and assent. He construed this approach as an appeal to the imagination. His theological method, then, encourages historical interpretation as a counterbalance to authoritative teaching in the Church.

The final division of essays pursues the emphasis upon *interpretation*, examining the implications of Newman's approach to theological inquiry for doctrinal development vis-à-vis the authority of the Church. C. J. T. Talar ("Receiving Newman's *Development of Christian Doctrine*") examines the different receptions of *An Essay on the Development of Christian Doctrine* (1845).[9] These receptions indicate a legitimate diversity of interpretation that can be illumined by literary theory as discussed earlier. The work of Hans Robert Jauss is also helpful in this regard. Like Ricoeur's distinction between the structured text and the personal commitment to interpret it based upon one's provisional position of value, Jauss distinguishes the original text from the interpreter's horizon of expectations. The horizon of expectations refers to the activity of the reader, influenced by dominant conventions and assumptions, as the context for interpretation. This approach is akin to Heidegger's horizons and forestuctures of understanding for interpretation. For Jauss the meaning of a text arises from the convergence of the structure of the work and its ever-changing interpretations within different historical contexts. His method is helpful for appreciating the diverse interpretations of Newman's essay on doctrinal development.

For example, such a shift in the horizon of expectations explains the different receptions of Newman's essay in France. Its authorized translation by Jules Gondon in 1848 had little impact upon French theology. Yet at the turn of the century there was a sudden revival of interest in Newman's essay on doctrinal development. Literary theory helps us to see that the context for reception underwent significant change, altering the range of interpretations of the text. In general, there was a shift from a classicist neo-scholasticism to a more progressive, historically oriented culture. In particular, Auguste Sabatier's conception of development (1897) was similar to Newman's, and Alfred Loisy expanded upon Newman's organic metaphors for development (1898), illustrating a productive reception of Newman's essay with normative power. Not surprisingly, however, the condemnation of modernism in 1907, in which Newman was implicated with Loisy's thought, introduced a new context of interpretation, bringing a cloud over Newman's thought.

Newman died before the period of the modernists (about 1890–1910). However, Lawrence Barmann ("Theological Inquiry in an Authoritarian Church: Newman and Modernism") argues that some of Newman's principles, methods, and conclusions can be construed as analogous to those of the modernists: for example, the comparison with Loisy's thought on doctrinal development. Loisy and George Tyrrell were condemned in 1907 by the encyclical *Pascendi dominici gregis*. They were not disciples of Newman, nor was Friedrich von Hügel; yet they were influenced broadly and deeply by the spirit in which Newman argued, especially by his emphasis upon history and upon human and real experience. An appropriate way to interpret historically the relation of Newman to modernism is to inquire whether Newman represented an earlier analogue of the later tension between Catholic intellectuals and ecclesiastical authority that led to the condemnation of modernism. That is, the condemnation of modernism provided a new historical context for a constructive interpretation of Newman's approach to the tension between theological inquiry and ecclesiastical authority. This interpretation provides insight into Newman's religious outlook and vision for ecclesiology today.

Newman, Tyrrell, and von Hügel attempted to make religion the integrative, existential factor of their experiences and lives. In doing so, each encountered confrontation with ecclesiastical authority in historically different ways. Reasoning on religious outlook, then, Newman's efforts to understand faith, with the consequent theological confrontation with ecclesiastical authority, provide the strongest links with the modernists. On ecclesiology, Newman analogously applied Christ's offices (prophet, priest, king) to the Church's offices of teaching (theology), sacred ministry (liturgy), and ruling (political structure); von Hügel later focused the three offices in religion rather than the Church. In this trilogy of offices, Newman identified theology as the regulating principle and normative interpreter of the whole Church system, including the ruling office of political authority. Defending the rights of intellectual inquiry in theology, he put limits to authority and the manner in which it is expressed in the Church. Hence, he accepted papal infallibility with a minimalist interpretation in his *Letter to the Duke of Norfolk* (1874),[10] astutely recognizing that the historical genesis of the doctrine was more political than theological. The creative tension that Newman encouraged between theological inquiry and ecclesiastical authority provides an insightful model for the study of religious experience and of ecclesiology today.

In sum, the intellectual ethos that pervades Newman's interdisciplinary interests reflects the fundamental interplay between discourse and context in his thought. The title of this book, *Discourse and Context*, expresses an underlying theme throughout his writings. Each essay in this collection indicates the breadth of Newman's intellectual accomplishment in a diversity of fields. From an interdisciplinary perspective, and in critical dialogue, the contributors indicate the enduring prominence of Newman's works today.

Notes

1. *Fifteen Sermons Preached before the University of Oxford, 1826–43*. See the edition, *Newman's University Sermons: Fifteen Sermons Preached before the University of Oxford, 1826–43*, with introductory essays by D. M. MacKinnon and J. D. Holmes (London: S.P.C.K., 1970). Page references are to the third edition (1873).
2. John Henry Newman, *The Idea of a University*, edited with introduction and notes by I. T. Ker (Oxford: Clarendon Press, 1976).
3. John Henry Newman, *Apologia Pro Vita Sua*, edited with introduction and notes by Martin J. Svaglic (Oxford: Clarendon Press, 1967).
4. John Henry Newman, *An Essay in Aid of a Grammar of Assent*, edited, introduction, and notes by I. T. Ker (Oxford: Clarendon Press, 1985).
5. *The Letters and Diaries of John Henry Newman*, ed. Charles Stephen Dessain et al., 31 vols. Vols. I–VI (Oxford: Clarendon Press, 1978–84); vols. XI–XXII (London: Oxford University Press, 1961–72); vols. XXIII–XXXI (Oxford: Clarendon Press, 1973–77).
6. John Henry Newman, *The Arians of the Fourth Century* (London: Longmans, Green, 1901).
7. John Henry Newman, *Lectures on the Doctrine of Justification* (London: Rivingtons, 1885).
8. John Henry Newman, *The Via Media of the Anglican Church*, edited with

introduction and notes by H. D. Weidner (Oxford: Clarendon Press, 1990), based on the 1889 edition of Newman's *Via Media*, vol. I.

9. John Henry Newman, *An Essay on the Development of Christian Doctrine* (Notre Dame, Ind.: University of Notre Dame Press, 1989).

10. John Henry Newman, "A Letter Addressed to His Grace the Duke of Norfolk on Occasion of Mr. Gladstone's Recent Expostulation" (1874, published 1875), in *Certain Difficulties Felt by Anglicans in Catholic Teaching*, vol. II (London: Longmans, Green, 1898).

Part 1

Individuality

1

Identity and Discourse: A Study in Newman's Individualism

EDWARD E. KELLY

If he were to become a Jesuit in 1846, Newman feared that "no one would know that I was speaking my own words; or was a *continuation*, as it were, of my former self" (*LD*, XI, p. 306).[1] Perhaps it is impossible to imagine Newman a Jesuit. But he admired the Society of Jesus in many ways (*LD*, XI, pp. 19, 103) and seriously considered a Jesuit vocation after his conversion to Catholicism in 1845 (*LD*, XII, p. 12). He decided against it in good part for the very reason already implied: he, John Henry Newman, was an individual person, while the Jesuits were, in his own words, all in the same groove or cast, a phalanx of soldiers (*LD*, XII, p. 113). Once, when he misnamed a certain Roman Jesuit and was corrected by his friend Ambrose St. John, Newman retorted: "It's all the same, all Jesuits have the same cut about them" (*LD*, XI, p. 275). In a semifictional work of 1854, Newman allowed the antagonist-character to remark: "What a great idea . . . is the Society of Jesus! what a creation of genius is its organization; but so well adapted is the institution to its object, that for that very reason it can afford to crush individualities, however gifted" (*HS*, III, p. 70–71).[2]

Although there were other issues involved, a basic consideration in Newman's vocational quest in 1846, then, was his own individuality, his own personal way of thinking and living (see *LD*, XI, p. 295). A certain amount of this was inevitably sacrificed in his conversion, but he could not prosper in the Church without it guarded carefully. He claimed that it was impossible to join an order whose ethos was so very different from his own, which he described as a "domestic one—easy, familiar and not rigid" (*LD*, XI, p. 304). The Oratory would eventually offer that ethos. But before that, the Dominicans would be rejected, for Newman believed they demanded unity of thought and were rigorists in doctrine (*LD*, XII, pp. 6, 25). His own philosophy would stand in confrontation with the "received dogmas" of both Jesuits and Dominicans (*LD*, XII, p. 6). Even though their rules would never do for Newman and his convert-friends, the Redemptorists were more attractive because they were not rigid and were "without a dominant imperious theology" (*LD*, XII, pp. 6, 8). It is clear that Newman felt that there would not be much room for individual views, for personal, real assents in such established systems. Later, in the *Grammar of Assent*,[3] he would characterize the unity of thought in intellectual schools as esoteric, the intellectual expressions of assemblage of minds as passwords or tokens or symbols that are notional rather that real (*GA*, p. 309). But Newman required the real in order to be himself, the individual John Henry Newman.

Newman's lifelong relations with the Jesuits have been well researched by Peter L'Estrange, an Australian Jesuit, and his Oratorian identity well documented by Placid Murray, an Irish monk.[4] Not so satisfying are some of the approaches to Newman's basic individual personality. Without pretending to be a psychologist, I hope in the rest of this essay to explore several aspects of that individuality that kept Newman from the Jesuits and other groups or schools and, in a sense, even from Rome. First, I need to confront the very idea and value of searching for Newman's individual personality.

I. Newman as Individualist

Something deep in Newman's personality, not just his formalized thought, directed him more than most other persons toward realizing his individual self. Some Newman scholars have readily granted that we need to know that self, that personality, if we can hope to know his thought. Maisie Ward demonstrated some of her father's wisdom when she wrote that "Newman's opinions have been too much abstracted from Newman's self. . . . To understand the thought we must first know the thinker."[5] Edward Miller more recently has insisted that "to understand Newman's theology and especially his ecclesiology requires one to understand a good deal about his temperament," his "personal tendencies," his "style."[6] Ward made some progress in trying to characterize the young Newman, but Miller was content to discuss only Newman's ideas fairly much abstracted from his individual personality. Even Ian Ker's recent 745-page biography concerned itself only in a minimal way with that personality. Ker seemed satisfied—even insistent—that only Newman tell us who he was! (Of course, Ker's selections and judgments to some extent determine the so-called self-portrait).

J. H. Walgrave was more confident in sketching a psychological portrait of Newman. He had no hesitation in categorizing Newman as typically introverted in the Jungian system and secondary in the analysis of the School of Groningen and Le Senne. These easy categories have some value, but, unfortunately, Walgrave supported them with almost no evidence from Newman's life. Nor did he explore very much the consequences of those personality traits on Newman's thought. He was more concerned with eagerly asserting that Newman was a completely balanced genius with a "perfectly integrated personality."[7] But he did some service for Newman studies by refusing to allow what he called the "order of nature" in Newman's personality to be swallowed up in spiritual or supernatural considerations; he was not presenting "an analysis of a saint."[8] For some spiritual analysts of Newman, there scarcely is a natural personality, a fallen nature with natural inclinations for both good and evil.

Newman himself was satisfied, as a true picture of his life, with his own documents from the past and his own third-person autobiographical biography (!) for all of which no interpretation from others was wanted. To some extent, then, he controlled our biographical search for his individual self by his own autobiographical writings, by editing some letters and journals and destroying others, and by his own personalistic epistemology and spiritual influence over his followers. I have written elsewhere about the unfortunate effects of all of this on the biographical tradition.[9] Here I want to suggest that this should be evaluated and seen as part of Newman's self-protective personality. It should be seen in conjunction with a number of passages from the *Grammar of Assent* where Newman offers a kind of theoretical defense or justification for his autobiographical-biographical self-assurance (see *GA*, pp. 342, 362, 386). And all of this needs to be questioned when we find research that shows inaccuracies in Newman's account of things. For example, Thomas Gornall, meticulous coeditor of six volumes of Newman's *Letters*, has revealed that Newman's statements regarding his "failure in the Schools" and his tutorial quarrel with Hawkins cannot be taken simply at their face value. They contain errors of fact. Newman's fervor "had a tendency to melt objective fact into what he thought it ought to be."[10] On these and other occasions, Gornall claims, Newman "became the victim of an obsessive self-protectiveness."[11]

As could be expected, an unusually perceptive and self-reflective mind like Newman's often keenly observed his own and others' personalities in the natural order, even though without any formal psychological categories. He was clearly aware of psychic activities on subconscious levels; he specifically noted those of a religious nature: for example, that under the garb and color of Christianity some writers in the "state of unconscious or semi-conscious unbelief scatter infidel principles" (*Idea*, p. 63).[12] More basically, in the *Grammar of Assent*, he acknowledged that "we cannot well see intellectual motives which are so intimately ours" (*GA*, p. 336).

Newman's private journals contain some acute and harsh analyses of his own wayward inclinations. But in his letters, he is more defensive about himself while outspoken about others. He often equivalently denies the complexity of his own feelings and motives with preemptive words like "I am not conscious of . . . "[13] In a reply to Manning in 1843, Newman denied feelings of "disappointment, irritation, or impatience" at the time of his resigning St. Mary's (*Apo.*, p. 199).[14] And in response to Bishop Wiseman in April 1845, Newman wrote: If you knew me, you would acquit me of "controversial rivalry or desire of getting the better, or fear lest the world should think I had got the worse, or irritation of any kind" (*Apo.*, p. 165). These are especially interesting contentions in view of what I will explore later in this essay on the subject of Newman and controversy.

It could easily be shown that Newman's sensitivity about judgments of others and analyses of motives and emotions is consonant with his views of the unique integrity of individual minds, especially his own. Yet he did judge others, like his brothers and sisters. When Blanco White published his Unitarian beliefs in 1835, Newman commented that "it is as bad as can be. He evidently wishes to be attacked. . . . He is not contented till he is talked about—and he has a morbid pleasure in being abused" (*LD*, V, p. 123). This is interesting in view of Newman's own indulgence in complaints about his being abused at various times in his life. Five months after his analysis of Blanco White, Newman wrote to a friend about himself and the other Tractarians: "Our persecution is on the eve of beginning. The first stroke will have fallen, if Hampden or other such [forerunner of Antichrist] . . . be placed in the Divinity Chair" (*LD*, V, p. 210).

Newman may not always have understood his own personality, then, but it can be shown that the kind of guarding of his own individuality that he exercised in seeking his religious vocation in the Catholic Church can be discovered in many other moments of his life. It probably began in his boyhood. The new Romantic age into which he was born certainly carried the message of individualism, and his father seems to have been a messenger of it to his specially gifted son. Every reader of the *Apologia* can readily see that Newman's early Calvinistic Evangelicalism was an undoubted source of his individualism. He tells us that it helped to isolate him from the reality around him (*Apo.*, p. 18). But it is plausible to think that the fifteen-year-old Newman was naturally drawn toward the individualism of Calvinistic religion by his already private vision of the world, his "childish imaginations" (*Apo.*, p. 18). In any case, the 1816 conversion, with the boy's conviction that he was personally elected by God, was his own unique experience, not the usual Evangelical conversion from sin. Newman often affirmed an assurance of personal election in his life and frequently interpreted Providence to explain that election in individual experiences. In the *Grammar of Assent* he even gives as an example of an indefectible certitude a man's being able to so "hold the doctrine of personal election as a Calvinist, as to be able still to hold it as a Catholic" (*GA*, p. 251).

But I do not want to dwell on Newman's religious experience as such, since I am convinced that even it had a natural dimension to it that is often overlooked. His natural personality and his religious identity were both involved in his insistence on his individual self. Even a sermon from 1836 on the "Individuality of the Soul" has this dual source of insight. Newman preached that "every man has a distinct soul," and he "is as whole and independent a being as if there were no one else in the whole world but he. . . . He is everything to himself, and no one else is really anything" (*PS*, IV, p. 81).[15] It is not surprising, therefore, to find Newman often appealing to his own way, even to the point of appearing self-centered. "I am too indolent and like my own way too well to wish [the Divinity Professorship]," he wrote Hurrell Froude in 1836 (*LD*, V, p. 219). And even his individualistic conversion to Roman Catholicism involved natural personality issues as well as religious convictions: "My own soul was my first concern, and it seemed an absurdity to my reason to be converted in partnership. I wished to go to my Lord by myself, and in my own way, or rather His way" (*Apo.*, p. 198). That is a pattern for Newman in most areas of life. No a priori position, no religious or political party, no school or thought would supersede his individual way of thinking or expressing himself. Even in the Oxford Movement, where he worked with his closest friends, he made claims for his individualism. And later in life he could not be a traditional Catholic theologian, for "I like going my own way, and having my time my own" (*LD*, XXIV, pp. 212–13). Newman seemed to think that in 1864 his real individual person escaped the artistic grasp of Richmond, the great portrait painter: "I was the only person he could not draw out" (*LD*, XXVI, p. 219).

Newman no doubt had a strong sense of his special individual self even in his preconversion boyhood; this includes a strong will, even self-will. His sister Jemima remembered how once he failed to get his way with his mother who reminded him: "You see, John, you did not get your own way." "No," he admitted, "but I tried very hard."[16] Self-will is a strong motif in many of Newman's writings, including his journals where he indicates this problem in terms of pride and vanity (*AW*, pp. 175, 177).[17] Mrs. Newman saw the inclination of self-will in all of her sons; John Henry, she thought, "was surrounded by admirers and had everything [his] own way" (*LD*, V, pp. 313–14). His sister Harriett insisted that he cannot "bow to any authority, collected or individual."[18] But Newman himself straightforwardly acknowledged his determination to have his "own way" on many occasions: in addition to those already mentioned, there is the instance when he could have been dean of Oriel College (*LD*, III, p. 83), and there are the many self-guarded conditions he made in later life for going to London.[19] Newman most dramatically portrayed the evil of extreme self-will in the character of Juba in his novel *Callista*. Juba, who would be independent in every thought and action, who insisted that "I am my own master" and "I'll have my own way," found himself unable to "escape from [himself]" in a hell-on-earth—exactly the hell described by Caecilius (St. Cyprian) to Callista ("you will be yourself, shut up in yourself"; *Call*., pp. 146, 148, 122).[20]

As readers have discovered and Newman himself admitted, he possessed some personality traits opposite from strong will or self-will: he was often shy, anxious, defensive, sensitive, and diffident. A. Dwight Culler has noted that Newman's choice of topic for his English essay in the Oriel examination in 1822 pointed toward the very qualities of his self that he was concerned with in his letters at the time to his family. That topic was: Knowing oneself can help one avoid the evils of both diffidence and self-conceit.[21] I agree with Culler but add that these traits—better expressed as anxiety and self-assurance—remained with Newman much, if not all, of his life.

Diffidence expressed itself, as Newman wrote in his Oriel essay, as fear of shame and failure, of being in the wrong. When the seventeen-year-old Newman discovered that he was not the most advanced undergraduate in Oxford, he wrote his father that "there are several who know much more than I do in Latin and Greek—and I do not like that" (*LD*, I, p. 48). On his twenty-third birthday he recorded in his journal: "I am a great liar, a mean liar . . . from pride, lest I should confess myself wrong" (*AW*, p. 189). And when he was twenty-five years old, he wrote that he was "cautious from fear of turning out wrong" (*AW*, p. 173). Of course, no young man relishes failure, but Newman tended to focus on the unpleasant experience. He wrote his mother from Trinity College that he did not want to try for a scholarship at the same time as taking his preliminary examinations, for then "I should stand a great chance of failing, and that I cannot say I should relish" (*LD*, I, pp. 50–51). Perhaps his very fear of failure was one of the operative factors in his "failure" in the bachelor's examination. Afterwards, he was blunt about it: "It is all over; and I have not succeeded. . . . my nerves quite forsook me and I failed." But he took a kind of facetious consolation in the possibility that at least he might be "honored as a hero" for falling "on the field of literature" (*LD*, I, p. 94).

An anxious person herself, Mrs. Newman noted her son's tendency toward anxiety. And the words "anxious" and "anxiety" appear very frequently in Newman's writings, public and private. In the first two paragraphs of the ninth discourse of the *Idea of a University*, for example, Newman acknowledges his anxiety four times and his fear of being wrong three times. When he was planning an answer to Gladstone in 1874, he expressed his anxiety to a number of friends: to Lord Emly he wrote that "a failure would be terrible" (*LD*, XXVII, p. 146), and to another correspondent, that "I am nearly knocked up" (*LD*, XXVII, p. 176).

While fear of failure, of being in the wrong, was an important element in Newman's personality, self-assurance was perhaps even more central to it. This need not, or should not, be explained in religious terms; it was a natural confidence in his own intellectual gifts. When Newman was just five years old, his father wrote, praising his ability to read but warning that he "must learn something new every day or you will no longer be called a clever Boy" (*LD*, I, p. 3). Newman himself recorded in his journal—as if merely objective fact—his "quick apprehension" and that, according to his school Master, "no boy had run through the school, from the bottom to the top, so rapidly as John Newman" (*AW*, p. 29). And even after his failure in the bachelor's examination, and as correction of his alleged diffidence, Newman wrote his father with no pretense at modesty: "I assure you that they know very little of me and judge very superficially of me, who think I do not put a value on myself *relatively* to others. I think (since I am forced to speak boastfully) few have attained the facility of comprehension which I have arrived at" (*LD*, I, p. 125). In another place he expressed pride in his logical and rhetorical powers: "I have a vivid perception of the consequences of certain admitted principles, have a considerable capacity of drawing them out. . . . [I have] a rhetorical and histrionic power to represent them."[22]

At Oriel College Dr. Whately more than any other person helped to build up Newman's self-assurance—by teaching him to think correctly and to rely upon himself. Newman seems proud to note that Whately thought him the "clearest-headed man he knew" (*AW*, p. 12) but also that he began to express his differences from his Master. His self-assurance at Oriel can be seen in one of his earliest scholarly publications, "Poetry, with Reference to Aristotle's Poetics," written in 1828 for the *London Review*. Newman not only disputed the *fact* of Aristotelian plots in the great Greek dramas but was still bolder and questioned "even the sufficiency of the rules of Aristotle for the production of dramas of the highest order" (*Ess.*, I, p. 257).[23] The twenty-seven-year-old Newman had his own literary theory that he applied not only to Greek literature but also to English poetry and fiction, including popular writers like Scott and Byron. This allowed him to keep up his attack on Aristotle ("The inferior poem may, on his principles, be the better tragedy") and to make strong judgments from moral and religious perspectives on Byron and Southey. Bold the essay was, and criticism of it by Blanco White did not deter Newman from reprinting it in 1871. Perhaps the most significant remark in it for my purposes concerns "originality." Newman defines it as the "power of abstracting for one's self, and is in thought what strength of mind is in action. . . . minds of original talent feel a continual propensity to investigate subjects, and strike out views for themselves—so that even old and established truths do not escape modification and accidental change when subjected to this process of mental digestion" (*Ess.*, I, p. 270). Add boldness to this determination to be original in this sense, and I think we have a good picture of Newman's self-assured intellectual character during the Oxford Movement but also later in his life. This will be further explored under the category of Newman as individual theologian.

Newman's self-assurance revealed itself in both denying error and positively claiming truth. He did not often admit to being wrong; he usually claimed to be right. I have found this to be a fairly universal pattern. Whatever deficiencies he allows in his writings in terms of completeness or expression, he still maintains that they are nevertheless true. Rather typical are his remarks of 1847: "What perhaps I feel some anxiety about is the fate of my writings, Essay on Development etc. I have no reason to feel misgivings about their substantial correctness" (*LD*, XII, p. 14). Of course, the great exception was his anti-Catholic remarks; he retracted or corrected them, though not always as fully as one might expect. But Newman's self-assurance is seen in a most dramatic way in his refusal, on the whole, to address (or sometimes even read) criticism of his works. He often asserted that he had faith that the truth would eventually be seen, but it looks very much as if he meant *his own* version of the truth (see, for example, *LD*, XXII, p. 44). His self-confidence seems to be based both on God's special personal providence over him and on his natural habits of real assent and indefectible certitude. Most people, he thought, do not have the latter (see *GA*, p. 88). Newman was probably writing of himself when he claimed that the more convinced of the truth a person is, the less need or even ability he has to engage in controversy. In the *Grammar of Assent* he maintained that "those who are certain of a fact are indolent disputants; it is enough for them that they have the truth; and they have little disposition, except at the call of duty, to criticize the hallucinations of others" (*GA*, p. 201). And in *The Via Media* he wrote: "As we advance in perception of the Truth, we all become less fitted to be controversialists" (*VM*, I, p. 69).[24]

II. Newman as Controversialist

These citations naturally lead to a discussion of Newman as controversialist, and here we find one of the traits that most characterizes the individual person, John Henry Newman, in both his public and private lives. Engaging in controversy, perhaps because it was so central to Newman's psyche, was one of the things that he did best, and he knew it. It became part of his own self-identification: "I am a controversialist, not a theologian," he wrote to W. G. Ward in 1866 (*LD*, XXII, p. 157). And in the *Apologia* he complained that certain acts of Church authority effectively tie the "hands of a controversialist, such as I should be" (*Apo.*, p. 236). Close to this identification is that which he gave himself in the early years of the Oxford Movement when he wrote to Hurrell Froude: "You and Keble are the philosophers and I the rhetorician" (*LD*, V, p. 225).

When he admiringly described Cicero as a kind of soldier and statesman, not of great deeds, but of language and reasoning (*Idea*, p. 212), Newman was also pointing to his own achievement. Cicero was obviously a model and an impetus for Newman's own rhetoric and controversy. Later, Whately and the Oriel common room played important roles. But Newman's own gifts of logic, mathematics, and argumentative thinking were responsible, so he thought (*AW*, p. 184), for his winning the Oriel fellowship to begin with. Earlier, in 1819, his propensities for disputation can be seen from a letter he wrote to his own Oxford periodical, the *Undergraduate*, advocating the founding of a debating society; he even suggested the subjects for disputation (*LD*, I, p. 63).

But we must go back still farther to see that Newman's controversial mode apparently began in the Newman home and at Ealing School, where the unathletic boy was deficient in boy's sports and camaraderie but most proficient in intellectual pursuits and games. It appears from family letters and journal remarks that argument and even forms of formal controversy were part of the life of the Newmans—often for amusement but sometimes with seriousness and unpleasantness. Newman easily "conquered" his sisters with witty argumentative letters and wrote a series of very long, rather pompous, controversial letters to his brother Charles over a five-year period. Newman wrote his sister Jemima about Charles's "controversial naiveté" and laughed at Charles's accusation that he, John Henry, exulted in the "vigor of his arguments" (*LD*, II, p. 286). John Henry and Frank Newman clearly had serious arguments about many matters, but Frank maintained that he would not allow John to get the upper hand by refusing to state his position.[25] In 1823 Newman wrote in his journal: "This evening I argued with my father with very unbecoming violence. . . . I have got into a way of asserting things very strongly . . . my manner is hasty and authoritative." He worried that this proceeded from pride and contempt (*AW*, p. 193). Even his mother was offended by his argumentative remarks concerning her view of his sermons; she readily admitted to him: "I know I am a very weak arguer." But she reminded him that some of his very intelligent friends did not always agree with him (*LD*, V, p. 25).

One of the things that has most struck me about Newman's letters of his Oxford years, right up to 1841, is the spirit of verve, excitement, and genuine fulfillment in which he engaged in controversies of all types. He simply liked to argue, sometimes for argument's own sake. He even admitted to using false rhetoric at times and that in the early years of the Oxford Movement he was a kind of controversial snob, contemning the "controversial position" of the Low Church. He even played for sport with dull opponents: "I was not unwilling to draw an opponent on step by step, by virtue of his own opinions, to the brink of some intellectual absurdity, and to leave him to get back as he could" (*Apo.*, p. 51). He was actually disappointed, controversially, with his letter-battle with the Abbé Jager, for "he is so weak that so far it is no fun" (*LD*, V, p. 25).

On the other hand, Newman thrived on winning skirmishes against more substantial opponents like Hampden, Fausset, and the Evangelicals generally (see *LD*, V, p. 89; VI, pp. 258, 270; VI, pp. 12, 177). Owen Chadwick has concluded that Newman "gives every sign of enjoying religious polemic . . . he shows signs of enjoying the demolition" both of the Church of Rome in 1837 and the Church of England in 1846–53.[26] Probably no one would deny that Newman exulted in his devastation of Charles Kingsley in 1864, thirty-nine blots and all. And he even valued the blows *he* received in his boxing-match type of life: "The truth is that it is my vocation to knock and be knocked. It has been such for now a good forty years—and I have taken it as my Cross. I might easily have a far heavier one, and do not want it changed" (*LD*, XXV, pp. 119–20).

I have been startled by the very forceful and bellicose nature of Newman's diction and imagery in passages of or about controversy. His frequent imagery of battle and warfare, of course, has a precedent in Scripture and Christian tradition, but he also uses it often in controversy generally. Moreover, he seems to delight in aggressive and even violent language in describing controversial triumphs: such words as smash, lash, cruel and malicious blows, crush and pound to dust, tear and hack, smack in the face, punch in the stomach, pounce upon his neck, and even murder (see *LD*, I, p. 219; II, p. 286; VI, pp. 53, 217, 287; XII, p. 158; *Idea*, p. 119; *Apo.*, p. 19). Frederick Roger's characterization of Newman's controversial manner as "flinty" really seems too weak.[27] The rougher, more violent manner revealed in Newman's own language, I maintain, is an important element in his individual controversial personality, sensitive, gentle, refined, spiritual, and otherworldly as he was in other areas of his life. I suggest, further, that very good but abstract studies of Newman as controversialist by Holmes and Jost are somewhat unreal in Newman's own terms because they neglect the person who writes the controversy.[28]

Everyone knows of Newman's opposition to controversy in matters of religious faith, but even here it must be stressed that he *argues* to that position against an opposite view. He also argues that bishops and the pope should not argue when they teach. Again, we all know that Newman often moaned over the anxiety and pain he experienced during controversies (even to the point of fainting), but it still appears as if he basically liked controversy and needed it. Almost everything he wrote is characterized by response to some antagonistic view, and antithesis is a basic ingredient of his prose style. Conflict, paradox, and challenging disjunctions are some of his rhetorical instruments for forcing readers to see *his* truth; they are the means by which truth is generally discovered. When the process of synthesis from conflicting views is neglected, as Newman thought was the case in the definition of papal infallibility in 1870, then some unsatisfactory, "miraculous" solution is adopted. In that particular case, he wrote, "the Pope and the bishops seem to have left everything to the Holy Ghost" (*LD*, XXV, p. 139).

Newman's poetic remarks as a new Catholic to a correspondent in 1846 are almost humorously ironic: "I have in a measure, at least for the time, forgotten controversy—for controversy is a means to an end—and when one has raised a building, why keep up the scaffolding? and when one enjoys the shore, why count the billows which preceded the landing?" (*LD*,

XI, p. 238). Also at that time he wrote conclusively to his sister Harriett that "Rome is the center of unity and the judge of controversies."[29] Newman would in fact have many more controversies as a Catholic and some of them with Rome itself. It is my view that his mind operated in an argumentative way and that controversy was all but inevitable. He was in Rome for preordination Catholic theology only a few months when he evaluated the leading theologian there, the Jesuit Giovanni Perrone, in this way: "I have been much pleased with Perrone's treatises on [reason and faith]—for whom I have as respectful an opinion in dogmatics as I think him often absurd in polemics. In polemics he does not understand the arguments he has to deal with" (*LD*, XI, p. 293). Also in Rome, Newman conceived and apparently began writing what was possibly the easiest and most natural book that he ever wrote—his novel *Loss and Gain*.[30] It is in good part a recreation of Oxford controversies of his own days there. So he could write what he enjoyed without the anxieties he usually experienced when he engaged in "real" controversy. After all, it was only a novel. Nevertheless, in 1864 Newman listed it as one of the controversial works of his Catholic years (*Apo.*, p. 421).

Back in England, Newman was back in controversy, forced on him, he claimed, by Bishop Wiseman. He was never happy with his performance in the *Difficulties of Anglicans* of 1850; this work is unfortunately the triumphalist polemics of a new Catholic. The next year he was much more comfortably engaged in lectures on Protestant prejudice against Catholics. While the *Present Position of Catholics in England* is not formal controversy, it is argumentative prose of the highest order, and Newman was very happy with this performance.

It should be no surprise now that Newman's second novel, *Callista, A Sketch of the Third Century* of 1855, is found to be full of remarks about argument and controversy. Newman's fictional characters think the way he does. So Agellius, a Newman-figure in several respects, yearns for Christian companionship, for conversation, and, yes, for "argument" (*Call.*, p. 15). He has some outlet with his pagan friends, however, and "in the debates which ensued, though there was no agreement, there was the pleasure of mental exercise and excitement" (*Call.*, p. 52). Even the eighteen-year-old Greek girl, Callista, enjoys argument on aesthetic questions, but not on religion: "She was not equal to a controversy, nor did she mean to have one, whatever might be the case with [Polemo]" (*Call.*, pp. 59, 171).

A full-length study of Newman as controversialist would have to confront the language and mode of development in all of Newman's Catholic writings, from the *Idea of a University, Apologia, Grammar of Assent, Letter to the Duke of Norfolk*, *On the Inspiration of Scripture*, to the articles against Fairbairn in the *Contemporary Review* of 1885–86 when he was eighty-five years old. Newman still thought of himself as a controversialist in his private letters of 1890, two months before his death (*LD*, XXXI, pp. 293–94). Finally, even Newman's Gerontius is scarcely up from his deathbed when he half argues with his Guardian Angel about the timing of Judgment.

I have been arguing that a primary element in Newman's individualism was a kind of addiction to controversy. Now I want to maintain that he was equally committed to an individualistic theology. Of course, many of his controversies were theological. But then almost everything he wrote was theological. In 1865 he wrote the Jesuit Henry Coleridge: "I have been too long in the groove . . . to write anything which [has] no theological meaning" (*LD*, XXI, p. 461). He made this remark three months after he had written "The Dream of Gerontius," a poem into which he wove a finer theology of judgment and purgatory than in any of his prose works.

III. Newman as Theologian

Newman was an anxious but bold, original, and self-assured theologian. His theological personality was at one with his general individualistic personality. "I had a way of inquiry of my own," he said of his method in Tract 90 (*Apo.*, p. 80; see also p. 254). And he insisted that he went wrong when he did not weigh the views of others "for myself" (*Apo.*, p. 115; also pp. 155, 184). He claimed the right to his own theological views throughout his life (*Apo.*, pp. 92, 123; *LD*, XXIII, pp. 274–76). Further, he often expressed confidence in their truth once they were formulated and published. Private judgment might not exist for the ordinary Catholic, but he as a Catholic theologian had the right to it, and the Church was enriched by it from individual theologians like himself (*Apo.*, p. 237).

Newman often very favorably used words like "bold," "original," "speculative," and "free" of some of the fathers of the Church like Origen and Athanasius and of contemporary thinkers like Thomas Scott, John Keble, and Hurrell Froude. Those words and those persons expressed his own ideals. He would be the first to admit that as an Anglican theologian he was very independent and self-assured, though always with his personality trait of being anxious at the same time. In 1852, in his introductory lecture in Dublin, he confessed that "it has been my lot for many years to take a prominent, sometimes a presumptuous, part in theological discussions" (*Idea*, p. 2). Since he had as yet written almost no theology as a Catholic, he must have meant his *Arians, Tracts, Prophetical Office, Lectures on Justification, Oxford University Sermons*, and his *Essay on the Development of Christian Doctrine*. Let us hear from Newman at the time of those works.

In 1833 Newman admitted that he and the other Tractarians were deficient in theological learning, but that did not stop him from writing many Tracts and his first important theological work, *The Arians of the Fourth Century*. Three years later, he acknowledged that "except that [the matter of the Arians] is true, I have long thought it just the most imperfect work that was ever composed" (*LD*, V, p. 399). Again, in 1838, Newman acknowledged his deficiencies in learning: about Palmer's *Treatise on the Church* Newman remarked to a friend that "it is a stupendous magazine of learning and has quite made me feel ashamed" (*LD*, VI, p. 217). At that same time he was preparing his *Lectures on Justification* for publication and was unusually anxious: "I am so afraid of [making] some floors in my Lectures." But he so typically added this remark—which has almost been the main motif of my essay: "It seems as if I must venture, and depend on myself and my good luck—and I only trust that I may be carried through as heretofore. Yet I so fear this is presumption—at least I have an indefinite sort of evil conscience on the subject" (*LD*, VI, pp. 182–83). Newman *should* have been worried about writing on the difficult topic of justification, for he really did not know either the German language or Luther. Yet he was both anxious and bold at the same time. He was a "good deal fussed" about the lectures, for "it is the first voyage I have yet made proprio marte, with sun, stars, compass, and a sounding line, but with very insufficient charts. It is a terra incognita in our Church, and I am so afraid, not of saying things wrong so much, as queer and crotchety—and of misunderstanding other writers for really the Lutherans etc. as divines are so shallow and inconsequent, that I can hardly believe my own impression about them" (*LD*, VI, pp. 188–89).

Newman's bold self-assurance in theological matters carried him through the presentation of one of the most original theological theories of modern times, that of development of Christian doctrine. Although this work was criticized from many sides, Newman kept faith in his view (*LD*, XII, p. 14), and he revised and published it again in 1878 with self-assurance. But the theological subject on which Newman was perhaps the boldest and most insistent on having his own view or interpretation was that of infallibility. He often refused the title of theologian, but he nevertheless claimed both the theologian's right and duty to theologize on that difficult subject before, during, and after the Vatican Council of 1870. He quite acknowledged that he was "writing on such nice theological subjects"

(*LD*, XXVII, p. 270). There was a strong personal element in his determination to have his own opinion. It is possible to see his views as part of a personal conflict with Manning, Ward, and others. He felt it important to point out that neither Manning nor Pope Pius IX was really a theologian (*LD*, XXVII, p. 212). He was genuinely angry and expressed himself with strong emotions in opposing the Ultramontanes. His opponents were labeled "a violent ultra party" (*Apo.*, p. 233), "an aggressive and insolent faction," and a "clique of Jesuits, Redemptorists and converts" (*LD*, XXV, pp. 18–19). There was something very personal and resentful about Newman's remarks on infallibility from 1864 on that should not be explained as merely concern for the scandal given to lay Catholics.

There is a curious irony, and perhaps inconsistency, in Newman's controversial approach to infallibility. On the one hand, the Church's gift of infallibility secured for him the validity of his theory of doctrinal development and helped him to his conversion of 1845. And it was also crucial to the logical framework of his ubiquitous apologetic disjunction between atheism and Catholicism.[31] On the other hand, his analyses of infallibility in the *Apologia*, his letters, and the *Letter to the Duke of Norfolk* are so negative and minimalist as to leave very little meaning for real, operative, errorless truth in the Church. He seems intent on undermining all positive meaning to the concept of infallibility, especially its papal form. Some of his remarks sound reckless.

Whatever is passed, Newman wrote before the Council, "will be in so mild a form as practically to mean little or nothing" (*LD*, XXV, p. 150). And after the Council he insisted that "nothing has been passed of consequence" (*LD*, XXV, p. 224) and that we do not know the meaning of what was passed because it is based on the Church's infallibility, which has never been defined (*LD*, XXVI, pp. 59–60). Newman himself adopted a kind of supernaturalist explanation in saying that the action of the pope and bishops is infallible, not their minds (they in fact could be heretics [*LD*, XXVI, p. 198]). The pope's "words would be infallible one moment, not the next" (*LD*, XXVI, p. 171). That is, neither pope, nor bishops, nor theologians can tell us infallibly what was defined infallibly. Theologians must try to explain infallible decrees, but that process will go on forever. Newman's final solution to infallibility as lying with the whole body of the Church is certainly bold and unique and also questionable, but that is a philosophical question beyond the scope of this essay.[32]

What I am interested in here is the self-assurance of the individual person, John Henry Newman, who claimed he was not a theologian, as he opposed Manning, Ward, Veuillot, the Roman Jesuits, and others, and as he proposed views that held so little positive meaning. It might be correct to see a parallel between what Newman did to the Thirty-Nine Articles as an Anglican and what he did to infallibility as a Catholic. In both cases, without much self-recognition, he took great risks in expressing his bold views. It seems impossible to imagine that he could not have anticipated unfavorable reaction in Rome to his views on infallibility. He already had a bad name there. He had no savior in the Church of England in 1841, but, ironically, a prime defender who helped to save him in 1874 was his old nemesis from Dublin, Cardinal Cullen, who Newman claimed was a good theologian (*LD*, XXVII, pp. 220, 231).

In concluding this exploratory study of some of the effects of Newman's individualism on his self-identity and various forms of discourse, I should return to the point where I began—his decision against the Jesuits as a vocation in his Catholic life. He was grateful for their support at various times in his life, but he must have always been aware that he could not have tolerated what he thought was their overly cautious and traditional life. He felt rejected by them for not taking the so-called true Catholic line, and he even ventured to suggest that they were "too powerful for the health of [the Church]" (*AW*, p. 271). It is tempting to look down the road not taken and speculate what Newman's life would have been like if he had entered the Society of Jesus in 1846. Would he still have made a significant contribution to religious and educational thought, or would he have become one of those crushed individualities he wrote of in 1854 who only subserve a set notional theology?

What is more tempting is to speculate more generally about Newman being less of a retiring individualist and more of a participant in the intellectual public forum, a regular contributor to various ecclesiastical and philosophical groups and gatherings in England, an active theological consultant in the discussions in Rome at the Vatican Council—in short, ironically, more of a persistent public controversialist. Would Newman have had to revise or even abandon some of his individualistic views, or would his contributions have been even greater? Of course, we are more than grateful for what he has given us in his inimitable prose, but my final conclusion is that all of his great gifts must always be interpreted in the light of the individualistic personality that offered them to us.

Notes

1. *The Letters and Diaries of John Henry Newman*, ed. Charles Stephen Dessain et al.

2. John Henry Newman, *Historical Sketches*, 3 vols. (London: Longmans, Green, 1897).

3. John Henry Newman, *An Essay in Aid of a Grammar of Assent* (London: Longmans, Green, 1891).

4. Peter L'Estrange, "Newman's Relations with the Jesuits," *Heythrop Journal* XXIX (1988): pp. 58–85, and Placid Murray, O.S.B., *Newman the Oratorian: His Unpublished Oratory Papers* (Dublin: Gill and MacMillan, 1969).

5. Maisie Ward, *Young Mr. Newman* (London: Sheed and Ward, 1948), p. 23.

6. Edward Jeremy Miller, *John Henry Newman on the Idea of Church* (Shepherdstown, W.Va.: Patmos Press, 1987), p. 3.

7. J. H. Walgrave, "A Psychological Portrait of Newman," in *John Henry Newman: Theologian and Cardinal* (Rome: Urbaniana Press, 1981), pp. 155–71, at p. 171.

8. Walgrave, "A Psychological Portrait," pp. 155–56.

9. Edward E. Kelly, "Newman's Reputation and the Biographical Tradition," *Faith and Reason* XV (1989): pp. 151–70.

10. Thomas Gornall, "Newman: The Tutorial Quarrel," *Clergy Review* LXIV (1979): pp. 205–209, at p. 209.

11. Thomas Gornall, "Newman's Failure in the Schools," *Clergy Review* LXII (1978): pp. 65–68, at p. 66a.

12. John Henry Newman, *The Idea of a University*, ed. Martin J. Svaglic (New York: Holt, Rinehart and Winston, 1960).

13. For example, see Anne Mozley, ed., *Letters and Correspondence of John Henry Newman*, 2 vols. (London: Longmans, Green, 1891), vol. II, p. 398.

14. John Henry Newman, *Apologia Pro Vita Sua*, ed. Martin J. Svaglic (Oxford: Clarendon Press, 1967).

15. John Henry Newman, *Parochial and Plain Sermons*, 8 vols. (London: Rivington, 1875).

16. Mozley, *Letters and Correspondence*, vol. I, p. 16.

17. *John Henry Newman: Autobiographical Writings*, ed. Henry Tristram (London: Sheed and Ward, 1956).

18. *Newman Family Letters*, ed. Dorothea Mozley (London: S.P.C.K., 1962), p. 165.

19. See Ian Ker, *John Henry Newman: A Biography* (Oxford: Clarendon Press, 1990), pp. 611–12.

20. John Henry Newman, *Callista, A Sketch of the Third Century* (London: Burns and Oates, 1962).

21. A. Dwight Culler, *The Imperial Intellect: A Study of Newman's Educational Ideal* (New Haven: Yale University Press, 1955), p. 33.

22. Mozley, *Letters and Correspondence*, vol. I, p. 416.

23. John Henry Newman, *Essays Critical and Historical*, 2 vols. (London: Longmans, Green, 1907).

24. John Henry Newman, *The Via Media*, 3d ed., 2 vols. (London: Longmans, Green, 1885).

25. Francis W. Newman, *Contributions Chiefly to the Early History of the Late Cardinal Newman* (London, 1891), p. 45.

26. Owen Chadwick, *The Spirit of the Oxford Movement: Tractarian Essays* (Cambridge: Cambridge University Press, 1990), p. 178.
27. Meriol Trevor, *Newman the Pillar of the Cloud* (New York: Doubleday, 1962), p. 221.
28. Derek Holmes, "Personal Influence and Religious Conviction—Newman and Controversy," *Newman Studien*, ed. Heinrich Fries and Werner Becker (Nuremberg: Glock und Lutz, 1948ff.), vol. X (1978), pp. 26–46, and Walter Jost, *Rhetorical Thought in John Henry Newman* (Columbia: University of South Carolina Press, 1989).
29. Sean O'Faolain, *Newman's Way: The Odyssey of John Henry Newman* (New York: Devin-Adair, 1952), p. 300.
30. John Henry Newman, *Loss and Gain: The Story of a Convert* (Oxford: Oxford University Press, 1986).
31. See Edward E. Kelly, "Atheism or Catholicism: Stark Disjunction from Complex Newman," forthcoming in *Newman the Theologian*, ed. Michael E. Allsopp and R. Ronald Burke (New York: Garland, 1992).
32. I have explored this matter in "Newman, Ward, and Modernism: Problems with Infallible Dogmatic Truth," *John Henry Newman and Modernism*, ed. Arthur Hilary Jenkins (Sigmaringendorf: Regio-Verlag Glock und Lutz, 1990), pp. 168–179.

2

Newman's Individualistic Use of the Caroline Divines in the Via Media

KENNETH L. PARKER

In the last days of 1836, John Henry Newman penned words that defined the gravest challenge facing the Oxford Movement. Acknowledging the firm ground on which its two great rivals stood, Newman observed, "Protestantism and Popery are real religions; no one can doubt about them; they have furnished the mould in which nations have been cast: but the *Via Media*, viewed as an integral system, has never had existence except on paper" (*VM*, p. 16).[1] In his *Lectures on the Prophetical Office of the Church*, Newman attempted to lay the foundations for this "integral system," claiming as its cornerstones the Scriptures, primitive Christian tradition, and the writings of the Caroline divines. These seventeenth-century theologians were crucial to his argument that the Oxford Movement was supporting and reviving the authentic Anglican tradition, which had suffered from the vicissitudes of Evangelicalism on the one hand and Latitudinarianism on the other. He stated, "Our champions and teachers have lived in stormy times; political and other influences have acted upon them variously in their day, and have since obstructed a careful consolidation of their judgments" (*VM*, p. 24). He went on to observe, "We have a vast inheritance, but no inventory of our treasures. All is given us in profusion; it remains for us to catalogue, sort, distribute, select, harmonize, and complete" (*VM*, p. 24).

In the last twenty-five years, scholars have differed over how well Newman knew this "vast inheritance" of seventeenth-century divinity. In his study of the origins of Newman's interest in patristics, T. M. Parker boldly stated, "There seems no evidence at all that Newman had read the Carolines before he became involved in the Oxford Movement."[2] He speculated that it was Martin Joseph Routh, the famous patristics scholar and president of

Magdalen College, who encouraged Newman to read more seriously the works of those theologians. Reflecting on an unrecorded conversation in early February 1834, which is thought to have focused on Newman's book *Arians of the Fourth Century*, Parker wondered about what they discussed during those two hours and concluded that Routh may have used the opportunity to exhort the "clever young gentleman of Oriel" to read the works of Laud, Bramhall, and Stillingfleet.[3]

These speculations have been rejected by H. D. Weidner, in his neglected but praiseworthy doctoral dissertation "Newman's Idea of the *Via Media*."[4] Noting Newman's use of Richard Mant's edition of *The Book of Common Prayer* in 1824, with its catena of Anglican divinity, and his reading of works by the Caroline patristics scholars James Ussher and John Pearson in 1828, Weidner demonstrates that Newman had been introduced to these divines during his twenties. He also points to Newman's correspondence in 1826 and 1827 with Samuel Rickards, the noted high churchman, which focused on the importance of the Caroline divines in the theological controversies of the period.[5] In an interesting study entitled "Newman and the English Theologians," Philip Rule has presented further evidence that supports Weidner's argument that Newman was reading those theologians long before the beginning of the Oxford Movement. Perhaps most impressive is a letter, thought to date from 1829, in which Newman supplied detailed references from Caroline works to his friend and colleague Edward Pusey.[6] These sources suggest that Newman may well have had an active interest in the divines of the seventeenth century dating from his mid-twenties.

Yet it remains unclear when the Caroline divines became an important part of Newman's theological development. In searching for an answer, his *Lectures on the Prophetical Office of the Church* is a logical point of reference, for it was a theological synthesis of the work he had pursued since the Oxford Movement began. In that study he appealed to the precedents established by "our standard divines" and supported his arguments with references to "our great divines" and the "most eminent divines" of the Anglican tradition.[7] However, if one studies the references to the Caroline heritage in the work, there are hints of an unreflective appeal to a theological tradition that was not well known or thoroughly digested: doctrines supported with mere references to Caroline luminaries and lengthy quotes intended to establish a direct link between his own system and those of the seventeenth century.[8] Most perplexing is the infrequent appeal to the greatest names of the Caroline tradition. Lancelot Andrewes is referred to once, in a list of Anglo-Catholic divines. Bishops John Cosin

and Joseph Hall appear on one occasion, in reference to differing opinions
concerning the end of primitive Christian tradition. Henry Leslie, William
Beveridge, William Chillingworth, John Pearson, and Simon Patrick are
also mentioned only once, while Herbert Thorndike and Robert Sanderson
are not cited at all.[9] If one is to judge the significance of a theologian by
the number of times his name in invoked, it is clear that John Bramhall,
Henry Stillingfleet, Jeremy Taylor, and William Laud played the most
important role in forming Newman's understanding of Caroline divinity;
yet even those luminaries seem neglected when one considers Newman's
professed devotion to them.[10]

   This is all the more interesting given Newman's early enthusiasm for
harmonizing and systematizing Anglican doctrine. In November 1826
Newman wrote to Samuel Rickards, suggesting that he use his considerable
knowledge of "our old Divines" to prepare a compendium of Anglican
theology. He stated:

> I would advise taking them *as a whole*, a corpus theologicum et ecclesiasticum,
> *the* English Church—stating indeed *how far* they differ among themselves, yet
> distinctly marking out the grand bold scriptural features of that doctrine in
> which they all agree.—They would then be a band of witnesses for the truth,
> not opposed to each other (as they now are) but *one*—each tending to the
> edification of the body of Christ, according to the effectual working of their
> gifts and the variety of circumstances under which each spake his testimony.
> (*LD*, I, p. 310)

Responding in January 1827, Rickards doubted whether such a work
would be effective and observed:

> My impression is, that our old writers are excellent men to keep company
> with, if you wish to strengthen your own powers by conversing with great
> and original thinkers; they will help you greatly to form a solid judgment for
> yourself, but they seldom give you a conclusion so wrought out, as that you
> can use it for an argument in the shape in which they present it to you. Hooker
> and Bishop Sanderson are almost the only exceptions to this.[11]

Rickards went on to conclude that "in these days the way to draw attention
and to make oneself useful, is rather by possessing oneself of the matter of
those old venerable men, [than] by leaning upon their names."[12]

   It would appear that Newman took at least part of Rickard's advice, for
later in 1827 he quoted passages from Richard Hooker's writings in a
sermon.[13] Observations concerning Hooker in his correspondence illustrate
that the great Elizabethan divine had made a deep impression on the young

theologian.[14] Clearly, his reading and personal contacts were working a great change in him, for as an old man Newman referred to this period as the time when he became "eagerly, but not very logically, High Church" (*LD*, II, p. 25n).

However, Newman's scholarly work during this period was far removed from the issues of the post-Reformation English Church. During 1827 and 1828 he was occupied with researching and writing articles on "Greek Tragedy" and "Aristotle's Poetics" for the *London Review*. In 1827 Edward Pusey brought back from Germany a collection of the writings of the Fathers, and by the summer of 1828 Newman began a chronological study of ante-Nicene sources.[15] When he was deprived of students by Edward Hawkins in the tutorial controversy of 1830, Newman turned to the Fathers and gave himself more fully to mastering their works.[16]

This is not to say that he had lost interest in the theological problems raised by the first two centuries of Anglican divinity. Through the intercession of a friend early in 1831, Newman proposed to Hugh James Rose that he prepare a work on the Thirty-Nine Articles for a new series of basic theological studies being edited by Rose and William Lyall. He suggested a thematic approach, not examining each article in turn, but collecting their substance under topic headings "with a view both to clearness of statement and fullness in the proof from Scripture." Rose and Lyall made a counterproposal that he prepare instead a study of the Councils. In March 1831 Rose stated: "Will you think me very unreasonable if I venture to suggest to you that as a preliminary to a work on those Articles in which all the great doctrines of Christianity are treated, a *History of the Councils*, in which so many of them (one may say *all*) were discussed would be very valuable."[17]

Newman was not to prepare a study of the Thirty-Nine Articles for another decade—a work that marked a turning point in his life. Instead, he devoted himself to the controversies of the early Church. In the first months of that research, he did not lose sight of the connection between the two projects, for he made repeated references to it in correspondence with Rickards and Rose.[18] Yet as the work progressed, he became preoccupied with the Arian controversy of the fourth century, and it was on that subject that he wrote his first book.

When his manuscript was rejected by Rose and Lyall in October 1832, it was because of the unsuitable nature of the subject, not the quality of the work. However, Lyall did express reservations about Newman's concept of the *disciplina arcani*, observing:

Mr. Newman's notions about tradition appear to me directly adverse to that which Protestant writers of our own church have contended for—according to them a "secret tradition" is no tradition at all—quod semper, quod ubique, quod ab omnibus, is the very definition of authentic tradition. Mr. Newman's views seem to me more favorable to the Romanist writers, than I should like to put forward in the *Theological Library*.[19]

Others, including a bishop, shared Lyall's objection when the work was published in November 1833.[20]

By that time Newman was a man who polarized opinion for other reasons, for his role as the most charismatic leader of the Oxford Movement and his aggressive promotion of its cause forced others to take sides. His early tracts on the threefold ministry in the catholic tradition of the English Church, the authority of primitive practice, and Apostolic Succession in the Anglican tradition were all calculated to challenge the positions of rival theological systems within the Church of England. Contrary to the advice offered by Samuel Rickards many years before, Newman used the names of the "old venerable men" of the seventeenth century and won polemical battles in the process. He condensed John Cosin's work against the doctrine of transubstantiation and published it as Tracts 27 and 28 in March 1834[21] and doubtless had a role in editing Beveridge's works on public prayer and frequent communion as well.[22] At the end of March 1834, he observed to R. F. Wilson, "I see a system *behind* the existing one, a system indeed which will take time and suffering to bring us to adopt, but still a firm foundation" (*LD*, IV, p. 227).

With this comment in mind, one ponders with some perplexity the fact that Newman began a new field of research at the beginning of that same month, not a study of the Caroline divines, but an edition of the works of Dionysius Alexandrinus.[23] Despite his professed devotion to the teaching of the seventeenth-century theologians, the recurring question of this essay remains: When did Newman seriously study the works of the Caroline divines?

The obvious solution of this mystery would be to determine what Newman was reading during the 1820s and 1830s, yet this line of enquiry is fraught with problems and unknown variables. His letters and diaries offer some evidence but do not provide a complete catalog of his reading. It would be difficult to ascertain what he was collecting in his personal library in any given period, and the loaning of books between friends remains another unknown variable. In his biography of Edward Pusey, David Forrester notes the revival of interest in seventeenth-century divinity in the 1820s and the republication of the collected works of William Beveridge, George Bull, Jeremy Taylor, and others.[24] This adds to the difficulty of determining exactly what Newman read and studied.

However, a partial solution to the problem has been found. By studying the library registers of the Bodley and the Oriel College Library, it has been possible to establish at least what Newman did not have in his personal library or receive in loan from friends.[25] This chronological bibliography is a fascinating overview of the young Newman's scholarly interests and a reliable measure of where his interests led him. The discussion here must be limited to his use of Caroline sources.[26]

Weidner was correct in arguing that Newman had early knowledge of Caroline divinity, though not necessarily for the reason he gave. There is no evidence from the library registers that the young fellow of Oriel turned to the Caroline sources cited in Richard Mant's catena for broader reading. Samuel Rickards's encouragement in early January 1827 to turn to the Caroline divines was followed six weeks later by the perusal of a volume of Hammond's works. Newman did not consult another work from that period for two years. As one works through the registers, the most striking aspect is the virtual absence of interest in seventeenth-century divinity. On the surface this seems highly improbable when, for example, one considers his role in directing Pusey in 1829 to Caroline sources for evidence in support for his views on biblical inspiration.[27] However, what one finds in the library registers is that Newman had not been reading Hall, Beveridge, Chillingworth, and Laud but instead, on June 19, had signed out of the Oriel College Library John Dick's *Essay on the Inspiration of Scripture* with the note "For Pusey" beside it.[28]

While it is possible to accurately follow Newman's scholarly interests as he worked on Greek tragedy, Aristotle's poetics, and the early Church Fathers, his interest in the Caroline divines appears to have been casual and unsystematic at best. Two weeks after Keble's famous sermon on "National Apostasy" in July 1833, he took out of the Oriel College Library Richard Field's *Of the Church* (1635), yet three months passed before he examined another work from that period. While Parker's speculations about Routh's influence in this matter are picturesque, the only Caroline divinity Newman examined shortly after that conversation was Cosin's *History of Popish Transubstantiation*, a work he was editing for the Tracts, and a collection of Andrewes's *Sermons*. Both were works he had previously used.

Weidner states that from the summer of 1834 to the end of 1836 Newman was working out his concept of the *Via Media*, as he carried on the controversy with Abbé Jean-Nicholas Jager and prepared his weekly lectures for the Adam de Brome chapel of St. Mary the Virgin.[29] While this is certainly true, seventeenth-century divinity remained a neglected subject for much of this period. During the summer of 1834, as he wrote Tracts 38 and 41 on the *Via Media*, the works of none of the Caroline luminaries were consulted. Indeed, from the fall of 1834 to July 1836, the library registers reveal that he consulted only eight works by distinguished seventeenth-century theologians. It would appear from Newman's selection of reading that there was no great enthusiasm for their works, much less a systematic study of their thought. With this in mind, it seems ironic that Newman used their names so effectively as he promoted his own vision of the Anglo-Catholic tradition.

Defending himself to Rickards in July 1834, Newman stated that his opponents would "find it was a very difficult thing to convict me of running counter to the great stream of our Divines. Sit anima mea cum Hammondo and such like" (*LD*, IV, p. 314). It is interesting that he mentions Hammond specifically, for he was the only Caroline divine that Newman consulted with any frequency from his mid-twenties to the time of the Oxford Movement.

Yet two years later, having made no close study of Caroline divinity, Newman observed to Rose in May 1836 that "the Anglican system of doctrine is in matter of fact not *complete*—that there are hiatuses which never have been filled up—so that, though one agrees with it most entirely as far as it goes, yet one wishes something more" (*LD*, V, p. 291). In July of that year he reported to Keble that he was preparing his lectures on Romanism for publication, the work that became his *Lectures on the Prophetical Office of the Church*.

At this point it would be reasonable to object and to suggest that Newman had personal copies of Caroline divinity or was using volumes loaned by friends. However, evidence from the library registers effectively challenges this assumption; for from August 8 to September 8, 1836, Newman was engaged in a frenzied reading of Caroline divinity. In the space of that month, he collected in his rooms the works of Sanderson, Andrewes, Hammond, Ken, Beveridge, Thorndike, and Stillingfleet. He reread Field and, most important, discovered the works of John Bramhall. After a week of those studies, he wrote to James Bliss:

> I have been going through Bramhall lately, and am astonished how far he goes and how clearly he lays down his lines. What pleases me most perhaps is his agreement with Laud, Taylor, etc.—for it seems to make it a more hopeful

project to *systematize* their writings, which is what we ought to aim at doing. At present the Romanist says, "What does your Church hold? etc."—I do trust we shall be able to produce a Consensus Doctorum. (*LD*, V, p. 340)[30]

Twelve years after suggesting the project to Samuel Rickards, the harmonization of Anglican divinity remained only a hope and dream for Newman. Because of his primary scholarly interests in patristics, he had been unable, or unwilling, to devote the necessary time to master their theology and achieve that goal. Perhaps most telling was the order in which he listed Caroline theologians when he wrote to Routh concerning the *Lectures* in January 1837:

> I cannot venture to hope that there is nothing in my volume of private and questionable opinion—but I have tried, as far as may be, to follow the line of doctrine marked out by our great divines, of whom perhaps I have chiefly followed Bramhall, then Laud, Hammond, Field, Stillingfleet, Beveridge, and others of the same school. (*LD*, VI, p. 7)

It would appear from those comments that Newman was most influenced by a Caroline divine whose work he had only recently discovered, and his understanding of that "school" of theology seems to have been superficial at best. Occupied as he was with so many projects and responsibilities, Newman had not made a close reading of Caroline divinity a priority. He was therefore largely dependent on what others had written about that school of theology and his own speculations about where it might lead the Oxford Movement, as he sought a firm foundation for his theology of the *Via Media*.

Without denigrating Newman's enthusiasm for the Caroline divines, one appreciates better why many High Church Anglicans of his day questioned Newman's interpretations of their tradition. Weidner observed that Newman's conclusion that the *Via Media* had never existed "except on paper" was due to not having been born High Church and commented that "if the *Via Media* had been more extensive in the actual life of the Church of England, it would not have cost Newman so much to find it."[31] One might also observe that if he had taken more seriously the advice received from Samuel Rickards in 1827, to possess himself of "the matter of those old venerable men, [than] by leaning upon their names," he might not have been so easily disenchanted with a system he professed to be reviving.[32]

Notes

1. John Henry Newman, *The Via Media of the Anglican Church*, ed. H. D. Weidner (Oxford: Clarendon Press, 1990); the page numbers used are those of the uniform edition.

2. Thomas M. Parker, "The Rediscovery of the Fathers in the Seventeenth-Century Anglican Tradition," in *The Rediscovery of Newman: An Oxford Symposium*, ed. John Coulson and A. M. Allchin (London: Sheed and Ward, 1967), pp. 31–49, at p. 41.

3. Parker, "The Rediscovery of the Fathers," p. 45.

4. H. D. Weidner, "Newman's Idea of the *Via Media*: An Introduction to the Lectures on the Prophetical Office of the Church" (D.Phil. diss., University of Oxford, 1984).

5. Weidner, "Newman's Idea of the *Via Media*," pp. 11–16, 26n; *The Book of Common Prayer*, ed. Richard Mant (Oxford, 1820); John Henry Newman, *The Letters and Diaries of John Henry Newman*, ed. Charles Stephen Dessain et al., vol. I, pp. 309–11, and vol. II, p. 81.

6. Philip Rule, "Newman and the English Theologians," *Faith and Reason* XV, no. 4 (1990): pp. 65–90, 82–83; Newman, *LD*, vol. II, p. 169.

7. Newman, *VM*, pp. xii, 8, 12, 23, 192, 194, 205, 207, 266, 280, 282, 335.

8. Newman, *VM*, pp. xii–xiv, 17, 280.

9. Newman, *VM*, pp. 17, 206, 195n, 207, 275, 280.

10. Newman, *VM*, John Bramhall, pp. xii–xiv, 124, 205, 274n, 280, 345n; Henry Stillingfleet, pp. 77n, 138n, 206, 207; Jeremy Taylor, pp. 77, 228n, 299, 335; William Laud, pp. 13, 17, 207, 322n.

11. From Samuel Rickards, in Newman, *LD*, I, p. 311.

12. Newman, *LD*, I, p. 311.

13. Sheridan Gilley, *Newman and His Age* (London: Darton, Longman and Todd, 1990), p. 67; Newman, *LD*, II, p. 25n.

14. Newman, *LD*, II, pp. 131, 164, 255.

15. *Newman Studien*, ed. Heinrich Fries and Werner Becker (Nuremberg: Glock und Lutz, 1948), vol. I, p. 287; Weidner, "Newman's Idea of the *Via Media*," p. 16; Gilley, "*Newman and His Age*," p. 71; John Henry Newman, *Apologia Pro Vita Sua: Being a History of His Religious Opinions* (London: Longmans, Green, Reader, and Dyer, 1881), p. 25.

16. Ian Ker, *John Henry Newman: A Biography* (Oxford: Clarendon Press, 1988), pp. 40–41; Gilley, "*Newman and His Age*," pp. 74–75.

17. From Hugh James Rose, in Newman, *LD*, II, p. 321.

18. Newman, *LD*, II, pp. 340–41, 352–53, 371.

19. From William Rowe Lyall to Hugh James Ross, in Newman, *LD*, III, p. 105.

20. Gilley, "*Newman and His Age*," p. 119; Newman, *LD*, IV, p. 169n.

21. Newman, *LD*, IV, p. 202.

22. *Tracts for the Times*, vol. 1 (London: Rivington, 1834), Tract 25 and Tract 26.

23. Newman, *LD*, IV, p. 202.

24. David Forrester, *Young Doctor Pusey* (London: Mowbray, 1989), pp. 86–87.

25. I am grateful to David Forrester for suggesting this line of research.

26. Oxford, Oriel College Library, *Register of Books Borrowed from the Library by the Provost and Fellows*, MS DCV 5; Oxford, Bodleian Library, MSS LR d.1274, LR d.1275. In the absence of pagination, all references from manuscripts are identified by date in the text.

27. Forrester, *Young Doctor Pusey*, pp. 85–86.

28. On the same day Newman borrowed Thomas Horne's *On the Holy Scriptures* as well.

29. Weidner, "Newman's Idea of the *Via Media*," p. 22.

30. It should be noted that while Newman referred to Taylor and Laud as authorities with whom he was familiar, evidence from the library registers and the *Lectures* suggests that Newman was only familiar with Taylor's *Dissuasive from Popery* and *Rule and Exercises of Holy Living/Holy Dying* and Laud's *Conference with Fisher* and *On Tradition*.

31. Weidner, "Newman's Idea of the *Via Media*," p. 24.

32. From Samuel Rickards, in Newman, *LD*, vol. I, p. 311.

Part 2

Understanding

3

Economies of Reason: Newman and the Phronesis Tradition

MARY KATHERINE TILLMAN

I. The *Phronesis* Tradition and the Indeterminateness of Human Discourse

In the great poem of Parmenides, the young inquirer is called forth by the Goddess and travels as far as his desire can take him, all the way to the limits of his mind. There, in the region of the Sun, the Goddess receives him kindly and reveals to his direct perception the motionless heart of well-rounded truth, wherein to think and to be are one and the same. Being appears to him "like a sphere in space / perfectly round and balanced / from every perspective / in precise equipoise."[1] Within the vision of eternal truth, the Goddess gives the young man an instruction for his return. He is to make his way back through the complex cosmos where light and darkness mix, where opposites harmonize and clash, where partial understandings seem to rule the day, the world of common opinion. He is never to forget the fractured and deceptive order of this world or the fullness of the truth that he has seen. When the youth returns to where his journey began, he sees a man and woman making love, and the formation of an embryo. An isolated fragment reads: "Where I begin is all one to me / Wherever I begin I will return again."[2]

As an old man, Parmenides instructed the young Socrates, who as an old man instructed the young Plato, who as an old man instructed the young Aristotle. Thus was established what I am calling "the *phronesis* tradition," which, despite other discontinuities from Parmenides to Plato to Aristotle, is strikingly whole in its main insights. The *phronesis* tradition of antiquity provides, I shall argue, one of the best clues overall to John Henry Newman's view of the economizing activity of human reason.

The topic of Plato's dialogue, the *Meno*, is whether human excellence or virtue can be taught. Socrates tells Meno that before they can answer that question they first need to know what virtue is. Together they must search among the many particular examples of virtue for the one idea of virtue, its essence or very reality. All of Meno's proposals are gradually undermined by the Socratic elenchus until Meno finally arrives at the point of no return. The realization of his ignorance and the crisis of perplexity create for Meno an opening for true learning. Socrates steps into the clearing and discloses the doctrine that he has heard from the tradition. The "priests and priestesses" and "the divine among the poets" have revealed to him, he says ("see whether you think they speak the truth"), that what is most true about reality lies buried and sleeping deep within our souls.[3] This privileged but shadowy knowledge or "sense" of what is true and good, if we diligently seek to draw it out, can tacitly guide us in our search for excellence, becoming ever more clear and explicit as it is "re-collected" again and again, remembered and energized in human discourse and action.

Phronesis, the peculiarly Socratic knowledge, is the activity of the collected, concentrated soul whereby its inner eye is focused, however veiledly, on the image within, while the mind is carried into and judges this or that particular word or deed. In the *Republic*, Plato calls *phronesis* the science of right choice, claiming that it is the most important thing in life to get this knowledge, that it cannot be learned from anyone else, and that, if the soul of the inquirer is guided in the right ways, the knowledge will arise of its own accord.[4]

For Aristotle, as for both Socrates and Plato before him, the *polis* is the large field within which *phronesis* operates and develops. Practical reason can no more exist in isolation from the discursive community that constitutes it than an individual can have self-definition or reality apart from it. In fact, human community is formed from the moral disposition, instinct, or "sense" out of which *phronesis* arises. Aristotle writes: "And it is characteristic of man that he alone has any sense of good and evil, of just and unjust, and the like, and the association of living beings who have this sense makes a family and a state."[5] The *phronimos*, says Aristotle, is the one "who is without qualification good at deliberating," the one "who is capable of aiming in accord with calculation at the best for man of things attainable by action."[6] The practical realm, the locus of contingency and change, is the field where wisdom plays, is exercised and grows. David Wiggins puts Aristotle's view this way: the person with practical wisdom

> is able to select from the infinite number of features of a situation those features that bear upon the notion or ideal of existence which it is his standing aim to

make real. This conception of human life results in various evaluations of all kinds of things, in various sorts of cares and concerns, and in various projects. It does not reside in a set of maxims or precepts, useful though Aristotle would allow these to be at a certain stage in the education of the emotions. In no case will there be a rule to which a man can simply appeal to tell him what to do.[7]

According to the *phronesis* tradition, then, practical reason is the mediating power of the mind. It moves, Hermes-like, in the middle region between the invisible and the visible, between the universal and the particular. The insight of this tradition rests in its recognition, on the one hand, of the indeterminate, time-bound nature of all human endeavor, including thought and speech, and, on the other, of the hope and pledge of genuine progress in understanding, even through error, due to the predisposition and desire, the inklings and ingenuity with which the human pilgrim comes equipped.

II. The Illative Sense: A Kind of Calculus

For the moment, I am not concerned with questions of particular influence upon Newman by one or the other of the above-named philosophers—influence that runs through Cicero, the Alexandrian Fathers, Augustine, the seventeenth-century Anglican divines, the British empiricists, the romantic poets, and the Oriel Noetics. I am interested rather in the bearing of the *phronesis* tradition *as such* upon Newman's thought. It is clear that he was entirely familiar with it, for the tradition formed and informed his mind from his teens to his early thirties: from Ealing School, through Trinity College, and for the duration of his years as fellow and tutor of Oriel College.

According to the *phronesis* tradition, one judges what to do in everyday actions by means of a "sense" of something more important and ultimate. Very simply, this is Newman's "illative sense." In the tradition, the predisposition and desire to make explicit the originating "sense" preserves the conception, anticipatingly interprets and guides the action, and helps to create the full realization or embodiment of the original sense or image. Very simply, this is what Newman means by "the method of antecedent probability." His early writing on "implicit reasoning" and his late description of "informal inference" come into view here as well.

For Newman, the illative, or inferential, sense is the directing or regulating principle of *all* our reasonings, active "in the beginning, middle and end of all verbal discussion and inquiry, and in every step of the process"

(*GA*, p. 233).[8] That sense guides by means of "tacit understandings," by the "vague and impalpable notions of 'reasonableness' . . . that make conclusions possible, and are the pledge of their being contradictory" (*GA*, p. 237). No "general faculty," the illative sense is "the elastic logic of thought" in every subject matter. Like the discourse of Parmenides' Goddess, the revelation of the Socratic divines, and the reasoning of Aristotle's prudent sage, the development of thought for Newman might be described as "circular," that is, returning and conserving, at the same time that it is "linear," or dialectically progressive. The inferential sense is always checking back with itself, as it were, taking the measure, correcting and readjusting in relation to what it always already knows, even as it deliberatively enters into the profusion and variety of elements in its immediate field. It aims solely at the explication, development, and realization of the original idea or latent sense in and through the particulars at hand. The following passage from Newman's fifteenth Oxford Sermon strikingly recalls the *phronesis* tradition in all of the subtlety of its insight.

> Though the Christian mind reasons out a series of dogmatic statements, one from another, this it has ever done, and always must do, not from those statements taken in themselves, as logical propositions, but as illustrated and (as I may say) inhabited by that sacred impression which is prior to them, which acts as a regulating principle, ever present, upon the reasoning, and without which no one has any warrant to reason at all. Such sentences as "the Word was God" or "the Only-begotten Son who is in the bosom of the Father," or "the Word was made flesh," or "the Holy Ghost which proceedeth from the Father," are not a mere letter which we may handle by the rules of art at our own will, but august tokens of most simple, ineffable, adorable facts, embraced, enshrined, according to its measure, in the believing mind. For though the development of an idea is a deduction of proposition from proposition, these propositions are ever formed in and round the idea itself (so to speak), and are in fact one and all only aspects of it. (*US*, p.334)[9]

Perhaps taking his cue from Aristotle, who wrote of practical wisdom as "aiming, *in accord with calculation*, at the best . . . attainable by action,"[10] Newman understood our ordinary judgments to attain their conclusions "by the method of reasoning that is the elementary principle of that mathematical calculus of modern times" (*GA*, p. 231). As a kind of calculus, practical reason functions "economically"; that is, it adjusts its methods to whatever matter it enters.[11] Deliberation moves back and forth dialectically, within maxima and minima, testing the poles and the limits of each view it inhabits, using symbols to approximate, making progress through error, self-correction, and continual adaptation, "saying and unsaying to a positive result" (*TP*, I, p. 102).[12]

Because "mental" inference, in contrast with merely "verbal" argumentation, is "the personal action of the ratiocinative faculty," our thinking adjusts or economizes too in relation to the whole person who reasons and the community of discourse within which thought develops. Writes Newman, "the human person is "a being of genius, passion, intellect, conscience, power"; and "man is a social being and can hardly exist without society" (*Idea*, pp. 174–75, 188).[13] Thus, the complex reality of individuals in their personal and sociohistorical particularity is always at the agent-pole of thinking's attunement, while the object of thought in all of its regional complexity provides the other pole or limit.

> Various distinct instruments, keys, or *calculi* of thought obtain, on which their ideas and arguments shape themselves respectively, and which we must use, if we would reach them. The cogitative method, as it may be called, of one man is notoriously very different from that of another; of the lawyer from that of the soldier, of the rich from that of the poor. The territory of thought is portioned out in a hundred different ways. (*US*, p. 344)

In his *Philosophical Notebook*, Newman experiments with various methodologies and subjects to see better how reason always works economically, in its ordinary as well as in its more specialized activities. He tracks reason through differential calculus, geometry, and algebra; in chemistry, optics, biology, physics, and music; and he illustrates the economizing activity of the mind with examples from everyday experience: the reflection of a face in a spoon as the spoon is moved; the answer given to a child who asks what an ox is, "The ox is the calf's uncle"; the way we make allowance for shadows in what we see; microscopes, telescopes, and, especially, kaleidoscopes; fables and parables.[14]

For Newman, the various "calculi" or notions in a given economy are held together by means of a particular "view." Walter Jost proposes the rhetorical art of *topics* as a key to understanding Newman's sense of "view." According to the rhetorical tradition dating back to antiquity, Jost emphasizes, *topics* function as discursive tools that "range across the middle ground of imagination," finding the particular circumstances, problems, and arguments that are relevant to a given concrete case, thereby providing "enabling ideas and dispositions by which we live."[15]

As Jost notes, *topics* function most often for Newman as dialectically structured pairs by means of which a view is opened out, tested and explored to its limits. Each correlation—for example, reason and authority, the notional and the real, liberalism and ultramontanism—is discovered by imagination as a limiting range or field of exploration for the formation of a view. "That two things may possibly be combined is enough [for the philosopher] to theorize and imagine the combination" (*TP*, I, p. 118).

Newman shifts from pole to pole and from one register to another, exploring the entire range of possibilities in relentless inquiry. "We can only set right one error of expression by another. By this method of antagonism we steady our minds, not so as to reach their object, but to point them in the right direction" (*TP*, I, p. 102). Thinking makes progress by being alive to its fallibility and indeterminateness: "With how many swayings to the right and to the left—with how many reverses, yet with what certainty of advance . . . part answering to part, till the whole truth 'self-balanced on its centre hung' " (*US*, p. 317). Even "mistakes carry information; for they are cognate to the truth" (*Dev.*, p. 224).[16] Newman's relatively brief discussion of the illative sense in his *Essay in Aid of a Grammar of Assent* is disproportionate to its tacit preponderance in all of his writings. Operative in *all* inferences, the illative sense is "the moral sense" when Newman shifts into the ethical register, and it becomes "conscience" when he shifts into the religious dimension of thinking. Again, when he shifts from the individual seat of judgment to that of the ecclesial community, the illative sense becomes the sense of the faithful, and conscience is translated into the principle of tradition in the Church.[17]

Just as *phronesis*, "the elastic logic of thought," has as its indispensable correlate and counterpart, the *phronema*, the "instinct" or memory buried deep within the soul, so is there "a sort of instinct, or *phronema*, deep in the bosom of the mystical body of Christ" (*Cons.*, p. 73).[18] The individual and the Church are figured by Mary, who keeps and ponders in her heart the inmost sense of God's word. "In all ages," writes Newman, "the Catholic Church is promised an instinctive perception of the Christian truth, detecting the grosser or the more insidious forms of heresy, though at a distance, as if by some subtle sense; and thus transmitting the fiat of the Gospel pure and inviolate to the latest times" (*SD*, p. 172).[19]

III. The Economy of Reason

The economy of organic growth is used by Newman to mediate his hypothesis or view of doctrinal development in the Church. The economy of the calculus is used more extensively, from the Oxford sermons to the *Grammar of Assent*, to translate the complex sense of inferential development. Perhaps the biological economy, basically Aristotelian, is more appropriate for unfolding the development of a body, the Church, while the mathematical economy, characteristically Platonic, works best to interpret the processes of reasoning. In the end, however, it would seem to be the economy of music that Newman sees as most accommodating of the energy of thought in all of its intricate, subtle, and elastic processes. In music the sensuous and the spiritual are united in that same "middle realm" where practical reason plays, and in which Newman most comfortably lived and thought. "Perhaps thought is music," he wrote (*LD*, XII, p. 9).[20]

The very idea of "economy" came to him from the Alexandrian Fathers like music, Newman recalled, striking an immediate chord within him. "The broad philosophy of Clement and Origen carried me away. . . . Some portions of their teaching, magnificent in themselves, came like music to my inward ear, as if the response to ideas, which, with little external to encourage them, I had cherished so long. These . . . spoke of the various Economies or Dispensations of the Eternal" (*Apo.*, p. 34).[21] Newman writes poetically, even mystically, of musical sounds as they are exhibited most perfectly in the economy of instrumental harmony.

> There are seven notes in the scale; make them fourteen; yet what a slender outfit for so vast an enterprise! What science brings so much out of so little? . . . yet is it possible that inexhaustible evolution and disposition of notes, so rich yet so simple, so intricate yet so regulated, so various yet so majestic, should be a mere sound, which is gone and perishes? . . . No; they have escaped from some higher sphere; they are the outpourings of eternal harmony in the medium of created sound; they are echoes from our Home. (*US*, pp. 346–47)

Music's disclosure of what lies beyond it—indeed, the disclosure of every economy—is for Newman the fruit of *phronesis*. Inquiry reaches its "breakthrough," or transcending insight, the moment the particular economy's limits are realized. In an instant the mind has circled back through remembrance, gathering up the economy's deepest sense into the plenum of an entirely new significance. In the end, all economies—that is, the entire dispensation of human reason and endeavor—are gathered up or "re-collected" in the bosom of the Father where the original sense or idea eternally abides, yet is ever made explicit and realized for us in the Word made flesh, is ever made sense of and interpreted for us by the guiding, mediating, "illative" Spirit of God, Hagia Sophia.

> To Him must be ascribed the rich endowments of the intellect, the irradiation of genius, the imagination of the poet, the sagacity of the politician, the wisdom (as Scripture calls it), which now rears and decorates the Temple, now

manifests itself in proverb or in parable. The old saws of nations, the majestic precepts of philosophy, the luminous maxims of law, the oracles of individual wisdom, the traditionary rules of truth, justice, and religion, even though imbedded in the corruption, or alloyed with the pride, of the world, betoken His original agency, and His long-suffering presence. . . . He speaks amid the incantations of Balaam, raises Samuel's spirit in the witch's cavern, prophesies of the Messias by the tongue of the Sibyl, forces Python to recognize His ministers, and baptizes by the hand of the misbeliever. . . . Even on the unseemly legends of a popular mythology He casts His shadow, and is dimly discerned in the ode or the epic, as in troubled water or in fantastic dreams. All that is good, all that is true, all that is beautiful, all that is beneficent, be it great or small, be it perfect or fragmentary, natural as well as supernatural, moral as well as material, comes from Him. (*Idea*, pp. 49–50)

Notes

1. Parmenides, *Parmenides and Empedocles*, trans. Stanley Lombardo (San Francisco: Grey Fox, 1979), frag. viii.
2. Parmenides, frag. v.
3. Plato, *Meno* 81a–e, trans. G. M. A. Grube (Indianapolis: Hackett, 1976).
4. Plato, *Republic*, especially 618c–e.
5. Aristotle, *Politics* 1253a15, trans. Benjamin Jowett, *The Basic Works of Aristotle*, ed. Richard McKeon (New York: Random House, 1941).
6. Aristotle, *Nicomachean Ethics* 1141b10, trans. W. D. Ross, in Richard McKeon, ed., *The Basic Works of Aristotle*.
7. David Wiggins, "Deliberation and Practical Reason," *Essays on Aristotle's Ethics*, ed. Amélie Oksenberg Rorty (Berkeley: University of California Press, 1980), p. 236. Books VI and VII of Aristotle's *Nichomachean Ethics* are on practical wisdom. For additional, authoritative discussions of *phronesis*, see Hans-Georg Gadamer, *Truth and Method* (New York: Seabury, 1975), pp. 280–87; Werner Jaeger, *Paideia: The Ideals of Greek Culture*, 3 vols. (New York: Oxford University Press, 1943–44); Alasdair MacIntyre, *Whose Justice? Which Rationality?* (Notre Dame, Ind.: University of Notre Dame Press, 1988), pp. 91–102; and Eric Voeglin, *Anamnesis* (Notre Dame. Ind.: University of Notre Dame Press, 1978), pp. 61–70.
8. John Henry Newman, *An Essay in Aid of a Grammar of Assent*, ed. I. T. Ker (Oxford: Clarendon Press, 1985). See also Ker's note 228 (p. 380) for references to *phronesis* in Newman's letters. In this essay, I am disregarding the minor distinctions between Newman's and Aristotle's views on *phronesis* in favor of the dominance and importance of their larger agreement.
9. John Henry Newman, *Fifteen Sermons Preached before the University of Oxford, 1826–43* (London: Rivingtons, 1890).
10. *Nichomachean Ethics* 1141b10, emphasis added.
11. The concern of this essay is, obviously, not with "the Economy," but with "economy" as a philosophical notion and methodological principle. Newman's writings on the Economy are the main subject of Robin C. Selby's work, *The Principle of Reserve in the Writings of John Henry Cardinal Newman* (Oxford:

Oxford University Press, 1975). See also Rowan Williams, "Newman's *Arians and the Question of Method in Doctrinal History*," *Newman After a Hundred Years*, ed. Ian Ker and Alan G. Hill (Oxford: Clarendon Press, 1990), pp. 263–85. On the Economy and "the sacramental principle," see Alf Härdelin, *The Tractarian Understanding of the Eucharist* (Uppsala: Almquist and Wiksells, 1965).

12. *The Theological Papers of John Henry Newman on Faith and Certainty*, ed. Hugo M. de Achaval, S.J., and J. Derek Holmes, vol. I (Oxford: Clarendon, 1976).

13. John Henry Newman, *The Idea of a University*, ed. Martin J. Svaglic (Notre Dame, Ind.: University of Notre Dame Press, 1982).

14. John Henry Newman, "On Economical Representation," *The Philosophical Notebook*, ed. Edward J. Sillem, vol. II (New York: Humanities Press, 1970), pp. 110–20.

15. Walter Jost, *Rhetorical Thought in John Henry Newman* (Columbia: University of South Carolina Press, 1989), pp. 156–57, 117, 17.

16. John Henry Newman, *An Essay on the Development of Christian Doctrine* (London: Longmans, Green, 1897).

17. See Günter Biemer's study *Newman on Tradition*, trans. Kevin Smyth (London: Burns and Oates, 1967).

18. John Henry Newman, *On Consulting the Faithful in Matters of Doctrine* (Kansas City: Sheed and Ward, 1969).

19. John Henry Newman, *Sermons Bearing on the Subjects of the Day* (London: Longmans, Green, 1869).

20. *The Letters and Diaries of John Henry Newman*, ed. Charles Stephen Dessain et al.

21. John Henry Newman, *Apologia Pro Vita Sua*, ed. David J. DeLaura (New York: Norton, 1968).

4

Philosophic Rhetoric: Newman and Heidegger

WALTER JOST

A good deal of exciting work has been done on John Henry Newman over the last few decades, but scholars have only begun to explore how Newman anticipates many of the leading themes of twentieth-century philosophy and, in particular, the hermeneutic and rhetorical thinking that derives from Kierkegaard and Heidegger. In the short compass of this essay, I should like to point out, if only in a programmatic way, how Newman and Heidegger can illuminate each other's methods of thought broadly conceived, as well as correct excesses and deficiencies in their reflections on method. Unfortunately, their own different emphases have obscured the fact that these thinkers are indeed closely allied and that their common ground is what might be called "philosophic rhetoric." After first explaining briefly what I mean by rhetoric, I will turn to Heidegger, and then to Newman, to see what we might learn.

I. From Rhetoric to Poetic

In point of fact, Heidegger understood perfectly well the connection between hermeneutics and rhetoric. In the first part of *Being and Time* (1927), taking up the question of what it means for *Dasein* (roughly, human being) to be "in" a world, Heidegger discusses the ontological importance of the fact that we cannot be in the world except in some state of mind and feeling, some mood (*Stimmung*) or other.[1] For Heidegger this is not merely a psychological observation but rather points to the essentially affective and interested nature constituting all of Dasein's knowing and doing, that is to say, its Being. And it is here, in this section of *Being and Time* on mood, that Heidegger notes that Aristotle's *Rhetoric*, and particularly Book II on the emotions, is "the first systematic hermeneutic of the everydayness of Being with one another" (*die erste systematische Hermeneutik der Alltäglichkeit des Miteinanderseins*; *BT*, pp. 178/138). Now, to call the *Rhetoric* a hermeneutic obliquely suggests that, in some ways at least, it is similar to *Being and Time* itself. Naturally, I cannot begin to suggest here all of the complex relations between rhetoric and hermeneutics,[2] but I can hope to specify certain salient aspects of rhetoric— that is, rhetoric understood now less as a discrete field and more as an intellectual function, as a *dynamis* or intellectual power or capacity in Aristotle's terms—as the link between Heidegger and Newman, as well as their point of difference.

Consider, first of all, that for Aristotle (as for Cicero, Quintilian, and much of the rhetorical tradition after them), we argue and deliberate persuasively about things that are not fixed, that "admit," as Aristotle says, "of turning out one way or another" (*Rhetoric* 1357a). Such matters we call contingent, meaning that their very definition and character depend upon the values, beliefs, and emotions of those whose problems they are. The interpretation of such matters, second, presupposes a stable and enduring yet dynamic framework of values, beliefs, laws, and practices within which, and by means of which, the rhetor seeks to strengthen the judgment of his or her audience regarding some shared public matter of concern. In other words, for Aristotle the goal of rhetoric is not winning at all costs but rather finding and communicating "good reasons" for inquiry, argument, and judgment. Third, the rhetor seeks for these good reasons by means of topics—more or less indeterminate general terms and propositions used as heuristic devices for locating all of the circumstances of a given case, those facts and beliefs that can be employed to create converging, probable arguments. Finally, rhetoric's orientation to the contingent and indeterminate, to *praxis*, is similar to that of ethical deliberation and its culminative excellence in *phronesis*. Like ethical knowledge, rhetorical topoi constitute a general set of resources for deliberation, and both sets are *incomplete* in the sense that they require application to specific and more or less unique cases. Unlike practical ethical knowledge, however, the scope of rhetoric after Aristotle (particularly in contemporary theory) has been extended to encompass the presuppositions upon which *phronesis* (or any body of knowledge) operates, and in that way transforms the art into a "philosophic rhetoric."[3]

Something like those four points is at the center of Aristotle's *Rhetoric* and the tradition following it. But they are also at the center of the early Heideggerian (and, we shall see, of the Newmanian) projects. Allow me to focus on three points: the "horizon-al" character of being-in-the-world; "being-in" as grounded in the forestructures of understanding; and both horizon and forestructures, essential to Dasein, as disclosed in, but also transcended by, the insight and language of the "poet" broadly understood. To speak of horizons, forestructures, and the poetic word is to locate Being amidst the contingent, interpretive, topical, and incomplete knowledge of the rhetorician and yet also to propose what for Heidegger is the insufficiently radical character of the rhetorician's characteristic stance.

In the first place, then, for the Heidegger of *Being and Time*, all of that which Dasein knows comes to presence within historically specific horizons of understanding. Although Heidegger worked to conceal his own historical horizons,[4] he rejected the various Enlightenment notions of an ahistorical "mirror of nature" found in Descartes, Kant, and Husserl, in favor of what I have elsewhere called the "indeterminacy of the real." In this conception the ground of human knowing and doing is neither demonstrative foundations nor subjective (Romantic) "empathy," but rather what Otto Pöggeler has called a "topology" of Being mediated by human experience with language and time. Allow me to work this out in more rhetorical terms.

To say that everydayness (*Alltäglichkeit*) is horizonal is to say that we are "thrown" or "ventured" into a situation "in which," as Heidegger himself says, "matters may turn out one way or another": not only are the consequences unpredictable, but the very meaning of the situation is indeterminate, dependent for its definition upon just those horizons of understanding within which it "is" at all.[5] By the same token, those horizons themselves are necessarily incomplete, in the sense that they, in turn, come to be only within that everydayness with respect to which they function as horizons of understanding. The understanding of which we speak, in other words, is not a rational demonstration, nor an irrational empathy, but rather a tacit interpretation whose persuasiveness is transparent, taken for granted, natural. In addition, those horizons are necessarily topical (at least in part), seeking their completion in the unique everydayness that they themselves disclose; and they are necessarily ethical and political in the broad senses of those terms, constituted by always already interpreted traditions, beliefs, and nondiscursive "practices."[6]

Heidegger expresses this rhetorical-hermeneutic situation by describing it as "ready-to-hand" and "equipmental"—terms not unlike Kenneth Burke's rhetorical description of literature as "equipment for living"—and by contrasting it to the isolated (abstract) present-to-hand. For Heidegger, we understand "as" or "in terms of" a totality of practices and uses, needs and beliefs, all of which have their integrity in temporal traditions and their receptivity in their own temporal incompleteness. Thus, we can speak of a topology—we can even say a "topics"—of Being, since all things come to be within the indeterminate, incomplete "places" of our horizons.[7] For Heidegger, to be human is to be "thrown" (*geworfen*) into existence, not as an objective *res cogitans* standing over against some value-free *res extensa*, but rather as one for whom self and world already "belong together in the single entity, Dasein."[8] That is, subject and object, knower and known, compose "*immer schon*," the engaged, interested, value-laden realities of one's "being-in." For this reason Dasein always interpretatively understands from out of its historical placement.[9] In fact, it is just our being-in-the-world in this mode of engaged, interested "everydayness" that Heidegger argues is the overlooked starting-point for the recovery of the question of Being, since Dasein is the only being for whom the question of Being arises, and since such engaged everydayness simply is Dasein's fundamental mode of being-in-the-world. Before we ourselves can understand how all of this relates to poetic speech, indeed to language generally, we need to consider the second point, namely, the forestructures of understanding.

Reflecting the temporality of its nature, Dasein's horizonal understanding is ineluctably structured in terms of an "equiprimordial" and nonsequential "past," "present," and "future" and is understood by Heidegger as a "fore-having," "fore-sight," and "fore-conception." "Fore-having" refers to the fact that Dasein is always already "thrown" into an existing equipmental and "involvement" totality—that is, a "world." Dasein always "has" an emotion-laden orientation toward this world in advance, as it were, of its moving within it—an established set of beliefs, values, practices, and so on that it uses to encounter the new. Such openness to the new comprises its own "fore-sight," that circumspective attention to the particulars of the present situation that are made salient by its fore-having and that offer themselves as candidates for relevance and importance in the situation. Said otherwise, by virtue of its past, Dasein gathers together the circumstances of the present. But such fore-having and fore-sight, in turn, make possible, *while they themselves are organized by*, a "fore-conception," a grasp of the possibilities of past and present "as" a meaningful whole. In this way, past-present-future are codependent, copresent, and mutually informing. I have never seen it remarked anywhere, but Heidegger's account of these fore-structures is in fact an anatomy, so to speak, of rhetorical invention, for in just these ways the rhetor draws on past tradition to survey his current problematic situation and the possible ways it can be meaningfully organized and argued.

But here we should pause. Rhetoric is one thing, while "poetry" and poetic "thinking" (the difference between these two is not clear)—the results of Heidegger's celebrated "turn" in the 1930s and thereafter—are another. How are we to understand Heidegger's shift from a rhetorical hermeneutics to poetry, and how, in any event, will such matters aid us in understanding Newman? In order to answer those questions, we need to appreciate Heidegger's different attitudes toward language, first in *Being and Time* and then afterwards, particularly the relation of language to Dasein and to Being itself. In lieu, however, of that special "meditative" or poetic thinking that the later Heidegger looked forward to in some unspecified future, and in lieu of that lengthier treatment that these issues obviously deserve and that others before me have undertaken, allow me to hazard two broad sets of comments.

My first set of comments begins with the simple observation that, in *Being and Time*, language performs but a small role in the author's existential analytic of Dasein. This is not to say that Heidegger's distinctions about language are unhelpful; they are not trivial, nor are they particularly new. But recall that in sections 29–33 Heidegger is laying out what he calls the constitutive "existential structures" of Dasein—those abiding factors that are presupposed in Dasein's being-in-the-world. And recall that Heidegger locates three such structures: (1) "mood" (*Stimmung*) as mentioned earlier, which here we can call that "affective concern" or state of mind within which Dasein moves and has its Being; (2) "understanding" (*Verstehen*), which we can define as the always already perspectival and implicit grasp of the possibilities of Dasein and its "world" ("interpretation" is the later explicit appropriation of understanding in action and/or language); and (3) Discourse (*Rede*), often translated as "speech" or "talk" or "telling," but which we might do better to think of as that constitutive ability to discriminate the "jointed" or "articulated" intelligibility of world, sometimes in words but sometimes nonlinguistically, in behavior and conduct.[10]

Now, language is noticeably *not* a constitutive element of Dasein, although it presently comes into focus, in section 34, as that which *inter alia* is used to make manifest and communicate the articulated intelligibility of the world (Heidegger's account of language here is avowedly fragmentary; *BT*, pp. 206/162–63). If Dasein is the concernful (mood) grasp of possibilities (understanding) of the significant (meaningful) discriminated world (Discourse), then language is the means by which Dasein manifests to itself and others, and thereby discloses for its own appropriation, the possibilities grasped in understanding. The question for us specifically, then, is how, with what presuppositions, does Heidegger discuss language, and what is the gist of his analysis when viewed from the perspective of rhetoric?

Perhaps most obviously, Heidegger's approach is in no way inimical to "rhetoric" understood (superficially) as the communication of one person to another, since the three functions he ascribes to assertions in section 33—"pointing out," predication, and communication (*BT*, pp. 196–97/ 154–55)—play similar roles in any number of rhetorical theories of language. Thus, Dasein is conceived in standard fashion as the agent of speech who expresses some kind of content and communicates it in words to another. This account does not, to be sure, rest solely on a "hypodermic needle" model of communication, in which some fixed content is linearly passed along from one person to another without alteration by form or medium (though this model does appear to apply to "apophantic" assertion as explained below). As would be expected of one so distrustful of the allegedly technologizing consciousness of the West, Heidegger avoids that social scientific approach to communication that was soon to popularize this model in America.[11] Still, his early account is standard, even common-sensical, in seeing individuals as initiators and agents of communication and its contents—an approach whose imperialistic scope, at least, he came later to disavow.

More interesting for our purposes here is Heidegger's distinction between what we can (less superficially) call "rhetorical" and "non-" or even "anti-rhetorical" uses of language, where rhetoric means the power to interpret indeterminacies persuasively. Like Wittgenstein at the time and Kenneth Burke soon after, like Newman eighty years before, Heidegger anchored all "seeing" as a "seeing-as": "That which is *explicitly* understood—has the structure of *something as something*" (*BT*, pp. 189/149). On this insight Heidegger constructs his distinction between the "hermeneutic 'as'" and the "apophantic 'as'" (*BT*, pp. 201/158), a distinction that fully extends to the expression in words of these types of "seeing." Specifically, the hermeneutic-as pertains to the concrete ready-to-hand and the apophantic-as to the abstract present-to-hand, and the difference is roughly equivalent to the following.

1. First is the *rhetorical* use of ordinary language to re-present, not only the "object" of attention (for example, Heidegger's infamous example of the hammer), but the contextual web, the equipmental totality, in which the object has its being, from the perspective of the one acting or inquiring. Such use is "rhetorical" as well as hermeneutic (interpretive) precisely because no fixed and determinate "content" preexists the representation;

"truth" in this account cannot be, therefore, a one-to-one correspondence between word or predication and fixed matter but is rather *the persuasive disclosing of one's interpretation of the object of attention in its equipmental setting*. What is required, accordingly, is a language of assertion in the ordinary sense, but also one of questions, commands, ironies, metaphors, imagery, emotion—in short, the entire range of rhetorical resources—to evoke the nuances and felt components of the real.

2. In contrast, the apophantic-as and its expression in (ideally) unequivocal and fixed categorical speech remove themselves from the felt particularities of the concrete situation in order to isolate the object from its equipmental environment, the totality of Dasein's engagements with it, in order to view or study it as an example of a (logical) type. And "truth" becomes the correspondence, the "adequation," of concept and object: "If the phenomenon of the 'as' remains covered up, and, above all, if its existential source in the hermeneutical 'as' is veiled, then Aristotle's phenomenological approach [for example] to the analysis of the λογος [logos] collapses to a superficial 'theory of judgment,' in which judgment becomes the binding or separating of representations and concepts" (*BT*, pp. 202/159).

In this latter case, to be sure, the "hypodermic" model of communication appears to fit handsomely, as if Heidegger were arguing that, even in such "scientific" (or "technological") thought and expression, no trace of the equipmental and "worldly" (and rhetorical) entanglements of Dasein are involved.[12] Yet, while Heidegger often appears to say just this, and while especially in his later work he often attributes to "science" and to the *Ge-Stell* (the "framework" or "En-framing") of technology so one-sided a view,[13] *Being and Time* at least actually makes some effort to establish a *continuity* within the evident difference between the apophantic and the hermeneutic, by speaking of "gradations" (*Zwischenstufen*) between these two "extreme opposites" (*extremen Gegen*; *BT*, pp. 201/158). This is, I believe, significant, since Heidegger's later "turn" to the poetic as something *sui generis* gains credibility only if we see the apophantic and hermeneutic on one side of a linguistic chasm and the poetic on the other.

Thus, to give an example by way of summary, as equipmental or *ready*-to-hand, an individual we meet is always constituted by the shifting relations and associations (the involvement and equipmental wholes) within which we place him or her, and any attempt to convey such a reality in words involves the fullest range of interpretative and linguistic resources. (Not surprisingly, the "poetical" is at this time also assigned to the hermeneutic expression of Dasein; *BT*, pp. 205/162). By contrast, as *present*-to-hand apophantically presented, that same individual is, to the calculative or "technological" mind, little more than the categorical predicate under which he or she is slotted.

From this perspective it should be clear that, because all hermeneutic interpretation is "horizonally" located (that is, historically relative and "negotiated"), it is appropriate to link it with the public, topical, and ethical-political persuasiveness of rhetoric. Indeed, were this the end of Heidegger's thought on the matter, we might be tempted to think of it as merely a warm-up to the more concrete analyses of the sometimes rhetorical Wittgenstein and the supremely rhetorical Kenneth Burke. But of course Heidegger did not end with these reflections, and, though in some ways his shift or "turn" (*Kehre*) marks a decisive break from his earlier study (particularly with respect to language), his thought overall evinces a deepening or radicalizing of his interests in *Being and Time*. Specifically, while he is focused there ostensibly on the Being of Dasein, Dasein itself had been selected for study as the most direct route to the study (we can say the Being) of Being itself, since only in Dasein is the question of Being an issue (*BT*, pp. 27/7). As a result, Heidegger's "turn" manifests two important components: the turn away from (or "through") the analytic of Dasein to Being; and the turn toward what one critic has termed "aestheticism," that is, "the tendency to see 'art' or 'language' or 'discourse' or 'text' as constituting the primary realm of human experience."[14] In Heidegger's case, the latter point translates into the attempt to specify the essence of "art" and "language" in the "poetic" broadly (and indeterminately) conceived, as a transcendent creative principle organizing all "authentic" meditative thinking whatever.[15] My second set of comments, therefore, briefly considers how the poetic essence of language generally, and the poet in particular, could come to perform for Heidegger such expansive roles.

Throughout his work, we have seen, Heidegger's consistent search, before and after his celebrated "turn," has been to attempt to "think Being" as he puts it, that is, to thematize the "ontological difference" between beings and Being. According to Heidegger, the entire Western tradition of metaphysics conceals this difference (and thus fails to think Being), chiefly because (1) it reduces all beings to fixed "essences" and truth to adequacy of judgments, both of which reductions are manifestly inadequate even to the existential "world," to say nothing of Being; and (2) in doing so, the tradition "freezes," as it were, its inquiry at the apophantic level of existents-as-present-to-hand and neglects to inquire how beings themselves come to "appear" as such. As we have additionally noted, however, it is Heidegger's argument, against the grain of this tradition, that, as the only being for whom the question of Being is a question—is its *own* question—

Dasein is that unique being *by virtue of which all beings come to appearance in the first place*; as Heidegger puts it, "Dasein *is its disclosedness*" (*BT*, pp. 171/133). In his excellent short summary of Heidegger's thought, and of this last insight in particular, William J. Richardson, S.J., repeats the point that Dasein is the "there" where *everything* happens, that is, comes to appearance:

> What is the fundamental structure of this [thinking of Being]? It is brought-to-pass by the nature of man conceived as ek-sistence, i.e., as endowed with the prerogative, unique among beings, of an ec-static open-ness unto the lighting-process of Being. Ek-sistence thus understood may be called the There (*Da*) of Being, because it is that domain among beings where the lighting-process takes place. Since the There comes-to-pass in a being, this privileged being is the There-being (Dasein), and, conversely, There-being must be understood always as the There of Being among beings, nothing more.[16]

Now, the problem with Heidegger's analysis in *Being and Time*, aside from his later recognition that his own conceptualizing was itself steeped in metaphysical categories,[17] is that, while it analyzed the existential structure of Dasein as "disclosure," it never problematized how that disclosure was possible or occurred. As Heidegger understood, hermeneutic interpretation itself presupposes a realm or "clearing" (*Lichtung*) within which existents can come to be known as existent, but *Being and Time* fails to make clear how this clearing comes about.[18] Negatively, to be sure, neither apophantic nor hermeneutic language is responsible for this clearing, since they can portray or communicate beings but not that Being that illuminates beings as beings. And here we arrive at the crux of nearly all of Heidegger's later writings: the disclosing of Being in the "there" of Dasein is achieved through "art," or more broadly "language," the essence of which is the "poetic" also broadly understood (and which includes "meditative" thinking), and the paradigmatic instance of which is poetry in the limited sense, the work of the poet. There are several points to highlight in Heidegger's position.

First, in his pivotal essay, "The Origin of the Work of Art" (1935–36), Heidegger gives one of his earliest and clearest accounts of the truth-value of art.[19] He begins by exploring variants of the view adumbrated previously, that representational-conceptual thought and speech miss what he calls the "thingly" aspect (*das Dinghafte*) of things—the ability of the artwork to symbolize, to bring together itself and something else—whether we think of the work of art or the things represented in the work of art. Specifically, to speak, for example, of the artwork in terms of essences and substances, and subjects and predicates, misses the existential, that is, the "feeling"-ful (*Gefuhl*) and "concern"-ful (*Stimmung*; *OWA*, pp. 25/9) dimension of things (quite in the manner of apophantic assertion). Or again, if we speak of the work solely as perceptions perceived by the senses, the thing itself "vanishes" (*verschwindet*; *OWA*, pp. 26/11).[20] Or if we speak finally of the artwork in terms of "matter" and "form," we feature the equipmentality of things (as in pragmatism, presumably) without grasping the "self-sufficient presence" (*selbstgenugsame Anwesen*; *OWA*, pp. 29/14) of the work.

These failures are significant, for Heidegger argues that all three approaches to the artwork bog down in things as things, and miss the "thingly" character of things, including how the artwork makes something else (the meaning or truth of beings) manifest. To be sure, Heidegger recognizes that, though Being is ontologically different from any other being, nevertheless, it can only be approached *by way of beings*—thus his famous example of Van Gogh's painting of the peasant shoes: "The art work lets us know what shoes are in truth" (*OWA*, pp. 35/21). We might say that what Heidegger is after may be distantly likened to a sacramental view of the world, for as he sees it, it is the job of the artist—later the poet, and all who use "language" (art, thinking, and so on) genuinely—to mediate in as full a way as possible the Being that "hails" us through the existent things of the world.[21] Through art-language the artist brings to presence the equipmentality of the world, its uses, which of course are equally present in the things on their own, but which are obscured by their very usefulness. Art "frees" equipment from this transparent utility; it brings things into manifestness for the first time: "To be a work means to set up a world" (*Werkseinheißt: eine Welt aufstellen*; *OWA*, pp. 44/30); "The work holds open the Open of the world" (*Das Werk hält das Offene der Welt offen*; *OWA*, pp. 45/31). And again, toward the end of the essay: "Language, by naming beings for the first time, first brings beings to word and to appearance. Only this naming nominates beings *to* their being *from out of* their being. Such saying is a projecting of the clearing, in which announcement is made of what it is that beings come into the Open *as*" (*OWA*, pp. 73/61).

Secondly, Heidegger seems to elevate "language" in such a way as to recapitulate the ontological difference between Being and beings as the difference between everyday language-use (presumably *both* apophantic and hermeneutic) and the "poetic": "Poetry proper is never merely a higher mode (*melos*) of everyday language. It is rather the reverse: everyday language is a forgotten and therefore used-up poem, from which there hardly resounds a call any longer."[22] Heidegger appears to posit a chasm between poetry (or the poetic) as the primordial essence of language and "ordinary" language, on the grounds that the latter may be able (more or less adequately) to convey beings, but only the former discloses Being. As early as *Being and Time*, Heidegger asserts that it is the task of philosophy properly understood to try to make sense of *primordial* truth: "The ultimate business of philosophy is to preserve *the force of the most elemental words* in which Dasein expresses itself" (*BT*, pp. 262/220). But the contrast that Heidegger is working with is that between *primordial* truth understood as "unconcealment"—in Greek, ἀλήθεια, "*a-letheia*"—and the derivative "*ontic*" truth-as-judgment, that is, of the *apophantic* present-to-hand (*BT*, pp. 261ff./218ff.).

But the "ontological difference," if it is that, between the *apophantic* and the *poetic* leads us to ask: What, then, is the ontological and truth status of hermeneutic-as-rhetorical interpretation and speech, which exists between the two? While there are, I believe, good reasons to understand the apophantic, hermeneutic-rhetorical, and poetic to reside for Heidegger *on a continuum*,[23] still it may be admitted that Heidegger's later writings consistently emphasize the removal of the poetic from the everyday and thus from the rhetorical as we have conceived it. The status of rhetoric, then, is seen as something other, and as something less, than primordial.[24] This emphasis often suggests that poetry is *not* a horizonal, historical communication but the "call" of Being;[25] that Dasein is *not* the agent of communication but the one who listens to and receives the call of Being;[26] that speech is *not* the expression of man ("equipment for living") but a gift of Being or language itself ("*Der Sprache sprichts*");[27] and that man's highest task is *not* hermeneutic-rhetorical "retrieval" (*Wiederholung*) of one's tradition (analyzed in *Being and Time*) but a passive, silent "waiting-for." On this reading of Heidegger, then, what we are left with from a rhetorical perspective is a sort of *transcendent* rhetorical *invention* in which man's inventive powers make way for the invitation to new worlds heretofore unseen, and where ethical-political communication is silenced on behalf of an ethical-political quietism.

Finally, the structure of Dasein as disclosure, and of disclosure in art and language as *aletheia*, unconcealment, is understood as the structure of Being itself. Unlike previous accounts, however, that formulate Being "theoretically" in terms of (for example) ideal Forms (Plato) or the historical unfolding of Reason (Hegel), Heidegger rather, in Otto Pöggeler's words, "determines the meaning of Being as abysmal groundless ground."[28] Less cryptically: because any disclosure or unconcealment of the Being of things (or of Dasein) is perspectival, historically placed and limited, it is necessarily also at the same time a concealment, a covering-up of what might otherwise be taken alone as the "ground" or "pure presence" of all that is. Like his romantic predecessors, Heidegger sees all existence in terms of an intense and ongoing interplay of opposing forces; but where most romantics see life as a journey through and beyond these oppositions, ending in reconciliation in some higher concept and the attainment of wisdom and self-knowledge,[29] Heidegger refuses the claim that there is anything above or "beyond" these processual tensions themselves. Where for others there is a "ground," in other words, for Heidegger there is "abyss." Walter Biemel writes:

> Truth is thus understood from the viewpoint of the openness in which both the thing and the man who comports with this thing find themselves. This openness, however, is in no way to be seen as a pure clearing in which what was in the dark before becomes gradually brighter and brighter, the eventual goal being maximum brightness. It might be understood, rather, as a medium that at each time lets certain determinate traits come to the fore so that the being is able to show itself according to the openness that has been achieved. Therefore, the openness is subject to change. . . . This change is, for Heidegger, the fundamental change of history.[30]

It is difficult to summarize this lengthy but all too sketchy overview of some of Heidegger's themes, but we might venture to describe it, from the perspective of our present interests, as a deepening exploration of language to its limits—a move from the rhetorical, to the poetical, to silence itself.[31] How, then, can we use Heidegger to illuminate Newman, and Newman, it may be, to correct and control Heidegger?

II. The Twofold Logos: Reason and Speech

I propose to extend this discussion of Aristotelian rhetoric and Heideggerian hermeneutics and poetics to Newman's epistemological interests. What I am suggesting, again, is that, first, many of Newman's most basic attitudes and concepts can be illuminated by, as well as illuminate, rhetoric and hermeneutics as we find them in Heidegger; second, that even Heidegger's radical turning to the poetic suggests a profitable line of inquiry into Newman, the tentative results of which speak, I believe—this is the third point—to the *powers and limits* of these two surprisingly similar enterprises.

Naturally—to pick up for a moment on my second point about poetics— the link between Newman and poetry is superficially easy enough to make. Not only did Newman write a considerable amount of poetry and fiction, but he produced early on a paper explicitly on poetry (1828),[32] an essay written in a Romantic-Platonic vein that eventually proved to be uncharacteristic of Newman's mature thought. More important, if only analogously, as Newman saw it, much of his mission in the Oxford Movement, for example, was to revitalize the symbolic life and ritual of his fellow Anglicans, and throughout his life, again like many of his romantic forebears, he considered "imagination" to be a central power of the mind, often for ill, it is true, but also for good.[33] Indeed, in much of his own prose, as John Holloway has shown, Newman regularly availed himself of metaphor and stylistic graces of many different kinds usually thought to belong to the poet and novelist.[34]

Still, we should recall that Newman's direct philosophical involvement with language, and even more with poetry proper, was quite limited. His primary task in life, as he understood it, was the "educational"[35] one of winning back a place for religious faith against that antireligious, antidogmatic liberalism of the age, and in this he relied in theory and practice on the discursive resources of "informal inference," on the strategies and calculations of rhetoric, and relatively little on poetry or "art" as it is usually conceived. In the fiercely argumentative context of nineteenth-century attacks on and defenses of religious faith, therefore, we might wonder what paths through Newman's thought Heidegger's insistence on the poetic can open to us.

We can begin to answer the question by taking a somewhat longer way around, through Newman's distinction between "real" and "notional" apprehension, inference and assent, and the primacy and privileges he awards to the former. In that primacy of the real we have, in fact, an insight that includes Newman with the likes of Kierkegaard, William James, and Heidegger. The evidence for this claim can be found as far back as the 1830s, in the early *Oxford University Sermons*, and in more sophisticated form in Newman's later magnum opus, *An Essay in Aid of a Grammar of Assent* (1870).[36] For Newman, all knowing begins in a real apprehension that he himself calls "interpretive" (*GA*, p. 13) and that we might call "horizonal." We might recall that, for Heidegger, to be human is to be "thrown" into a totality of involvements. Like Heidegger's "equipmental" and "involvement" wholes, Newman's "concrete" or "real" is mediated by the full experience—the traditions, values, beliefs, common sense and so on—of the knower so that "reality" emerges in what John Dewey calls an "interaction" of percept and concept, as something relative to the full life of those involved. It follows that the *expression* of the "real" in language requires, as I have argued elsewhere, an essentially rhetorical language—

emotional, polysemous, topical, and ethical-political—in which concepts do not function as rule-governed abstractions but rather as dynamic, situationally shaped and shaping attempts to persuade to a particular interpretation of the real (of the equipmental and involvement wholes), and style is not ornament but the very body of thought about the "real."[37] By contrast, abstract scientific (apophantic) thought, and its expression in logical language, cannot engage this complexity of the lived world. Now, such a rhetorical stance clearly includes for Newman both what Heidegger calls forestructures of understanding and poetic thinking in the following ways. First, all of Newman's sustained attention to what he variously called antecedent probabilities, antecedent considerations, prejudices, presumptions, principles, previous notices, and the like compose the material basis of Heidegger's "fore-having." Drawn from our past experience, and from the larger social and cultural frameworks in which we are always already thrown and have our being, those antecedent factors direct us toward and partly constitute our reality.

Such antecedent orientations, secondly, provide us with resources needed to be "circumspective"—"fore-sightful"—toward what is more or less novel and unique, by suggesting angles of approach to what is *similar* to the old and yet not mere *repetitions*-of-the-same.[38] Newman had no specific term or set of terms to describe what approximates to Heidegger's circumspective "fore-sight," but we need look no further than Newman's own practice of inquiry and argument to recognize that his celebrated openness to the evidence and arguments of his interlocutors, his willingness to start with their positions and concede many of their points, was not only a personal virtue but a rhetorical-hermeneutical requirement. Newman, in fact, was responding to the intrinsic incompleteness of antecedent probabilities and considerations, to the incompleteness of a "fore-having" which, unequal to the task of *dictating* to a contingent and indeterminate future, can nevertheless be "appropriated" and fore-sightfully "applied" to that future in ways that respect its uniqueness. In the *Grammar of Assent*, discussing the nature of ethical knowledge, Newman describes this necessary and valuable incompleteness of antecedent probabilities and openness to the new in a way that can apply to *all* concrete knowing:

> An ethical system may supply laws, general rules, guiding principles, a number of examples, suggestions, landmarks, limitations, cautions, distinctions, solutions of critical or anxious difficulties; but who is to *apply* them to a particular case? whither can we go, except to the living intellect, our own, or another's? (*GA*, pp. 228–29)[39]

Such "application" of the old to the new depends upon the ability not merely to draw on the past but to open oneself to the present and future.

Finally, we can see most clearly perhaps Heidegger's notion of "fore-conception" in Newman's repeated interest in getting what he (and other Victorians) called a "view." To be sure, to "get a view" sometimes signified reaching a final position. But more frequently and importantly for New-man, it referred to the need to organize and interpret our antecedent considerations (our fore-having) as well as the facts and arguments located, by means of them, in our circumspective openness to the new case (our fore-sight). Thus Newman could say, "It is difficult for me to take a step without what I should call *a view*,"[40] and even more tellingly, since a "view" is the organization of antecedent resources and the openness they make possible with respect to some chosen end: "If I have brought out one truth in anything I have written, I consider it to be the *importance of antecedent probability* in conviction" (*LD*, XV, p. 381). Newman's own views generally get organized as pairs of rhetorical topoi—either complementary or contra-dictory to each other—that generate, or as it were "exfoliate" into, further topoi, all serving the purpose of identifying, organizing, and interpreting the facts and arguments constituting some present, contested (or contesta-ble), concrete problem.

In summary, then, "antecedent probabilities and considerations," "open-ness," and "views" function as do Heideggerian forestructures of under-standing, as three interdependent dimensions of hermeneutic-rhetorical inquiry, argument, interpretation, and judgment in concrete, "real" ("hori-zonal") situations or cases. In this way Newman can be said to anticipate aspects of Heidegger's thought. It is true, of course, that Heidegger goes well beyond Newman, insofar as he focuses on Being and thematizes art and language (more on this presently). Yet I wish to argue that Newman indirectly anticipates even this area of Heidegger's thought, his "aestheti-cism" (as defined previously), insofar as Newman's talk (for example) about the power of music, about metaphor and analogy, about the sacramental view of the world—about "the poetic" conceived broadly—parallels Hei-degger's talk about Being and its call to the poet. A full-scale study of their similarities and their considerable differences is obviously not possible here, but my argument cuts, I believe, to the center of Newman's thought.

In his most significant statement on the nature of language ("Literature," 1859),[41] Newman subsumes what little he has to say about "literature" proper (poetry in particular) under his overriding interest in the expression of what he calls "thought." By that term he means "the ideas, feelings, views, reasonings, and other questions of the human mind" (*Idea*, p. 243) and contrasts such thought to "mere words," on the one hand (florid speech, bombast), and, on the other hand, to "things" and to "science." It is this second contrast that preoccupies him. Whereas thought and its expression are of people's "thoughts, feelings, imaginations, aspirations, . . . views of external things, [one's] judgments upon life, manners, and history" (*Idea*, p. 232), science abstracts from this personal and social realm, seeking "objective" truth, systematic study, of anything taken precisely "as" a fixed, isolated, and determinate thing, *sub specie aeternitatis*. The objects of such study "are not mere thoughts but things: they exist in themselves, not by virtue of our understanding them, not in dependence on our will, but in what is called the *nature* of things, or at least on conditions external to us" (*Idea*, p. 230).

It does not take long to recognize in this distinction between "thoughts" and "things" the same distinction—now on the linguistic level (for Newman is concerned with the *expression* of this thought)—between the "real" and the "notional" in the later *Grammar of Assent*. In truth it is a distinction operative at all levels and in all areas of Newman's writings: between the "moral" (or human) sciences and the natural sciences (for example, as he discusses them in *An Essay on the Development of Christian Doctrine*), between deductive theology and "inductive" religion (in "Christianity and Physical Science"), between deductive theology and Newman's own inductive theologizing, between "implicit" and "explicit" reason in the *Oxford University Sermons*. And this distinction is, of course, essentially the same as that between the hermeneutic and the apophantic in Heidegger. What, then, does such thought require by way of language?

What is crucial to note is that, throughout Newman's mature writings, thought and language are one. In one passage indispensable for appreciating this point, Newman writes:

> Thought and speech are inseparable from each other. Matter and expression are parts of one: style is a thinking out into language. . . . Call to mind . . . the meaning of the Greek word which expresses this special prerogative of man over the feeble intelligence of the inferior animals. It is called Logos: what does Logos mean? it stands both for *reason* and for *speech*, and it is difficult to say which it means more properly. It means both at once: why? because really they cannot be divided,—because they are in a true sense one. (*Idea*, p. 232)

In such a passage we possess, I believe, not only the yoking together of reason and speech customary to rhetorical thinkers since Isocrates, but the key to Newman's not-so-latent "linguistic turn," in which (1) the constructed nature of our knowledge and (2) the dependence of such knowledge on rhetorical speech come to the fore. Though it is not possible here to play out all of the implications of this stance, we can make three points in particular.

First, the passage points toward what is ultimately a skeptical or pessimistic attitude of Newman's regarding the ability of any language to capture the "real" or "concrete." Even language in its "full compass," as Newman puts it in "Literature," language using the extent of the rhetorical register, must fail to plumb the depths of any existent being or state of affairs (to say nothing of Being itself): "Thought is too keen and manifold, its sources are too remote and hidden, its path too personal, delicate, and circuitous, its subject-matter too various and intricate, to admit of the trammels of any language, of whatever subtlety and of whatever compass" (*GA*, p. 185).

Second, by virtue of its contextualized nature, the expression of concrete thought in rhetorically rich language (and in rhetorically flexible concepts, or "topoi") necessarily connects it with all three of Newman's key concepts earlier aligned with Heidegger's "forestructures of understanding." For example, antecedent probabilities and considerations will themselves be expressed (to the extent that they can be expressed) in a feelingful language of a particular time, place, and people, just as the choice and deployment of words will themselves be guided by such antecedents. Or again, to find language to manifest thought will require "openness" to one's situation and a perspective or "view" with respect to which one approaches one's problems. In sum, for Newman real apprehension, inference, and assent are incarnated within a rhetorical universe and language featuring action, effect, public concern and argument, the conflict of interpretations, the topicality of thought, and the suggestiveness of nuanced concepts and speech.

Third, as one would imagine, such an approach makes for a strongly rhetoricized notion of "literature" and "poetry" narrowly conceived, quite distinct from Heidegger's. It is characteristic of Newman, for example, in his essay "Christianity and Letters" (1854), to observe of Homer's poetry that "such poetry may be considered oratory also, since it has so great a power of persuasion; and the alliance between these two gifts had existed from the time that the verses of Orpheus had . . . made woods and streams and wild animals to follow him about" (*Idea*, p. 218). It is characteristic of him also to cite Shakespeare's *declamatory* powers and then to instance Cicero as an admirable example of what he has in mind regarding literature (*Idea*, pp. 235–36). In *The Idea of a University* (1853) Newman speaks of literature proper as the "Life and Remains . . . of the *natural* man" (*Idea*, pp. 193–94), and in "Literature" he calls writers the "spokesmen and prophets of the human family" (*Idea*, p. 245), emphasizing in each case the resolutely this-worldly aspect of such use of language. In "English Catholic Literature" (1854–58) Newman characteristically places his talk of literature in even more situated terms: "*National* literature is the untutored movements of the reason, imagination, passions, and affections of the natural man" (*Idea*, p. 261; emphasis added). All of Newman's stress, in short, is rhetorical, focusing on the situated, moral (or immoral) effect of literature, and we hear little even remotely like Heidegger's elevation of poetry as a "call" of Being. If anything, "poetry" for the later Newman is virtually the opposite of transcendence.

And yet, in spite of Newman's skeptical view of the ultimate powers of rhetorical language and in spite of his fairly didactic view of poetry and literature as such, throughout Newman's writings there is an unthematized aestheticism, that is, a turn to language, art, music—the "poetic" as the creative essence of human action—as the expression not only of human experience but of the transcendent. To be sure, this is not the evocation of Being we find in Heidegger; it is more usually the attempt rhetorically to communicate something about God. But it is a more hopeful attitude than a skeptical one, and it is broadly cast. Allow me to cite briefly two examples of what I mean.

1. In the fifteenth of the *Oxford University Sermons,* in the midst of speculating on the difficulty of credal formulations to express their object, Newman speaks of the evocative power of music:

> Can it be that those mysterious stirrings of heart, and keen emotions, and strange yearnings after we know not what, and awful impressions from we know not whence, should be wrought in us by what is unsubstantial, and comes and goes, and begins and ends in itself? It is not so; it cannot be. No; they have escaped from some higher sphere; they are the outpourings of eternal harmony in the medium of created sound; they are echoes from our Home.[42]

Replete as this passage is with romantic themes, it speaks to Newman's recognition and acceptance of the power of art to bring into presence the "Other."

2. In this same sermon Newman makes much the same point about symbolic language, metaphor in particular, conceding the undeniable limitations of human speech but advancing its power to evoke the transcendent. Anticipating much of the recent theorizing on the cognitivity of metaphor, Newman observes, "The metaphors by which they are signified are not

mere symbols of ideas which exist independently of them, but their meaning is *coincident and identical with the ideas*" (*US*, p. 338; emphasis added).[43]

> The various terms and figures which are used in the doctrine of the Holy
> Trinity or of the Incarnation, surely may by their combination create ideas
> which will be altogether new, though they are still of an earthly character. And
> further, when it is said that such figures convey no knowledge of the Divine
> Nature itself, beyond those figures, whatever they are, it should be considered
> whether our senses can be proved to suggest any real idea of matter. . . . Let,
> then, the Catholic dogmas, as such, be freely admitted to convey no true idea
> of Almighty God, but only an earthly one, gained from earthly figures. . . .
> Still, there may be a certain correspondence between the idea, though earthly,
> and its heavenly archetype, such, that idea belongs to the archetype . . . as
> being the nearest approach to it which our present state allows. (*US*, pp. 339–
> 40)

The same sentiments are repeated thirty years later in one of Newman's
notebooks:

> Such is the true answer, it seems to me, which is made to those who object
> that the doctrine of the Holy Trinity deals with figures, and with proofs and
> inferences from figures. I reply that, from the nature of the case, all our
> language about almighty God, so far as it is affirmative, is analogical and
> figurative. We can only speak of Him, whom we reason about but have not
> seen, in terms of our experience. When we reflect on Him and put into words
> our thoughts about Him, we are forced to transfer to a new meaning ready
> made words, which primarily belong to objects of time and place. We are
> aware, while we do so, that they are inadequate, but we have the alternative
> of doing so, or doing nothing at all.[44]

Our question is whether or not Heidegger's turn to the poetic allows
us to see something similar in Newman, and the answer can be at least
partly in the affirmative. Even in Newman, who from a distance can
appear so classically conservative and reactionary, modernist and even
postmodernist consciousness has emerged, though it remains in and of
itself unexplored. For Newman thought and language are two sides of the
same phenomenon, and one must turn to essentially artistic and "poetic"
devices—music, metaphor, imagery—to figure forth the transcendent.

Yet to say as much is to raise significant differences between Newman
and Heidegger, which I can only touch on here. Most obviously, Newman
is never concerned with Being as such, but rather with beings and with
God, for him the Supreme Being (and for Heidegger yet one more "onto-
theo-logical" formulation rooted in traditional metaphysics). Thus, in the

Apologia he cites "my mistrust of the reality of material phenomena, and [my] thought of two and two only absolute and luminously self-evident beings, myself and my Creator."[45] This is just the sort of religiously romantic metaphysics Heidegger sought to escape.

Secondly, for Newman there is no ontological divide between the "real"-as-rhetorical and the poetic. On the one hand, Newman certainly departs from the romantic elevation of "General Thoughts" (Wordsworth) above and beyond contingency and change, and, on the other hand, he resists Heidegger's neoromantic severance of poetry from the everyday, political-ethical strife and conflict that always surrounds the poet. For Newman what we have broadly called the "poetic" after Heidegger is resolutely rhetorical in four ways.

1. All talk of the powers and limits of poetic language, such as metaphor and analogy, is consistently tied to the realities of historical audiences and their "antecedent considerations" and to historical change (as in the *Development of Christian Doctrine*). To Newman ideas are never "General Thoughts" but are time-bound, "living," above all imperfect human attempts to formulate what will never finally formulate: "In a higher world it is otherwise, but here below to live is to change, and to be perfect is to have changed often."[46]

2. For this reason the language of Scripture and its interpretations, to give an example, function as topoi, as rhetorical resources of specific communities, resisting reification in "final" form.

3. Newman ever sees religious faith and its evidence and expression (to give another of his central concerns) in terms of persuasion.

4. Newman consistently uses an approach to language and communication that features the personal expression of the speaker in his unique situation, the agent of communication, and the give-and-take with an audience's presuppositions and beliefs in dialogue or conversation. In this was he is far closer to Gadamer than Heidegger.

Finally, a third difference between Newman and Heidegger is that, for Newman, the "notional" can stand as a salutary corrective to the exaggerations of the "real" and the "poetic," just as the latter can invigorate and control the former. To give an example, Newman frequently noted how theology acts as a brake on religious superstition and excess. This attitude is diametrically opposed to Heidegger so long as we stress the differences between the apophantic and hermeneutic and the gap between both of these and the poetic. For Heidegger apophantic assertions are in no position to correct anything having to do with Being as such, and it is perhaps this difference that most deserves future examination.

What might we conclude from this brief comparison between two thinkers from whom we might not otherwise have been inclined to expect many similarities? By way of closing, I suggest that each is a challenge and a corrective to the other. Heidegger can be said to radicalize much that is present in Newman. Heidegger's aesthetic turn in his quest for Being is possible in part because the "ready-to-hand" and its hermeneutic expression have already defeated an objectivist view of the world, and in this Heidegger extends and elaborates Newman's own philosophic stance, though not in ways Newman could always approve. Though Newman would have sympathized, I believe, with Heidegger's turn to the poetic, still the onto-logical rift that Heidegger often seems to posit between the ordinary and the poetic risks serious obfuscation. Much of the criticism of Heidegger has focused on that point, although much of the criticism is itself superficial, claiming against the evidence, for example, that poetry for Heidegger is not referential. Perhaps one of Heidegger's staunchest defenders on this point, Fred Dallmayr, best indicates some of Heidegger's value:

> As I have tried to indicate, *homo loquens* is not merely a language-user—employing symbols to convey information or to express intentions—but is simultaneously maintained or sustained by language. Accordingly, the *bios politikos* cannot be preserved or recaptured through cognitive and practical-moral endeavors alone; in Arendtian vocabulary, the activities of "knowing" and "willing" must be undergirded and permeated by a more purposeless thoughtfulness or poetic thinking—which is the genuine abode of human freedom.[47]

At the same time, reading Newman helps us to restrain Heidegger from his own apparently irresistible urge to mystify and obfuscate. Newman's rhetorical emphasis prevents us from getting superstitious about what it is language can do, and his emphasis on time, history, audience, and commu-nity help us to return Heidegger's "topics" of Being to the "earth" as we know it. To be sure, no synthesis is possible between these thinkers: in most ways Newman's informal and programmatic studies are the very antithesis to Heidegger's rigorous professorial "thought," but, more im-portant, their interests and results are too widely divergent. And yet we have within each of these thinkers, I believe, a quite *similar* attitude toward existence and truth that will help us to remain "open" to their own call to fuller being. In Heidegger "truth" is an ongoing interplay between concealment and unconcealment, and mankind can and should accept both the instability of this fact and its infinite opportunities for creativity and growth. In Newman truth only emerges slowly out of what he calls a "principle of antagonism" by which "we steady our minds, not so as to reach their object, but to point them in the right direction." Individually and together, Newman and Heidegger conceal and reveal truth, and by using them as cooperative antagonists, we ourselves can further their paths "by saying and unsaying, to a positive result" (*TP*, I, p. 102).[48]

Notes

1. *Being and Time*, trans. John Macquarrie and Edward Robinson (New York: Harper and Row, 1962), sec. 29 (pp. 172/134ff.). Further citations appear parenthetically in the text as *BT*; the first number following the citation refers to the pages of the English translation; the second refers to the pagination of the German editions (Max Niemeyer Verlag).

2. It might be helpful to address at least briefly the question of the relation between rhetoric and hermeneutics. Several possibilities offer themselves. First, like philosopher Paul Ricoeur, who is putatively following Aristotle ("Rhetoric-Poetics-Hermeneutics," in Michel Meyer, ed., *From Metaphysics to Rhetoric* [Dordrecht: Kluwer Academic Publishers, 1989], pp. 137–49), we can choose to treat rhetoric, poetics, and hermeneutics as discrete fields of inquiry seeking similar and even overlapping but finally distinct aims. Or second, like rhetorician Michael Hyde, who is putatively following Gadamer ("Rhetorically, Man Dwells: On the Making-Known Function of Discourse," *Communication* 7 [1983]: pp. 201–20), we can view rhetoric and hermeneutics as supplements of each other. On this reading hermeneutics would deal with understanding and rhetoric with the "making known" function—the articulation—of understanding in interpretation. Or third, like philosopher Ernesto Grassi, who is putatively following Heidegger (*Heidegger and the Question of Renaissance Humanism* [Binghamton, N.Y.: Center for Medieval and Renaissance Studies, 1983]), we can collapse rhetoric and hermeneutics into each other under the rubric of nonmetaphysical, nontraditional philosophy: as rhetorical, all philosophy, including hermeneutic phenomenology, can be seen to be in the business of offering interpretations of interpretation; and all interpretations, philosophical or not, can be understood to be rhetorical. This last strategy, a kind of rhetoricizing of all understanding, is essentially the strategy of Kenneth Burke, and—according to Grassi and others—of many of the Renaissance humanists.

   My own view is pluralistically "aspectual" or "perspectival" in a way that I think Newman would approve. All three of the foregoing choices are, I believe, "aspects" of the truth and as such are variously useful, depending upon the kinds of discriminations, the kinds of knowledge, one desires. At the same time, however, the third option is the one that I see as the most fruitful for my purposes, and I therefore adopt it here. For examples of such an approach, see Michael Heim, "Philosophy as Ultimate Rhetoric," *Southern Journal of Philosophy* 19 (Summer 1989): pp. 181–95, and Calvin O. Schrag, *Communicative Praxis and the Space of Subjectivity* (Bloomington: University of Indiana Press, 1986).

3. On this concept (closely akin to the third option discussed in the preceding note), see Harold Zyskind, "A Case Study in Philosophic Rhetoric: Theodore Roosevelt," *Philosophy and Rhetoric* 1 (1968): pp. 230–31: "In broad terms applicable to thought and action alike, this is an operational rhetoric: a rhetoric because the end is to do and to say what has impact on the minds of men, and operational because the 'what' is conceived in terms of effect achieved by altering or adjusting to actual circumstances . . . in brief, a philosophic rhetoric." See also Richard McKeon, *Rhetoric: Essays in Invention and Discovery*, edited with an introduction by Mark Backman (Woodbridge, Conn.: Ox Bow Press, 1987).

4. See Allan Megill, *Prophets of Extremity: Nietzsche, Heidegger, Foucault, Derrida* (Berkeley: University of California Press, 1985), pp. 21, 115.

5. Martin Heidegger, "What Are Poets For?" in *Poetry, Language, Thought*, translation and introduction by Albert Hofstadter (New York: Harper and Row, 1971), p. 103. This collection of essays will be cited hereafter as *PLT*.

6. On the ultimately nonpropositional nature of our horizonal "background," see Hubert L. Dreyfus, *Being-in-the-World: A Commentary on Being and Time, Division I* (Cambridge: MIT Press, 1991), pp. 4–5, 10–12, passim; Mark Johnson, *The Body in the Mind* (Chicago: University of Chicago Press, 1987); and Ludwig Wittgenstein, *On Certainty*, ed. G. E. M. Anscombe and G. H. von Wright, trans. Denis Paul and G. E. M. Anscombe (New York: Harper and Row, 1969), passim.

7. Such a use of the term *topos* exceeds Aristotle's own application of it but not his grasp of its function. On Heidegger's topics or topology of Being, see Otto Pöggeler, "Metaphysics and the Topology of Being in Heidegger," in Thomas Sheehan, ed., *Heidegger: The Man and the Thinker* (Chicago: Precedent Publishing Company, 1981), pp. 173–85; and "Heidegger's Topology of Being," in Joseph Kocklemans, ed., *On Heidegger and Language* (Evanston, Ill.: Northwestern University Press, 1972), pp. 107–46. See also Michael Heim, "Philosophy as Ultimate Rhetoric."

8. Martin Heidegger, *Basic Problems of Phenomenology* (Bloomington: Indiana University Press, 1982), p. 297.

9. See *BT*, pp. 188–89/148: "In interpretation, understanding does not become something different. It becomes itself. . . . [Interpretation] is . . . the working-out of possibilities projected in understanding."

10. Thus Dreyfus, *Being-in-the-World*, p. 215, cites the example of our being able to "tell the time" or "tell the difference between different types of nails" without any intervention of words or even cognition.

11. See, for example, the "information theory" approach of Claude Shannon and Warren Weaver, *The Mathematical Theory of Communication* (Urbana: University of Illinois Press, 1949).

12. This is the thrust of the article by Robert E. Innis, "Heidegger's Model of Subjectivity: A Polanyian Critique," in Thomas Sheehan, ed., *Heidegger: The Man and the Thinker*, pp. 117–30.

13. See Martin Heidegger, "The Question Concerning Technology," in *The Ques-*

tion Concerning Technology and Other Essays (New York: Harper and Row, 1977), passim.

14. Megill, *Prophets of Extremity*, p. 2.

15. See Kocklemans, ed., "Preface," *On Heidegger and Language*, p. xiii: "Thus by *language* he [Heidegger] means everything by which *mankind* brings to light *in an articulated way*, regardless of whether it is done concretely, by means of the sentences of a language in the narrow sense of the term, or through a work of art, a social or religious institution, and so on."

16. William J. Richardson, S.J., "Heidegger's Way Through Phenomenology to the Thinking of Being," in Thomas Sheehan, ed., *Heidegger: The Man and the Thinker* (Chicago: Precedent Publishing, 1981), p. 82. See Michael E. Zimmerman, *Eclipse of the Self* (Athens: Ohio University Press, 1981), p. 23: "For common sense, it is outrageous to say that Being 'is' only so long as Dasein exists, for this seems to make 'reality' dependent on humanity. Yet Heidegger is no subjective idealist. The totality of natural beings persists whether or not Dasein exists. Without Dasein, however, these beings would not be manifest; all would be dark, hidden, unknown." See also, for example, *BT*, pp. 171/133 and pp. 269/226: "Before there was any Dasein, there was no truth; nor will there be any after Dasein is no more. For in such a case truth as disclosedness, uncovering, and uncoveredness, *cannot* be."

17. See, for example, "Letter on Humanism" [1946–47], in Martin Heidegger, *Basic Writings*, edited with introductions by David Farrell Krell (New York: Harper and Row, 1977), p. 208; and "A Dialogue on Language" [1953–54], in Martin Heidegger, *On the Way to Language* (New York: Harper and Row, 1971), p. 8.

18. *BT*, pp. 171/133: "To say that it [Dasein] is illuminated [*erleuchtet*] means that *as* Being-in-the-world it is cleared [*gelichtet*] in itself, not through any other entity, but in such a way that it *is* itself the clearing."

19. "The Origin of the Work of Art," in *PLT*, pp. 17–87. In German, "Der Ursprung des Kunstwerkes," in *Holzwege. Gesamtausgabe* (Frankfurt am Main: Vittorio Klostermann, 1977), vol. V, pp. 1–74. Hereafter cited in the text as *OWA*, with English and German pagination from the editions noted.

20. See *BT*, pp. 207/164: "It requires a very artificial and complicated frame of mind to 'hear' [for example] a 'pure noise.'"

21. It might be helpful in a small way to contrast this to the similar romantic views of a Wordsworth or Coleridge, on three counts: (1) where the latter posit a unifying principle (or ground) to reconcile all worldly tensions, Heidegger sees an "*Abgrund*" (*BT*, pp. 194/152) or "abyss," that is, Being as an ongoing tension of concealment and unconcealment without any "higher" unity; (2) whereas a Wordsworth, if not Coleridge, saw himself (for example in *The Prelude*) as a sage whose "high argument" it was to express the mystery of Nature and the mind of man, Heidegger eschewed all such sense of a special calling; and (3) whereas Wordsworth (and other romantics like Schelling) had the optimism and confidence to feel that "now" was the time for revelations, Heidegger considers the poverty of the times to have postponed such wisdom to some indefinite future. For an excellent overview, see M. H. Abrams,

Natural Supernaturalism (New York: W. W. Norton, 1971); and for an excellent critique, see Jerome J. McGann, *The Romantic Ideology* (Chicago: University of Chicago Press, 1983). For an analysis of a postromantic account of poetry and Being similar to Heidegger's, see my " 'It wasn't, yet it was': Naming Being in Frost's 'West-Running Brook,' " forthcoming.

22. "Language," in *PLT*, p. 208.

23. As George Steiner, himself a student of Heidegger, puts this point in *Real Presences* (Chicago: University of Chicago Press, 1989), p. 168: "Language as a medium, the interplay between social constraints and personal invention, the relations between artist, patron, and public, are radically social. They embody class and commerce. It is abstruse nonsense to try and experience Blake without knowledge, however imperfect, of the complicated solitudes within social class which fuel the inspired idiosyncrasies of his artisanship and vision." See note 25 below.

24. Heidegger has been attacked on these grounds by a variety of critics. See, for example, Allan Megill, *Prophets of Extremity*, p. 180, who speaks of Heidegger's "utopian idealism"; J. Glenn Gray, "Poets and Thinkers," in Edward N. Lee and Maurice Mandelbaum, eds., *Phenomenology and Existentialism* (Baltimore: Johns Hopkins University Press, 1967), pp. 109–11; Richard J. Bernstein, "Heidegger on Humanism," in *Philosophical Profiles* (Philadelphia: University of Pennsylvania Press, 1986). For a view of Heidegger that essentially accepts the idea of an ontological rift between, for example, metaphor as conceived by theorists like Ricoeur and Black, and Heidegger's notion of poetry, but that defends the poetic side of this rift as *helpful* to pragmatic political thinking, see Fred Dallmayr, *Language and Politics* (Notre Dame, Ind.: University of Notre Dame Press, 1984), pp. 174–92.

25. See, for example, Martin Heidegger, "Holderlin and the Essence of Poetry," in *Existence and Being*, introduction and analysis by Werner Brock (Washington, D.C.: Regnery Gateway, 1988), p. 283: "Poetry is the foundation which supports history, and therefore it is not a mere appearance of culture, and absolutely not the mere 'expression' of a 'culture-soul' "; but see also p. 289: "The essence of poetry belongs to a determined time. But not in such a way that it merely conforms to this time, as to one which is already in existence. It is that Holderlin, in the act of establishing the essence of poetry, first determines a new time"; and ". . . *Poetically Man Dwells.* . . . " in *PLT*, p. 219: "The poet counters this misgiving [i.e., that poetic dwelling 'flies fantastically above the earth'] by saying expressly that poetic dwelling is a dwelling 'on this earth.' " However, even when Heidegger attempts to bring poetry back to earth, as he says, the "everyday" is curiously transformed *back* into the poetical, the primordial "out" of time.

26. Thus, in the essay "Language" (1950) in *PLT*, p. 192, Heidegger resists the standard account of communication as expression, presentation of the real, and an activity of man.

27. "Language," in *PLT*, p. 190.

28. "Heidegger's Topology of Being," in Kocklemans, ed., *On Heidegger and Language*, p. 122.

29. For a succinct summary, see Abrams, *Natural Supernaturalism*, p. 255.

30. Walter Biemel, "Poetry and Language in Heidegger," in Kocklemans, ed., *On Heidegger and Language*, p. 74.

31. On this last point, see Gerald Bruns, *Heidegger's Estrangements: Language, Truth and Poetry in the Later Writings* (New Haven: Yale University Press, 1989).

32. John Henry Newman, "Poetry, with Reference to Aristotle's Poetics," in *Essays Critical and Historical*, 2 vols. (London: Longmans, Green, 1919), vol. I, pp. 1–29.

33. See particularly the essay in this volume by M. Jamie Ferreira.

34. John Holloway, *The Victorian Sage* (New York: W. W. Norton, 1965).

35. See *John Henry Newman: Autobiographical Writings*, ed. Henry Tristram (New York: Sheed and Ward, 1957), p. 259: "Now from first to last, education . . . has been my line."

36. John Henry Newman, *An Essay in Aid of a Grammar of Assent*, edited with introduction and notes by I. T. Ker (Oxford: Clarendon Press, 1985).

37. Walter Jost, *Rhetorical Thought in John Henry Newman* (Columbia: University of South Carolina Press, 1989), pp. 145ff.

38. See Thomas Langan, "Panel Discussion," in Kocklemans, ed., *On Heidegger and Language*, p. 271: "If . . . an utterance is only a repetition of what has been said before, it is small talk (*Gerade*), or in the region of merely calculative thinking."

39. For a similar approach, see Bernard Lonergan, *Insight* (New York: Harper and Row, 1958), p. 175, for whom "common sense" operates along the lines of the Newmanian "concrete" or "real" knowing explored here: "Common sense, unlike the sciences, is a specialization in the particular and concrete. It is common without being general, for it consists in a set of insights that remains incomplete, until there is added at least one further insight into the situation in hand; and, once that situation has passed, the added insight is no longer relevant, so that common sense at once reverts to its normal state of incompleteness."

40. John Henry Newman, *The Letters and Diaries of John Henry Newman*, ed. Charles Stephen Dessain et al., vol. XIX, p. 26.

41. John Henry Newman, "Literature," in *The Idea of a University*, edited with introduction and notes by I. T. Ker (Oxford: Clarendon Press, 1976), pp. 226–45.

42. *Newman's University Sermons: Fifteen Sermons Preached before the University of Oxford, 1826–43*, with introductory essays by D. M. Mackinnon and J. D. Holmes (London: S.P.C.K. 1970), p. 347.

43. To cite only two examples: George Lakoff and Mark Johnson, *Metaphors We Live By* (Chicago: University of Chicago Press, 1980); and George Lakoff and Mark Turner, *More Than Cool Reason: A Field Guide to Poetic Metaphor* (Chicago: University of Chicago Press, 1989).

44. John Henry Newman, *The Theological Papers of John Henry Newman on Faith and Certainty*, vol. I, partly prepared for publication by Hugo M. de Achaval, selected and edited by J. Derek Holmes, with a note of introduction by Charles Stephen Dessain (Oxford: Clarendon Press, 1976), p. 102.

45. John Henry Newman, *Apologia Pro Vita Sua*, edited by David J. DeLaura (New York: W. W. Norton, 1968), p. 16.
46. John Henry Newman, *An Essay on the Development of Christian Doctrine* (Westminster, Md.: Christian Classics, 1968), p. 40.
47. Dallmayr, *Language and Politics*, p. 191.
48. A shorter version of this essay was presented at the Saint Louis University Newman Centenary Conference, 1990.

5

Theory of Discourse: Newman and Ricoeur

ALAN J. CROWLEY

Walter Jost's *Rhetorical Thought in John Henry Newman*[1] advances the thesis that "Newman's intellectual stance is thoroughly and persistently rhetorical," by which Jost means that the key to an interdisciplinary integration of Newman's thought is to see Newman's rhetoric as not an incidental matter of style but rather as an enactment of an understanding of mind to which all other aspects of his theological, epistemological, and metaphysical theory answer. As Jost surveys the effect of such an understanding of Newman's rhetoric on his views of the human sciences, he advances a perspective on Newman's theory of liberal education as "a pluralistic rhetoric of invention requiring the ongoing discovery and formulation of a developing truth understood from the perspective of concrete existence" (p. 204).

In support of Jost's thesis, and to develop it more thoroughly in the context of contemporary literary theory and its relation to the problem of pluralism versus value, or tradition versus diversity, in liberal education, I would use Paul Ricoeur's vocabulary for a theory of interpretation of texts as a schema to envision Newman's rhetoric as an active balancing of the opposition of epistemology and metaphysics in what Ricoeur terms "the hermeneutical circle," a consideration of undecidability vis-à-vis the interpretation of texts that demands of the writer and reader the assertion of personal commitment to transform language into an exploratory tool for engagement with the text of the world.

In an essay entitled "The Model of the Text" from his *Hermeneutics and the Human Sciences*,[2] Ricoeur makes a claim for the personal, moral ends of reading and writing as that perspective from which analysis moves toward understanding, breaking the hermeneutical circle of distance from and belonging to meaning in language.

> The paradigmatic character of text-interpretation must be applied to this ultimate implication. This means that the conditions of an authentic appropriation, as they are displayed in relation to texts, are themselves paradigmatic. Therefore we are not allowed to exclude the final act of personal commitment from the whole of objective and explanatory procedures which mediate it.[3]

Ricoeur's theory of interpretation of texts points a way out of the impasse of viewing the text only as a structural entity by reconceiving it as a work, as an action done by a message giver that is a structured totality intended to deliver a message. By conceiving the text as a "work," he can reconceive distanciation, his term for the various aporiae experienced by reader and writer between word and act, word and meaning, word and world, as a problem of the personal giving and appropriation of meaning, while still maintaining attention to the structured representation of the text.

To consider Newman and the reading of his work as a performative rhetoric in studies like Jost's, I would argue that Newman's method in all of his works, explained and brought under closest scrutiny in the *Grammar of Assent*,[4] can be construed as a discovering of personal commitment, under the rubric of real assent, as the only architectonic by which a coherent resolution of the problem of distance from and belonging to meaning can be resolved. Using Ricoeur's criteria, Newman's work can be seen to assert that acts of thinking, writing, and interpreting are living acts of personal commitment and are yet ones that require the intellectual discipline of treating objects of inquiry, whether they be text or world, as themselves structured totalities susceptible of rational analysis and the test of concrete experience.

My previous study of Newman has argued for Newman's participation in an understanding of language rooted in the romantic tradition.[5] My reading of the *Grammar* as influenced by the poetic theory of the English romantic poets, an influence reinterpreted through the contemporary critique of deconstruction, is that Newman enacts the rhetorical method of the romantic poet in a "re-teaching" of the reader how to read the text. His rhetorical enactment of the problems of reading calls to attention the need for the assertion of personal commitment to the act of assenting to the meaningfulness of all propositions, including our acts of interpreting the world around us. Using essential insight from the contemporary analysis of deconstruction, I have claimed that Newman's rhetorical performance of the *Grammar* teaches the reader that he or she must rewrite the text, in a process of assenting to propositions and living out that assent in an inscription of one's life on the world. I have further argued that the rhetoric of "teaching the reader how to read" is a method by which both critical consciousness of language and personal appropriation of meaning can be preserved in the process of discourse.

The intriguing problem of using the terminology of deconstruction to understand Newman's achievement is the radical critique of subjectivity deconstruction can make of a writer like Newman, particularly of his idea of conscience, which deconstruction would identify as a self-constructed deception on his part.[6] Newman's subjectivity, Derrida would argue in the same manner he would deconstruct the writing of Rousseau, is revealed in a logocentric discourse, a discourse which predetermines inquiry by its implication in a "metaphysics of presence."[7] This metaphysics of presence involves the implicit establishment of an idea of the self that stands as a "transcendent signified," an unassailable self-justifying ground of being that precludes reflection on the personal and cultural influences on one's discourse.

Walter Jost investigates a similar criticism of Newman, one that he clarifies by placing the question of rhetorical solipsism in the *Grammar* in the context of the hermeneutical debate between Hans Georg Gadamer and Jürgen Habermas. In the debate Gadamer's claims for a historicized tradition of discourse that enables interpretation opposes Habermas's emphasis on reflection, the epistemological analysis of discourse that exposes the prejudices inherent in any tradition. Paul Ricoeur has named this opposition between reflection and interpretation as one between a hermeneutics of suspicion and a hermeneutics of belief. John Thompson, editor and translator of Ricoeur's *Hermeneutics and the Human Sciences*, describes this opposition as being between seeing the hermeneutic project as a "demystification of disguise" and as a "restoration of a message." The strategy of the first mode is to be suspicious, to be skeptical toward the given, to distrust symbol as a dissimulation of the real. As Thompson explains, the latter mode of restoration, analogous to our concept of belonging, requires faith in the messenger and message, the disposition to listen, the disposition to respect symbol as revelation of the sacred. Jost's rhetorical investigation of Newman acknowledges the challenge posed by contemporary literary theory's emphasis on the epistemological, reflective, or "suspicious" mode, when he applies Habermas's critique of Gadamer to Newman's work:

Newman is also open to the charge that his elevation of the importance of "antecedent probabilities and considerations" in informal inference is intrinsically conservative and even reactionary, as if the problem of coming-to-truth were merely a matter of returning-to-truths-already-established and making further inferences from them. Such a view may be said to enshrine entrenched ideologies (political, psychological, religious). . . . I have tried to indicate at least that this objection, while an important one, does not do justice to the power of "suspicion", "critique" and "reflection" in Newman's "rhetorical philosophy, . . . The rhetorical use of antecedent considerations derived from one's fiduciary framework, of tradition, or paradigm, of social practice, does not preclude reflection; on the contrary it makes reflection possible since it makes tradition answerable to ongoing testing. To be sure, this does not explain, how reflection escapes co-option by ideologies.[8]

My argument is that in the same manner that Ricoeur's theory of discourse attempts to mediate between Gadamer and Habermas's views of the hermeneutical project, Ricoeur can also help us understand the "how" that Jost would seek concerning the way Newman's rhetorical method escapes co-option by ideologies. My central thesis is that Newman's pluralism inheres in the balance his rhetoric achieves within the hermeneutical dialectic of structure and assertion that Ricoeur's discourse theory insists on.

In moving my search for a literary theory, or poetics, in Newman's work from the categories of romantic theory, through those of deconstruction, to those of Ricoeur's engagement with the hermeneutical tradition, I am first acknowledging significant limits on the usefulness of deconstruction for enabling a reading of Newman. It is not so much that I think that deconstruction's nihilistic roots and radically iconoclastic method is formally and substantively unsympathetic to Newman's thought. In fact, I have found deconstruction quite a useful tool to help discover the scope of Newman's achievement. My quarrel with deconstruction is that it is not capable of going as far as it would like, as far as it claims it can, in freeing discourse from both its self-inflicted and culturally influenced over-determinations. Like that of many of the postmodern and poststructuralist discourses of contemporary literary theory, the search for intellectual authenticity that motivates deconstruction's methodology of perpetual critique and infinite series of textual unravelings does not sufficiently succeed in its goal of demythologization and demystification. While meaning in the text, the idea of a text itself, is destroyed, in a discourse modeled after the figure of Nietzsche's hammer in *The Twilight of Idols*,[9] ideology finally eludes the hammer of analysis because the instrument itself is idolized, with no one empowered to name the forces that wield it.

It is, then, in their ability to "out-reflect" the iconoclasts that I read Ricoeur, and Newman, as appropriating a methodology that begins where deconstruction cannot go. And that despite, really because of, their concerns with the recovery of meaning, of historical tradition, and of value, they are able to be more successful than the methodologies of radical skepticism at preserving pluralism and freedom in intellectual discourse. Pure analysis by itself is not sufficiently iconoclastic to preserve intellectual freedom. Newman and Ricoeur share the insight that one must assert and assent to a provisional position of value in order to even begin interpretive acts and to project the experience of being on which inquiry is directed. To attempt intellectual freedom by making an idol of skepticism is both to lose the efficacy of discourse and to compromise one's ability to judge, as judgment occurs in choosing between competing claims to power and value that will always be part of culture, whether or not we decide to name them texts.

I discover Ricoeur and Newman pursuing a balance between icon building and icon breaking in their understanding that discursive acts exist in a mutual relation of will and structure. Their acknowledgment that willed acts of assent and understanding depend on meaning residing in structural articulation that can be separated from the intention of author or interpreter provides a view of how meaning can be built on structure, regulated by reason, and yet always remain responsible to the fact that it is oriented by personal desire and belief. As I try to develop this reading of Ricoeur as a lens through which to read Newman, I wish to show in method and concept that one of the central problems in liberal education, that of how we can maintain a pluralistic, diverse, and free consideration of knowledge while allowing for the assertion and exploration of value and belief, is of a parallel structure to this balance of assent and critique that is enacted in both by the interpretation theory of Ricoeur and the *Grammar of Assent* of Newman.

To establish the methodology to balance reflection and interpretation, Ricoeur must first point the way out of the impasse of viewing the text only as a structural entity by reconceiving it as a work, as an action done by a message giver that is a structured totality intended to deliver a message. In this way Ricoeur sees a sentence, a poem, or a paragraph as different in kind from a word, a phoneme, a morpheme, or any other minimalist linguistic unit. By conceiving the text as a "work," he can reconceive distanciation as a problem of the personal giving and appropriation of meaning, while still maintaining attention not on the ephemeral discourses of intention or reception, but on the structured representation of the text.

Appropriation remains the concept for the actualization of the meaning as addressed to somebody. Potentially a text is addressed to anyone who can read. Actually it is addressed to me, hic et nunc. Interpretation is completed as appropriation when reading yields something like an event, an event of discourse, which is an event in the present moment. As appropriation, interpretation becomes an event.[10]

Ricoeur's fundamental distinction between event and meaning enables him to distinguish the utterer from the utterance but at the same time recognize that each is indispensable in constituting language as discourse. Language is intended, a willed projection of the self that becomes communicable when put into the structure of a sentence, a structure that can be analyzed, judged, and built upon. For Ricoeur, the act of reading is also an event that demands an assertion of intention by the reader, who recreates an event of commitment or projection of self by building on the structure that has preserved a logical context for words that otherwise might be indeterminate because of the distance of time and culture between reader and author. Just as the "saying" of a sentence, or the authorship of writing, is an event, so is the interpretation of a text an event. As Newman argues that real assent is the only sufficient mode of knowledge for deciding on the truth of propositions, so Ricoeur's argument that reading is an event putting the reader's will on the line provides a way out of the undecidable hermeneutical circle, which is broken by a person's assertion of will in committing his life to the value of his interpretation.[11] Like Newman's understanding of the developmental power of ideas, Ricoeur's balance of will and structure involves a progressive projection of structure in time, enabling a sequence promising assent in structure, yet, because assent establishes itself in a grammar susceptible to the discourse of reason and experience, can grow through its successive reformulations.

To demonstrate the analytical function of this commitment to interpretation, Ricoeur parallels his displacement of the idea of language as code to language as act, when he displaces the idea of metaphor as trope to one of metaphor as heuristic. Analyzing metaphor as model or heuristic focuses the problem of interpreting metaphor as a function of predication and transformation, not a function of identification. His tension theory of metaphor helps us to understand how grammatical structure works within speech to enable interpretation. Metaphor works in the tension created between the literal absurdity preserved in the sentence's grammar (his example is the figure "Mantle of sorrow": how does one wear sorrow like a mantle?) and the real emotion or idea that motivated the event of saying by the author. The heuristic function of metaphor requires that the reader work to synthesize the distance between the literal but structured absurdity and the inaccessible private experience the author wishes to express. The reader essentially must produce (write) a story that can resolve the contradiction. Hence, Ricoeur can claim that the referential dimension of a metaphor is its heuristic value, in the creation of a heuristic fiction that enables discovery, so that metaphor works as a kind of scientific model.

This concept of scientific model is not so much a simile as it is the precise analogue of Ricoeur's interpretive method to scientific method. Thomas Kuhn's work on the structure of scientific revolutions,[12] for instance, shares a lexicon with Ricoeur's hermeneutics, in which the "models" and "paradigms" of scientific method function heuristically in relation to the world, as Ricoeur's "model" or "heuristic fiction" operates on written texts. Perhaps the most interesting word shared by Kuhn, Ricoeur, and Newman, for that matter, is the concept of "commitment," establishing the rubric of willed assent as both final and efficient cause in the act of knowing. Witness Kuhn's exposition of the idea:

> Normal science . . . often suppresses fundamental novelties because they are necessarily subversive of its basic commitments. Nevertheless, so long as those commitments retain an element of the arbitrary, the very nature of normal research ensures that novelty shall not be suppressed for very long. Sometimes a normal problem, one that ought to be solvable by known rules and procedures, resists the reiterated onslaught of the ablest members of the group within whose competence it falls . . . when . . . the profession can no longer evade anomalies that subvert the existing tradition of scientific practice—then begin the extraordinary investigations that lead the profession at last to a new set of commitments, a new basis for the practice of science. The extraordinary episodes to which the shift of professional commitments occurs are the ones known in this essay as scientific revolutions. They are the tradition shattering complements to the tradition-bound activity of normal science.[13]

This last concept is key and returns us to the promised discussion of how the analysis of ideology is better served by a process of assent and figuring of value rather than through acts of hyperanalysis. Ricoeur's comparison of the function of poetic language to that of scientific language rests on an understanding quite common today concerning the value of scientific models in the analysis of physical experience. Ricoeur points out that a scientific model enables one to cut through inadequate descriptions of reality while yet testing the model against reality itself:

> In scientific language, a model is essentially a heuristic procedure that serves to overthrow an inadequate interpretation and to open the way to a new and more adequate one.

> . . . poetic language has in common with scientific language that it only reaches reality through a detour that serves to deny our ordinary vision and the language we normally use to describe it. In doing this both poetic language and scientific language aim at a reality more real than appearances. . . . In the same way that the literal sense has to be left behind so that the metaphorical sense can emerge, so the literal reference must collapse so that the heuristic fiction can work its redescription of reality.
>
> In the case of metaphor, this redescription is guided by the interplay between differences and resemblances that gives rise to the tension at the level of the utterance. It is precisely from this tensive apprehension that a new vision of reality springs forth, which ordinary vision resists because it is attached to the ordinary use of words. The eclipse of the objective, manipulable world thus makes way for the revelation of a new dimension of reality and truth.[14]

Newman's project in the *Grammar of Assent*, conceived as a rhetorical performance of philosophy, can be read as enacting this same kind of heuristic process, first showing the inadequacy of the seemingly objective, manipulable world of notions, or notional apprehensions, thereby making room within language for a new dimension of reality and truth, the revealed reality of his tradition of faith. The parallel between Ricoeur's hermeneutics and Newman's *Grammar of Assent* is in their common rejection of the sufficiency of analysis (explanation for Ricoeur, doubt for Newman) for breaking open language and experience to have freedom from ideology or ignorance. For Ricoeur, a heuristic fiction must function as a model with which to engage language and experience. For Newman, the illative sense enables assent to propositions that can lead to propositional reasoning, which in turn can explore the possibilities of knowledge. Consider how Newman rejects radical doubt out of hand as itself bound by its incapacity to acknowledge its own vested interests:

> There are writers who seem to have gone far beyond this reasonable skepticism, laying down as a general proposition that we have no right in philosophy to make any assumptions whatever, and that we ought to begin with a universal doubt. This, however, is of all assumptions the greatest, and to forbid assumptions universally is to forbid the one in particular. Doubt itself is a positive state, and implies a definite habit of mind, and thereby necessarily involves a system of principles and doctrines all its own. Again, if nothing is to be assumed, what is our very process of reasoning but an assumption . . . the very sense of pleasure and pain, which is one of the most intimate portions of ourselves, inevitably translates itself into intellectual assumptions. (*GA*, p. 294)

I would argue that here Newman anticipates a postmodern understanding of the case of language, a Heideggerian (or even Derridean) understanding of how the nature of reason itself can predetermine discourse.[15] But given such knowledge, Newman does not propose a radical abandonment of discourse as inherently inauthentic but advocates a provisional assertion of believed, or received, or intuited value from which to begin the process of learning:

> Of the two I would rather have to maintain that we ought to begin with believing everything that is offered to our acceptance, than that it is our duty to doubt everything. The former, indeed, seems the true way of learning. In that case, we soon discover and discard what is contradictory to itself; and error always having some portion of truth in it, and the truth having a reality which error has not, we may expect, then when there is an honest purpose and fair talents, we shall somehow make our way forward, the error falling off from the mind, and the truth developing and occupying it.
>
> This I conceive to be the real method of reasoning in concrete matters. . . . First, it does not supersede the logical form of inference, but is one and the same with it; only it is no longer an abstraction, but carried out into the realities of life, its premises being instinct with the substance and the momentum of that mass of probabilities, which acting upon each other in correction and confirmation, carry it home indefinitely to the individual case, which is its original scope. (*GA*, p. 294)

This heuristic scope of belief corresponds to the rhetoric of invention that Jost argues characterizes Newman's writing. I have described this rhetoric as "teaching the reader how to read" in which Newman creates "a self-conscious process of assent in the reader which involves a re-writing of the text's meaning, a re-writing which imitates a process of extending ideas into a linguistic exploration of their implications."[16] This rhetoric can be understood in terms of Ricoeur's concepts of heuristic model and of language as willed act. The limits of the hermeneutics of suspicion or "explanation" in Ricoeur's theory of interpretation parallel Newman's rejection of a rhetoric of doubt. Ricoeur's emphasis on the necessity of commitment to interpretation to break the undecidable hermeneutical circle parallels Newman's insistence on real assent, the willed commitment to live out interpretation, as the only way to transcend the undecidable impasse between assertion and argument. As such, and insofar as this poetics of assent of Newman is the epistemology that can be seen to underwrite the concept of the development of ideas that holds together the sequence of Newman's major writings, from *An Essay on the Development of Christian Doctrine*, to the *Apologia*'s figuring of the writing of his own life, to the idea of liberal education figured in the *Idea of a University*, the rhetorical understanding of Newman can be employed to reframe contemporary problems concerning the relation of textual interpretation to the aims of liberal education.

The modern educator in a pluralistic society is exceedingly reluctant to make a moral demand in the structure of the classroom, and the history of modern literary criticism reveals a similar retreat from the moral dimensions of reading and writing. Any teacher's syllabus is always a provisional narrative of meaning, never neutral, to which the teacher makes a moral assent. Contemporary literary and philosophical critiques expose the naïveté or self-serving disingenuousness of not acknowledging such an impact on the minds and lives of students. But rather than embrace the techniques of hypercriticism and "negative dialectics" of many contemporary schools to prevent moral imperialism in the classroom, I would argue that a reappropriation of Newman's methodology reveals that pluralism and freedom will best be preserved by the positive structurings of "things hoped for" in the lives of students, structurings that can be examined and reformed by a developing poetics of liberal education.

In relating Ricoeur's theory of interpretation to Newman's and then to the construction of the liberal arts curriculum, my primary emphasis is that the question of liberal education must be approached through a willingness to name and create the ends of education in terms of personal commitment or assent to an ongoing construction of the world. In order not to be oppressed by the ideological constructions of others, it is not enough to deconstruct all modes of thought. One must counter the force of ideology by continually reconstructing meaning as a self-conscious naming of the values on which one's living and thinking coheres. This involves a process of breaking the idols by naming one's gods.

Newman's and Ricoeur's ways of resolving the opposition of epistemology and ontology through the focus on the interpretation of the text, and on interpretation of action in the world as text, creates a focus of inquiry limited by the text's existence as object. Rather than absolutize philosophical or historical narratives as the construction of cores, canons, or traditions, rather than exclude the historical, absolutize the present, ignore the diverse, an educator in the liberal arts tradition values the self-conscious participation of students in the dynamic of investigating the mode of saying, the purpose of saying, the context of saying, and the results of saying. The liberal arts tradition is not a pantheon of ideals that must be imparted in its purest form but an intensification of the awareness between the reception and the construction of a world through reading, writing, and talking about texts. Our goal is to combine freedom and value by helping students to become their own best teachers as they "figure forth" value and critique in a self-conscious appropriation of the means and ends of their own education.

Notes

1. Walter Jost, *Rhetorical Thought in John Henry Newman* (Columbia: University of South Carolina Press, 1989).
2. Paul Ricoeur, *Hermeneutics and the Human Sciences*, ed. John B. Thompson (New York: Cambridge University Press, 1981).
3. Ricoeur, *Hermeneutics*, pp. 220–21.
4. John Henry Newman, *An Essay in Aid of a Grammar of Assent*, introduction by Nicholas Lash (South Bend, Ind.: University of Notre Dame Press, 1979).
5. This reading of Newman is carried out in my dissertation's study of the relation of Newman's rhetoric to that of Samuel Taylor Coleridge's religious discourse and of the relation of Coleridge's rhetoric to the poetics of English romanticism as framed by his collaboration and conflict with William Wordsworth; see Alan J. Crowley, "Ezekiel's Wheels: Reading the Performance of Assent in Newman and Coleridge," (Ph.D. diss., Boston College, 1989), and "The Performance of the *Grammar*: Newman's Exercise in Reading and Assent," *Renascence* 43 (Fall 1990/Winter 1991): pp. 137–58.
6. Such a critique of Newman has been made in Michael Ryan's "Grammatology of Assent: The Question of Autobiography in Cardinal Newman's *Apologia Pro Vita Sua*," *Georgia Review* 21 (Fall 1977): especially p. 680.
7. Derrida's critique of Rousseau contextualizes a work like the *Confessions* in a tradition of romantic "self-writing," which obscures its own reliance on an idea of God as primary author, or primary writer of a pure, transcendent discourse; Jacques Derrida, *Of Grammatology* (Baltimore: Johns Hopkins University Press, 1974).
8. Jost, *Rhetorical Thought*, p. 106.
9. Friedrich Nietzsche, "The Hammer Speaks," in *The Twilight of Idols: How to Philosophize with a Hammer*" (1889), trans. R. J. Hollingdale (Baltimore: Penguin Books, 1968).
10. Paul Ricoeur, *Interpretation Theory: Discourse and the Surplus of Meaning* (Fort Worth: Texas Christian University Press, 1976), p. 92.
11. Hence, the orienting power of liberal education comes not only from its empowering of critical analysis or structural explanation but also from when, through the capacity to enact one's assent in writing or living, reading becomes an event of assent.
12. Thomas Kuhn, *The Structure of Scientific Revolutions* (Chicago: University of Chicago Press, 1962).
13. Kuhn, *The Structure of Scientific Revolutions*, pp. 5–6.
14. Ricoeur, *Interpretation Theory*, pp. 66–68.
15. The distinction between a "modern" and "postmodern" understanding of the

case of language might be simplified by the suggestion that the romantic or modernist question of language is whether language is adequate. The postmodern question is whether language is everything, or better, whether it is all there is.

16. Crowley, "The Performance of the *Grammar*," p. 137.

Part 3

Education

6

Christianity and Culture in Newman's Idea of a University

James C. Livingston

Over the past two millennia, the relationship between Christianity and culture has been fiercely debated within the Christian community. Tertullian, Aquinas, Luther, F. D. Maurice, Tolstoy, to name but a few, have taken radically opposing, irreconcilable positions on this vital question.

At the present time there is a significant debate under way among Christian theologians that goes to the heart of the matter. It is a debate between theologians who, taking their lead from a Tillich or a Rahner or a Lonergan, propose some form of a "theology of correlation." Their critics, called "postliberal," look to Karl Barth and the work of the Yale theologian Hans Frei. They are suspicious of "theologies of correlation" as having capitulated to Enlightenment modernity, thereby failing to preserve the particularity, the distinctive identity, of the Christian message.

The theologians of correlation, on the other hand, claim that it is intrinsic to a Christian *monotheistic* theology to seek to relate the substance of the Christian message to the ever-changing human cultural situation if Christianity is to make legitimate claim to a genuine universality and to avoid retreating into a cozy, intratextual form of life, a covert, though not acknowledged, cultural-linguistic relativism.

David Tracy, a leading Roman Catholic theologian of correlation, insists that "the fundamental loyalty of the theologian *qua* theologian is to that morality of scientific knowledge which he shares with his colleagues, the philosophers, historians, and social scientists. No more than they, can he allow his own—or his tradition's—beliefs to serve as warrant for his arguments."[1] The Christian, in other words, cannot appeal *solely* to authority, for example, to a so-called plain reading of the Bible or to the magisterium.

95

Tracy is sensitive to the charge that the correlationists are in danger of forfeiting Christian distinctiveness through suspect appeals to universality. He therefore begins theologically with the intratextual particularness of what he calls the "Christian Classic" or classics. Every text comes out of a particular tradition. But a "classic" text addresses profound and perennial human questions: it has, by definition, a broad, if not universal, resonance in human experience that transcends the community that produced it. You do not need to be a Russian to feel the "shock of recognition" in reading Dostoyevski.

The postliberal theologians are, on the contrary, suspicious of appeals to general experience—especially the experience of "modern" persons with all their Enlightenment assumptions about what constitutes the rational and the real. They propose to begin not with the assumptions of the modern world but with that "strange new world within the Bible." They say, in effect, let the Bible or the Christian tradition define what is real and true. We must fit our human assumptions into *that* framework, not the other way around. Experience, including religious experience, is always culture-specific, since it emerges out of particular linguistic formulations. It is from that conviction that the theologian George Lindbeck proposes a cultural-linguistic model of Christian theology in which doctrines function primarily "as communally authoritative rules of discourse, attitude, and action."[2] The Christian religion, or Buddhism for that matter, is a distinctive cultural-linguistic world-scheme, a kind of Wittgensteinian "form of life," incommensurate with other forms of life. The Bible has authority because the Christian community has so authorized it.

It appears that we are observing a new chapter in the old debate initiated by Tertullian and the Greek Fathers: What has Jerusalem to do with Athens, the church with the academy? Our question here is, What does Newman have to say on this matter? Can Newman instruct us? Or is his position finally anachronistic, "impossible" in our present situation?

In an attempt to answer this question, I want to explore Newman's exhaustive handling of the theme in *The Idea of a University*. And in so doing, I will contrast Newman's conclusion of the matter with the position of Matthew Arnold, his younger contemporary, and one who was, in so many ways, profoundly influenced by and in accord with Newman's subtle and complex ideas and sentiments. The comparison can, I believe, illuminate this crucial issue in a strikingly contemporary way. Matthew Arnold frequently declared or alluded to Newman's influence on his own intellectual development and on his role as a cultural critic. I need only briefly sketch this influence for our purposes here; it is detailed in masterful fashion by David DeLaura in his *Hebrew and Hellene in Victorian England: Newman, Arnold, Pater*.[3]

Speaking of Matthew Arnold's Oxford days, his brother Tom Arnold commented that "Newman['s] *teaching* never made an impression on him" (emphasis added).[4] Later evidence from Matthew's letters and essays is more complex. While writing *Culture and Anarchy*, he confessed that Newman's influence was "mixed up with all that is most essential in what I do and say."[5] In 1871, during his preoccupation with *Literature and Dogma*, Arnold gave what may appear to be a significant qualification. He wrote that Newman's influence upon him "consists in a general disposition of mind *rather than in a particular set of ideas*" (emphasis added).[6] But then, again, a few months later, he wrote to Newman confessing that he (Newman) was one of the four persons from whom he had especially "learnt habits, methods, *ruling ideas*, which are constantly with me" (emphasis added).[7]

The "ruling ideas" have been enumerated by DeLaura. They include the role of the cultural elite or remnant; the place of conscience and the affections in the life of reason; a skepticism with regard to the efficacy of metaphysical propositions and argument; the importance of edification as well as critical analysis, and the function of reserve and economy in religious discourse and apology; an abhorrence of positivistic rationalism and middle-class Philistinism; and perhaps above all, the qualities of disinterestedness and urbanity.

I would urge, however, that it was Arnold's deep preoccupation with those ideas and sentiments—the qualities that so attracted him to the *Apologia* and *The Idea of a University* and that were so critical in the development of Arnold's own cultural ideal—*that ultimately deepened the gulf between the two men on the question of Christianity and culture*.

In his Emerson lecture given in America in 1883, Arnold took the occasion to reminisce about Newman after almost a half century. He commented that Newman's "words and thoughts . . . were a religious music—subtle, sweet, mournful." Newman continued to haunt Arnold's memory as "that spiritual apparition." But despite this, Arnold concludes that, "[Newman] has adopted, for the doubts and difficulties which beset men's minds today, a solution which to speak frankly, is impossible." It represented, for Arnold, "the last enchantments of the Middle Age."[8]

Almost twenty years earlier in 1865, in the first of his lectures on Celtic literature, Arnold spoke of Newman's discourses on *The Idea of a University*. They were, he said, the championing "of a cause more interesting than prosperous,—one of those causes which please noble spirits, but do not please destiny, which have Cato's adherence, but not Heaven's."[9] This is a striking comment from one who so often is associated with Newman's idea of liberal learning.

I believe that the key to the deep opposition between Arnold and Newman is not found in Arnold's alleged move to a post-Christian ethical humanism, as some writers on Arnold either assert or imply. To so identify Arnold's intellectual and spiritual pilgrimage is wholly to minimize or misread his religious prose writings of the 1870s. David DeLaura is certainly correct when he says that "Arnold's developing vision of human perfection . . . extended along an unbroken continuum into social and religious problems."[10] That is to say, religion, and specifically Christianity, demands to be seen as deeply infused in Arnold's *developing* understanding of culture. And it is here that we see the emergence of Arnold's very modern, essentially dialectical, grasp of Christianity's relationship to culture.

It is simply too neat to see Arnold's rejection of Newman's "dogmatic" solution as signaling an either/or choice between commitment to a particular conception of what constitutes orthodox Christianity and a post-Christian, humanistic, cultural idea. Arnold did not believe that the future lay either with Medieval theology or some neoreligion of humanity. In a revealing letter of March 1881, Arnold declares that the future lies neither "with any of the orthodox religions, or with any of the neo-religious developments which propose themselves to supersede them." He suggests that the reason is that each, in its own way, gives to religion alone "too large and absorbing a place in human life; man," he continues, now "feels himself to be a more various and richly endowed animal than the old religious theory of human life allowed."[11] This statement requires comment, for it touches on the crucial difference between Arnold and Newman on the mutual bearing of Christianity and culture on one another.

It is during the decade or so following the mid-1860s that Arnold's essentially correlational and dialectical understanding of the reciprocation between Christianity and culture is first perceived. The balance and the tension between what Arnold now calls "the scientific passion" and "the passion for doing good," between "reason and the will of God," is, for example, present throughout *Culture and Anarchy* (1869). "Hebraism and Hellenism," Arnold insists, "are, neither of them, *the* law of human development, as their admirers are prone to make them; they are, each of them *contributors* to human development."[12] Different times and circumstances will, of course, mean that one will, necessarily, be called upon and will preponderate over the other. And, inevitably, the one falsely will presume itself to be *the* law of human perfection. The barbarians that overran the Roman empire needed "sweetness and light," not "fire and strength." Can it be said, Arnold asks, that Mr. Murphy, the Birmingham evangelical preacher—or, we might add, the televangelist Jimmy Swaggart—needs the "fire and strength" of Hebraism and not the light of Hellenism?

Arnold used the term *criticism* to denote culture, or "the free play of the mind." He saw culture not only in dialectical tension with religion but also in religion's service. First, it serves religion as the instrument of intellectual discrimination: in "justness of perception," in "critical tact," in a "sense of history." Culture is required for the right reading of religious texts. Second, culture or criticism explores what Arnold called the "want of correspondence" between the religious sources of our life and the modern spirit. It involves the dialectic between "the hermeneutics of suspicion" and "the hermeneutics of retrieval or recovery." It often implies the deconstruction or the demythologization of the antique and literal reading—which may be a debasement of the spiritual meaning. Criticism, of course, may preempt traditional, and agreeably conventional, readings of the ancient formulation, but it may also, for example, disclose meanings in Jesus' *logia* lost on the literalizing reporters and redactors. If space allowed, I would enumerate other important hermeneutical tasks of criticism elaborated by Arnold.

The point I wish to stress is that for Arnold religion does not merely subserve culture, nor is it simply a matter of the autonomy of criticism or culture, or of culture's dominance of religion, or of religion's sway over culture. Their relation is reciprocal and interdependent, one of tension and counterpoise. But a religion that turns its back on criticism, on culture, is in Arnold's estimation ultimately under the sentence of death.

Here I want only to suggest that what Arnold attempts to do is to conjoin the experiential, correlationist *and* the cultural-linguistic models of theological interpretation and understanding—that is, unite communal text and wider experience. As Nicholas Sagovsky has argued,[13] Arnold is committed to the biblical text, constantly quoting key words and phrases whose meanings are apparent only by their use in the biblical context. It is within the text, for example, that the meaning of the essential word "righteousness" is made known. The "Power that makes for righteousness" is revealed *to Israel*, and it is the Bible, and not in other books or with other teachers, where this "Power not ourselves" and its "righteousness" are incomparably revealed. Arnold constantly appeals to the biblical text to ground and substantiate his claims to authentic experience. But he also appeals to and finds in culture and in ordinary experience analogies to vindicate his claims regarding the distinctive authority of the biblical text and its necessary reconception. It is this dialectic of the imagination that represents Arnold's position.

It is, however, to Newman's proposal that we now must turn. *The Idea of a University* is Newman's fullest statement on the Christianity and culture question. And for all of its brilliant defense of the exigency of a liberal education, the critical later discourses of the book, especially, are a sustained exposition of the ways secular, humanistic knowledge has come to threaten and to supersede religion. Newman's unease about the university in Dublin hearkens back to some of the same concerns that preoccupied him in Oxford in the 1830s regarding liberalism and mixed education. But this worry is now couched in the urbanity of his paean of praise for the educated gentleman and liberal learning.

In the early discourses of the *Idea*, one notes that Newman does not appeal to authority and that his defense of theology as an intellectual discipline makes no essential reference to its moral role in education. He defends theology as a science whose absence from the curriculum would not only be prejudicial but would allow other sciences to intrude themselves into an area beyond their competence. However, as Peter Dale makes clear,[14] Newman's defense of theology entails dispensing with the Aristotelian duality between the physical and the moral or human sciences. Rather, Newman sees the circle of the sciences as subdivided into three segments: the physical, moral, and theological. He considers theological science to be a distinct way of knowing, an intellectual discipline, taking its place within the circle of the sciences. It is, he says, the science of Divine Agency. It is this idea of the "unity" of knowledge and the "circle of the sciences" that is a central theme of the first four discourses; it would appear critical to Newman's idea of the university.

The sciences proceed, Newman tells us, in terms of a division of labor, but that division is itself a mere abstraction. It is not, he insists, "a literal separation into parts." "It is not," then, "every science which equally, nor any one which fully, enlightens the mind in the knowledge of things, as they are, or bring home to it the external object on which it wishes to gaze" (*Idea*, p. 54).[15]

The several sciences that make up the circle—and Newman is arguing for the inclusion of theology among these sciences—have to do with "one and the same subject matter viewed under its various aspects;" they are "true results, as far as they go, yet at the same time separate and partial" (*Idea*, p. 54). By reason of their incompleteness, each science needs the external assistance of the others, and "they are able to afford it to each other, by reason, first, of their independence in themselves, and then of their connection in their subject-matter." Newman—with theology principally in mind—further insists that the sciences, "viewed together . . . approximate to a representation or subjective reflection of the objective truth, as nearly as possible to the human mind, which advances toward the accurate apprehension of that object, in proportion to the number of sciences which it has mastered; and which, when certain sciences are away, in such a case has but a defective apprehension" (*Idea*, p. 54).

Here Newman *appears* to stand for a real interdependent circle of the sciences, one which entails a genuinely dialectical view of theology and the other sciences. Theology is not immune. "Not even theology," he writes,

> so far as it is relative to us, or is the Science of Religion, do I exclude from the law to which every mental exercise is subject, viz., from that imperfection, which ever must attend the abstract, when it would determine the concrete. . . . For even the teaching of the Catholic Church, in certain of its aspects, that is, its religious teaching, is variously influenced by the other sciences. (*Idea*, p. 58)

Newman cites the fact that the Church's "interpretations of prophecy are directly affected by the issues of history; its comments upon Scripture by the conclusions of the astronomer and the geologist" (*Idea*, p. 58).

The genuinely interdependent circle of the sciences is insured, Newman insists, "because the subject-matter of knowledge is intimately united in itself, as being the acts and work of the Creator. . . . [They] demand comparison and adjustment. They complete, correct, and balance each other" (*Idea*, p. 94). In expansive terms, Newman proceeds to describe the university as "an assemblage of learned men, zealous for their own sciences, and rivals of each other . . . brought, by familiar intercourse and for the sake of intellectual peace, *to adjust together the claims and relations of their respective subjects of investigation*" (*Idea*, p. 95; emphasis added).

Newman's defense of the place of theology in the university is compelling. It is consistent with his notion of the circle, of the rivalry and adjustment of the sciences. Quite reasonably he observes: "If you drop any science out of the circle of knowledge, you cannot keep its place vacant for it; that science is forgotten; the other sciences close up, or, in other words, they exceed their proper bounds, and intrude where they have no right" (*Idea*, pp. 73–74).

Notice, however, that in the final clause a different note is struck—one that introduces ambiguities, indeed, I believe, an important shift in emphasis. Newman speaks especially of each science's "proper bounds."

But he now also speaks of Science (with a capital S) in distinction from Theology, as if Theology were not one of the sciences in the circle. And he speaks of Science's proclivity to reach beyond its proper boundaries. Theology must, then, be "present to defend its own *boundaries and to hinder the encroachment* . . . and if Theology is not allowed to occupy its own *territory*, adjacent sciences . . . will take possession of it" (*Idea*, p. 91).

Here, I believe, Newman backs off from his dialectical vision of the circle and retreats into a form of intratextual or, perhaps better, intrascientific language-game. He appears to envision the sciences as various habits "of *viewing* . . . the objects which sense conveys to the mind, of throwing them into system and uniting and stamping them with *one form*" (*Idea*, p. 75). We get the impression here, with his attention to boundaries, territories, forms of knowing, and encroachments, that Newman conceives of the various sciences (say, history, geology, ethics, theology) as having their own irrelative logic and criteria of the rational and the real.

In his irenic discussion of "Christianity and Scientific Investigation," Newman speaks of the breadth and capaciousness of the liberally educated mind, one feature of which is the ability to perceive that "principles, recognized as incommensurable, may be safely antagonistic" (*Idea*, p. 371). "Safely antagonistic," because, in the last analysis, the sciences are not dialectically interdependent but are disparate and incommensurate.

Here I speak with some hesitation, since Newman's words strike me as equivocal. I sense, however, that Newman does not appreciate that the imperialistic tendency of the natural and social sciences also has been an irresistible propensity of the science of theology. In all the illustrations Newman here offers of scientific encroachment and arrogation, never does he allude to the sorry tale of the science of theology's relation to the other sciences. In his reference to Lord Bacon's rebuke against the concepts of the sciences giving "all things else a *tincture* according to them *utterly untrue and improper*" (*Idea*, p. 77), no mention is made of theology's hermeneutical distortions.

The direction of Newman's thinking in the *Idea* is signaled by the shift that takes place from his use of the image of the circle of the sciences to that of a hierarchic principle and from the discussion of the intellectual role of theology to its moral function in the university. Both moves, I think, are crucial. Having argued persuasively for the inclusion of theology in the circle of the sciences, Newman now proceeds to seize on the fact that all knowing is subjective, is culture-specific, as we say. Every subject takes its color, its drift, its bias from the whole system to which it belongs. Hence, it is imperative that instruction be consciously guided by the principle of a system—in Newman's words, a clear, distinct "form." Newman writes:

> [A science] is the grasp of many things brought together in one, and hence is its power. . . . Well, then, this is how Catholics act towards the Sciences taken all together; *we view them as one and give them an idea*. . . . *Imagine a science of sciences*, and you have attained the true notion of the scope of a University. We consider that all things mount up to a whole, *that there is an order and precedence and harmony in the branches of knowledge* one with another as well as one by one, and that to destroy that structure is as unphilosophical in a course of education, as it is unscientific in the separate portions of it. (*Idea*, p. 423; emphasis added)

Earlier, Newman spoke of this as the role of Philosophy, "the science of sciences," or "the philosophical habit of mind." It was, in the early discourses, "the comprehension of the bearings of one science on another, and the use of each to each, *and the location, and limitation and adjustment and due appreciation of them all*" (*Idea*, p. 57; emphasis added). Now, however, he speaks of a particular *idea* or *form* or *center* that informs all the sciences. And in some passages in the later discourses this turns out to be Theology, which now is not a science, that is, a subjective reflection and approximation to objective truth; rather, it is the articulation in doctrinal form of Divine Revelation.

As early as the original fifth discourse[16] Newman asserts that, though theology be one branch of knowledge "and does not interfere with the real freedom of any secular science," it is, nevertheless, "the highest indeed, and the widest" (*Idea*, p. 428). Newman then writes: "We form and fix the sciences in a circle and a system, and give them a *centre* and an *aim*, instead of letting them wander up and down in a hopeless confusion. In other words, to use scholastic language, we give the various pursuits and objects, on which the intellect is employed a *form*" (*Idea*, pp. 423–24). Is it not true that for Newman there should, in the last analysis, be no philosophic form, "a science of sciences," but that of Catholic doctrine? "A University," Newman writes, "which refuses to profess the Catholic Creed is . . . hostile both to the Church and to Philosophy" (*Idea*, p. 434). In his communication to the Irish Bishops offering his model of university organization, Newman writes:

> As all academic instruction must be in harmony with the Principles of the Catholic Religion, the Professors will be bound not only not to teach anything contrary to religion but to take advantage of the occasion the subjects they

treat of may offer, *to point out that Religion is the basis of Science*, and to inculcate the law of Religion and its duties [emphasis added].[17]

If we recognize the exigencies of the Dublin assignment, Newman's claim for a Catholic form of education is not surprising. But it has, I believe, larger implications for his understanding of the relationship between Christianity and culture. His talk of an architectonic principle informing the sciences exposes the issue at stake. I believe that Newman's long and deep unease about the humanistic and naturalistic sciences causes him to slacken the dialectical interdependence of the circle. A significant psychological process follows. It is conspicuous in the changed tone of the later discourses. Discourse Nine on the "Duties of the Church Towards Knowledge" is often scornful, ironic, and dismissive. Its final appeal is to the imposition of Church authority. Newman's fear is that Liberal knowledge will throw Catholic teachings into the background, recast them, tune them, "as it were, to a different key." It is "Intellectualism" versus "the principle of dogmatism" (*Idea*, pp. 186–87), and Liberal Knowledge inevitably collides with the dogmatic principle.

But is Newman's deep and not wholly unjustified fear his real position? How does his unease translate into actual intellectual practice? Here, it strikes me, Newman is highly ambivalent and equivocal. In the discourse on "Christianity and Scientific Investigation," not only the tone but the substantive position *appears*, once again, altered. There is no longer mention of a *centre*, or *aim*, or *form*. The geologist, historian, or astronomer "should be free, independent, unshackled in his movements . . . he should be allowed and enabled without impediment, to fix his mind . . . exclusively on his special object" (*Idea*, p. 379). But, lest he be misunderstood, Newman proceeds. Regarding such theological opinions that concern, for example, geocentrism or the authorship of a sacred writing, Newman insists that there is no "direct intrusion into the province of religion, or of a teacher of Science actually laying down the law *in a matter of Religion*." Newman insists that the historian, for example, must not propose his historical conclusions as "the formal interpretation of the sacred text," but only as a scientific judgment, "leaving it to those whom it really concerns to compare it with Scripture" (*Idea*, p. 380).

My question is, does this not call for an impossible duality in the mind of the believing scientist, who may well be a Church theologian? There is a deep psychological conflict here. Newman, it would appear, calls for a suspension that requires adherence to a form of "double truth," since he appeals to the principle that the discoveries of the scientist cannot in principle be "contradictory to anything really revealed," but neither can he directly intrude into the sphere of religion. But, as history has taught us, the notion of what is "really revealed" often changes or, if one prefers, is radically reconceived—very often because of advances in the sciences. In the meantime, Newman counsels "religious writers . . . geologists, historians, to go on quietly . . . in their own respective lines . . . in a generous confidence that they will be ultimately consistent, one and all, in their combined result" (*Idea*, p. 375).

Does this not, tacitly and for all practical purposes, foster the notion of irrelative fields of inquiry? Newman writes that "the theologian speaking of Divine Omnipotence, for the time simply ignores the laws of nature as existing restraints upon its exercise; and the physical philosopher, on the other hand, in his experiments upon natural phenomena, is simply ascertaining those laws, putting aside the question of that Omnipotence" (*Idea*, p. 189). Can the theologian or the believing scientist operate in this dual fashion? Is it psychologically, let alone intellectually or ethically, possible or justified? Is it true, as Newman writes, that "he who believes Revelation with the absolute faith which is the prerogative of the Catholic . . . laughs at the idea, that anything can be discovered by any other scientific method which can contradict any one of the dogmas of his religion" (*Idea*, p. 376)?

If Newman is correct in his psychology and in his apologetic strategy, the effect, I fear, is not the freedom and sharing that he also appears to genuinely commend—not correlation—but a growing isolation and advocacy of irrelative forms of knowledge and life, an almost inevitable appeal to a submission of the understanding, and finally to sheer authority. Newman's fear of the perilous hegemony of Liberal Knowledge was one source, certainly, of the appeal for him of an economy and a reserve. Toward the close of "Christianity and Scientific Investigation," he characteristically counsels that great care be taken "to avoid scandal, or shocking the popular mind, or unsettling the weak." It is true, of course, that in some contexts this may be very wise advice. But it is also the case that such a temper of mind is, all too frequently, a check and curb to free and vigorous intellectual inquiry. Indeed, Newman concludes the above warning about "great care" with the call to "eschew secular history, and science, and philosophy for good and all, if we are not allowed to be sure that Revelation is so true that the altercations and perplexities of human opinion cannot really or eventually injure its authority" (*Idea*, p. 381).

I pose, again, the question once asked by Dwight Culler. If Newman, in the *Idea*, "set forth . . . the image of Civilization as a great, distinct, and objective fact . . . coextensive with Christianity and more than coeval in point of time, why did he not acknowledge the power of that fact?"[18] The answer is that Newman could not admit knowledge's power because he saw it as "stubbornly naturalistic." But does not such a position call for a too peremptory separation of the realms of nature and grace, or the assumption that natural knowledge is so "fallen" as inevitably to have a deleterious effect on moral judgment and action?

Newman's break with the Liberal Catholics in the early sixties over the role of historical studies in theology intensified his apprehension about the freedom of the sciences to pursue their work. In cases of conflict, silence and the hope for some future amelioration became the rule.[19] Is it not difficult to dismiss Lord Acton's judgment that for Newman the truth was to be silenced "if it injures religious interest"?[20] C. F. Harrold, a scholar deeply sympathetic to Newman, judges that "Newman always approaches history with his mind made up and solidly established on principles which, for him, . . . are indeed truer and more real than historical facts."[21] Again, Newman is correct that history goes wrong if it "assumes to be the *sole means* of gaining Religious Truth" (emphasis added),[22] or when "documentary testimony to Catholicism and Christianity may be so unduly valued as to be made the absolute measure of Revelation" (*Idea*, p. 90). But such one-sided excesses do not excuse the scholar-theologian from remaining genuinely open to the dialectical interdependence between theology and science.[23]

Indifference to the claims of scientific knowledge is possible only when it is wholly irrelevant to the theologian's belief. But in our modern world it is not possible, I believe, to isolate our histories or to speak simply of "internal" and "external" histories. We live at a time of competing internal histories. Hermeneutically, these multiple perspectives oftentimes logically interpenetrate. They coexist in the same mind and are not incommensurate. As Van Harvey puts it: "The historicity of the Christian historian includes the culture of the West as well as that of his own narrower community of belief. The Christian's mind is informed by the physical science, sociology, economics, and psychology of his time, as well as by his own Christian connections."[24] Hard perspectivism or a purely intratextual hermeneutic are today beguiling snares for Christian theology. The very logic of a monotheistic Christian theology demands a real conversation with natural knowledge; it demands, as David Tracy argues, the expression of theistic belief "in ways that will render it public not merely to ourselves."[25] Our pluralistic and conflictual culture is now also *within* us, within our very selves, and *within* our very tradition. That, I believe, was one of Matthew Arnold's enduring insights into our present history.

Notes

1. David Tracy, *Blessed Rage for Order: The New Pluralism in Theology* (New York: Seabury Press, 1975), p. 7.

2. George A. Lindbeck, *The Nature of Doctrine: Religion and Theology in a Postliberal World* (Philadelphia: Westminster Press, 1984), p. 18.

3. David J. DeLaura, *Hebrew and Hellene* (Austin and London: University of Texas Press, 1969); see especially "Arnold and Newman: Humanism and the Oxford Tradition," pp. 5–80.

4. Thomas Arnold [Jr.], *Passages in a Wandering Life* (London: E. Arnold, 1900), p. 57.

5. Henry Tristram, "Newman and Matthew Arnold," *The Cornhill*, n.s., LX (March 1926): p. 311.

6. Matthew Arnold, *Unpublished Letters of Matthew Arnold*, ed. Arnold Whitridge (New Haven: Yale University Press, 1923), p. 56.

7. Matthew Arnold, *Unpublished Letters*, pp. 65–66.

8. Matthew Arnold, "Emerson," *The Complete Prose Works of Matthew Arnold*, ed. R. H. Super, vol. X (Ann Arbor: University of Michigan Press, 1961–77), p. 165.

9. Matthew Arnold, "On the Study of Celtic Literature," *Complete Prose Works*, vol. III, p. 305.

10. David DeLaura, *Hebrew and Hellene*, p. 154.

11. Matthew Arnold, *Letters of Matthew Arnold 1848–88*, II, ed. G. W. E. Russell (London: Macmillan, 1895), p. 190.

12. Matthew Arnold, *Complete Prose Works*, vol. V, p. 171.

13. Nicholas Sagovsky, "Between Text and Experience: Arnold Among the Theologians," *Groupe de Recherche Litterature et Religion dans les Pays de Langue Anglaise*, (Université Paris, Nord, 1989).

14. Peter A. Dale, "Newman's 'The Idea of a University': The Dangers of University Education," *Victorian Studies* 16 (September 1972): pp. 5–36.

15. John Henry Newman, *The Idea of a University*, ed. I. T. Ker (Oxford: The Clarendon Press, 1976).

16. This discourse, entitled "General Knowledge Viewed As One Philosophy," was omitted from the published version of *The Idea of a University* because of its largely theological character.

17. Fergal McGrath, *Newman's University: Idea and Reality* (London: Longmans, Green, 1951), chap. 2.

18. A. Dwight Culler, *The Imperial Intellect: A Study of Newman's Educational Ideal* (New Haven: Yale University Press, 1955), p. 235.

19. See, for example, Wilfrid Ward, *The Life of John Henry Cardinal Newman*, vol. I (London: Longmans, Green, 1912), pp. 567, 641–42.

20. Lord [John] Acton, Cambridge University Library, Add. MS 4989.

21. Charles Frederick Harrold, *John Henry Newman: An Expository and Critical Study of His Mind, Thought and Art* (New York: Longmans, Green, 1945), p. 225.

22. John Henry Newman, *A Letter Addressed to His Grace the Duke of Norfolk* (London, 1875), pp. 104–5.

23. See Josef L. Altholz's criticism of Newman and historical science in "Newman and History," *Victorian Studies* III (March 1964): pp. 285–94.

24. This point is made very forcibly in Van A. Harvey, *The Historian and the Believer* (New York: MacMillan, 1966), p. 242. See especially his critique of H. R. Niebuhr's distinction between "inner" and "outer" history. On another aspect of this theme, also see David Tracy, *Plurality and Ambiguity* (New York: Harper and Row, 1987), chap. 4.

25. David Tracy, "Defending the Public Character of Theology," *The Christian Century* 98 (1981): p. 350.

7

Newman's Idea of a University: *Is It Viable Today?*

EDWARD JEREMY MILLER

To consider fully Cardinal Newman's views on education is to contemplate nearly everything he wrote and did, for it was he who said of himself, "from first to last, education, in this large sense of the word, has been my line" (*AW*, p. 259).[1] To assess the contemporary situation of colleges and universities is to undertake a practically endless effort, all of which is compounded by the constraints of a limited essay. To attempt too much will ensure that nothing is done well, and to select issues will invite overlooked aspects. I must chance the latter, however, with the conviction that Newman's educational philosophy has important views to contribute to some contemporary questions about our universities, while regarding other current issues it is surely dated.

Two recent discussions on university education invite a particular selection of topics in examining Newman anew. The discussions bore on the nature of *Catholic* colleges and universities and on the nature of *liberal arts* higher education. On August 15, 1990, Pope John Paul II issued his *Apostolic Constitution on Catholic Universities*, a document whose prior drafts engaged many Catholic educators during the previous decade. During that same decade, William Bennett, first as chairman of the National Endowment for the Humanities (NEH) and later as secretary of education, challenged the American university community to reexamine its undergraduate core curriculum, having been convinced that rightful disciplinary content and curricular cohesion in the liberal arts had been abandoned by most undergraduate institutions.[2]

In examining those issues, three theses shall emerge, and an advance view of them is helpful. They are as follows: (1) a discussion examining *truth* takes a different direction than if the discussion proceeded on *knowl-*

edge, and here is to be situated the pope and the cardinal; (2) a discussion about academic *content* concludes differently than if it were based on *process*, and here one finds William Bennett and John Henry Newman; and (3) Newman himself is best understood when his penchant for dialectics is appreciated.

Let us first turn to Newman's thoughts on university education, with some brief background about their historical context and about the primary materials themselves. In 1845 the British government established the non-denominational Queen's University in Ireland to provide an alternative to the Anglican-based Trinity College Dublin, opening college campuses in Belfast, Cork, and Galway. (In the Roman Catholic parlance of that day, both the Queen's colleges and Trinity College were considered *mixed education*, for Catholic youth would mix with non-Catholics in attending them). Under pressure from the Vatican, the Irish bishops at the Synod of Thurles (1850) prohibited involvement of Catholics at Queen's colleges, though some Irish bishops had been favorably disposed to them because they were nonsectarian. The Vatican enjoined the bishops to establish a Catholic University in Ireland, modeled on Louvain, and a funding drive was begun by Archbishop Cullen in 1851. Cullen, who first met Newman in Rome in 1847 while Newman was preparing for ordination, wrote him in April 1851 to invite him to lecture on education, to lecture in Dublin "against Mixed Education" (*AW*, p. 280), as Newman observed in his journal.[3] In a subsequent personal visit to Newman during the summer, Cullen offered him the rectorship of the new university, which Newman later and somewhat hesitantly accepted.[4]

Newman first conceived a trilogy of lectures, but the scheme grew into five public lectures, which he offered in the spring of 1852.[5] Later that summer and autumn in Birmingham, Newman wrote five more discourses, and the ten discourses were published at year's end as *Discourses on the Scope and Nature of University Education: Addressed to the Catholics of Dublin.*[6] After Newman was formally installed as rector on June 4, 1854, he gave occasional lectures at the university over the next four years. These lectures as well as some articles he wrote for the school newspaper, *The Catholic University Gazette*, were brought together as "Lectures and Essays on University Subjects" and published as a companion volume to an 1859 edition of the 1852 discourses; Newman deleted his original fifth discourse since he feared it went against the thinking of the pope.[7] In 1873 he brought both segments into one volume, calling it *The Idea of a University Defined and Illustrated*. Minor changes were made up until his last edition of 1889, and this is the text now known as *Idea*.

Newman wrote other essays for that university newspaper that are often overlooked by investigators, yet they are very important for concretely illustrating his conception of a university. He published those articles in 1856 under the title of *Office and Work of Universities*, and they are now tucked away in the third volume of his *Historical Sketches*. In addition to all of these "textual materials," one needs to be aware of Newman's pertinent correspondence and of various memoranda he wrote about the Dublin university venture.[8]

What aim lay behind these educational writings? There is no single fundamental objective. Newman had different audiences and goals in mind, and this fact invites confusion as he moves, both rhetorically and argumentatively, between goals. For example, many claim somewhat too facilely that Newman wanted fundamentally to justify the place of theology in the curriculum. That goal, I am convinced, was a secondary preoccupation. Newman surely had a primary concern to urge the value of *Catholic* education, "unmixed education" as he called it, since some of the Irish bishops and many of the laity saw no harm in the secularized Queen's colleges. Theology was to have its rightful and necessary place, as a discipline among disciplines, but more overarching was to be the "idea" that makes an institution a genuine university; this idea was possible, indeed strengthened in Newman's view, within a Catholic institution if the rights of the institution and the Church were mutually respected by each other. Furthermore, as shall be seen, other aims engage Newman's energies.

What about those laity, those potential professors and students without whom the new university would not march? In *Historical Sketches* there is a curious discussion of *public opinion*, which Newman calls the "main adversary" to the new enterprise. The university, he says, "has to force its way abruptly into an existing state of society which has never duly felt its absence," and it butts against a "reluctant or perplexed public opinion" (*HS*, III, p. 2).[9] Somewhat later, in describing the zeal and courage of Irish people, "springing fresh and vigorous from the sepulchre of famine" and religious oppression, "it sets me marvelling," he noted, "to find some of those very men, who have been heroically achieving impossibilities all their lives long, now beginning to scruple about adding one little sneaking impossibility to the list" (*HS*, III, p. 48). As is known, save for the medical school, the university venture failed, and one failure was its inability to recruit sufficient students.

Another major aim was to justify university education in the Oxford mode, that is to say, the cultivation of intellect vis-à-vis whatever is knowable. In one sense, the first eight discourses of *Idea* recapitulate the turn-of-the-century argument between Oxford and the "Edinburgh party,"[10] answering the latter's charges that (1) religion is not a suitable intellectual endeavor since religion at best is a matter of private opinions and (2) the only knowledge that matters serves the commonweal and is practically oriented; the liberal arts are simply not useful. I believe Newman used the discourses to state the Oxford case in his words and, along the way, sufficiently distanced himself from those aspects of Oxford, then in the 1820s and now in the 1850s, that troubled him.

One of those troubling matters was not developed in *Idea* but came under sustained treatment in *Historical Sketches*. It was the *college or tutorial* system in contrast to the *professorial or university* system. In Newman's view, the German schools educated through university professors without benefit of college residence; Oxford-Cambridge education was in the main sequestered into resident colleges, the university itself having an impotent structure. The professor-college contrast, or the metaphors *Athens and Rome* that Newman develops at length in these essays as illustrative of the contrast, are meant to describe the tension between freedom and regulation, inquiry and structure, in the education of students. After ably describing their characters and their competing aims, Newman's option is for both, if they are allowed to interact dialectically. To this important feature of dialectics I shall return.

In the preface to the discourses in *Idea*, Newman states his thesis that a university "is a place of *teaching* universal *knowledge*" (*Idea*, p. ix). After eight of those discourses he flatly states that everything to this point has been considering a university per se, not a university as *Catholic*. The latter is treated in the ninth discourse. For the moment, however, I wish to note the linchpin of every other discourse in *Idea*. It is his supple use of the word *knowledge*.

To sense his own struggle with the word and its correct notion, he uses other terms at times, though they are not quite synonymous. It is "mental cultivation," it is "enlargement," and it is "philosophy."[11] To speak in Thomistic categories, Newman strains to describe the perfection of a habit, as, for example, *virtue* is the word to describe the perfected habit of doing good, and *health* describes somatic well-being. He wishes to describe a cultivated mental excellence, and at one point in the second half of *Idea*, he calls it "the philosophy of an imperial intellect" (*Idea*, p. 462). Furthermore, and again to speak Thomistically, he uses the word *knowledge* materially and formally depending upon his aim at the moment. Knowledge, materially, refers to what is being known, and thus Newman will argue that no branch of knowledge, no academic discipline, as it were, can be a priori excluded from the curriculum. Knowledge, formally, refers to the mental capacity by which what is known is properly known. It is the capacity to discriminate facts and ideas, to order them, to perceive relations between them, and ultimately to judge them and act upon them. In this respect, perhaps, Newman's greatest commentator is Bernard Lonergan if one can sense this impress of Newman's educational psychology within the chapters of Lonergan's *Insight*.[12]

A reader of *Idea* might well object: Newman has much to say about theology, indeed about Catholic theology, in those first eight discourses, and therefore he has much therein that would affirm what constitutes a university as *Catholic*. I stand my ground. Every discipline, even theology, is subsumed under the more important discussion of what constitutes knowledge, in both its material and its formal sense.[13] In these discourses theology needs to be justified as an academic subject as does any other subject, and Newman argues its justification on the nondogmatic grounds of educational philosophy, not on the imperatives of revelation or magisterium nor on the precisely Catholic nature of the university as such.

As already noted, Newman began the discourses with the flat statement that a university is a place of teaching universal knowledge. He emphasized *teaching* in order to assert two matters: (1) the university is an intellectual service to students, not a moral or indoctrinating enterprise as might occur in a seminary; (2) it is a pedagogical enterprise and not per se a research endeavor. In Newman's day there were academies and royal societies whose business it was to extend the frontiers of knowledge, and he noted the quandary that obfuscates many contemporary tenure discussions: "To discover and to teach are . . . distinct gifts, and are not commonly found united in the same person" (*Idea*, p. xiii). Teaching, in other words, involves students in its very notion, and having asserted only this much in the opening pages of *Idea*, he leaves aside until the essays in *Historical Sketches* the fuller discussion of what he terms the "professorial system" to describe teaching. The remainder of *Idea* focuses on that illusive word *knowledge*.

The notion of knowledge is described variously. From one angle it is the *very aim* of the university, and in this respect he calls it "the cultivation of mind," "the force, the steadiness, the comprehensiveness and the versatility of intellect," having "a connected view or grasp of things, which allows entry into a subject with comparative ease" (*Idea*, pp. xvi, xvii). All such depictions of knowledge refer not to the accumulation of facts and ideas but rather to the digestion of such things and the making of them into a pattern or ordered configuration, into what may simply be called a view. If we today are inclined to term someone possessed of many facts and ideas a knowledgeable person, Newman is thinking rather of what we would term an insightful person.

Care needs to be taken of Newman's use of the word *view*. There is a spurious knowledge he termed "viewiness" (*Idea*, p. xviii), which he thought a chief evil of his day: "An intellectual man, as the world now conceives of him, is one who is full of 'views' on all subjects . . . of the day. It is almost thought a disgrace not to have a view at a moment's notice on any question" (*Idea*, p. xx). Periodical literature catered to this tendency, in Newman's opinion, and it served up superficial knowledge for genuine knowledge. He called such viewiness "nutshell truths for the breakfast table" (*Idea*, pp. xx).

The genuine knowledge that university education engenders, and that Newman at times simply calls "philosophy,"[14] is an active and formative power of the mind that reduces to order and meaning the sundry things one learns. He likens it to arriving at a center of thought or to "first principles," such first principles being practically a signature of Newmanian thinking.[15] In the essay, "Discipline of Mind," he writes:

> The result is a formation of mind,—that is, a habit of order and system, a habit of referring every accession of knowledge to what we already know, and of adjusting the one with the other; and, moreover, as such a habit implies, the actual acceptance and use of certain principles as centres of thought, around which our knowledge grows and is located. Where this critical faculty exists, history is no longer a mere story-book, or biography a romance; orators and publications of the day are no longer infallible authorities; eloquent diction is no longer a substitute for matter, nor bold statements, or lively descriptions, a substitute for proof. (*Idea*, p. 502)[16]

Newman draws an analogy with a blind person to whom sight miraculously returns and into whom pours a confusing world of colors, lines, hues, and shapes, without drift or meaning, and "like the wrong side of a piece of tapestry or carpet" (*Idea*, p. 495).[17] Only by degrees and through trial and error does that person arrive at ordered and meaningful perceptions. In similar fashion must the arduous task of intellectual cultivation proceed.

Some implications follow from the vision of knowledge as centered thought or philosophy. The individual mind cannot grasp the whole at once; it progresses by grasping aspects of the whole and arranging those aspects into ever more fundamental views that approach the understanding of the whole in itself. Discourse Three transposes this personal mental law to the communal mind of a university and portrays the aspects of the universal knowledge as the disciplines: history, physics, theology, and others. Secondly, to ignore an aspect (that is, a discipline) leads to deficient knowledge, much as if Newman's man-born-blind chose to ignore a particular color in describing a rainbow, and here of course is situated Newman's famous argument for the necessity of including theology in a university's purview. One cannot understand the total universe without reference to its Creator any more than one can view a muscle and call it an explanation of motion without considering free will. Indeed, the a priori exclusion of any discipline invites not only deficient knowledge but, more alarmingly to Newman, erroneous pontification, for wherever there is an excluded discipline, other disciplines will encroach on its land and opine on its issues from their own inadequate first principles.[18] The psychologist will play the ethicist; the physicist will play the theologian of nature.

A third implication follows that is particularly germane to the discussion involving Pope John Paul II. The knowledge of which Newman speaks, and which is described in terms of moving ever closer to centers of thought, is of its very nature a progressive coming to know. It is not ready-made insight; it is not without false steps; and there are not to be sanitized topics for the sake of "pious ears." Of the latter, one recalls Newman's famous statement that "it is a contradiction in terms to attempt a sinless Literature of sinful man" (*Idea*, p. 229). Such knowledge, whether considered formally as a mental habit to be attained, or considered materially as subject matter, enjoys within the university context the freedom to be wrong, if I may so put it. Newman did not wish erroneous knowledge, to be sure, but he wished the free play of ideas to have elbowroom in the interest of getting at truth. "It is the very law of the human mind in its inquiry . . . to make its advances by a process which . . . is circuitous. There are no shortcuts to knowledge. . . . In scientific researches error may be said, without paradox, to be in some instances the way to truth, and the only way" (*Idea*, p. 474). Such faith in the merits of open and free inquiry, I am arguing, is best provided for by setting up the discussion on the word *knowledge* rather than *truth*, which is what Newman did.

Note some of the things he had to say. In *Historical Sketches*, the university, he writes,

> is the place to which a thousand schools make contribution; in which the intellect may safely range and speculate, sure to find its equal in some antagonist activity, and its judge in the tribunal of truth. It is a place where inquiry is pushed forward, and rashness rendered innocuous, and error exposed, by the collision of mind with mind, and knowledge with knowledge. (*HS*, III, p. 16)

Is one to fear this collision of knowledge with knowledge? In describing the "imperial intellect," hear him again:

> If he [the true university person] has one cardinal maxim in his philosophy, it is, that truth cannot be contrary to truth; if he has a second, it is, that truth often *seems* contrary to truth; and, if a third, it is the practical conclusion, that we must be patient with such appearances, and not be hasty to pronounce them to be really of a more formidable character. (*Idea*, p. 461)

Furthermore, for Newman, if there is any academic discipline that from its sovereign position ought to bear calmly the collision of knowledge with knowledge, it is theology. For he says that an objection posed to Christian faith could (1) be unproven in the end, (2) turn out not to be contradictory, or (3) be uncontradictory to anything *really revealed*. Yet, if at this moment it appears contradictory, then one "should be content to wait, knowing that error is like other delinquents; give it rope enough, and it will be found to have a strong suicidal propensity" (*Idea*, p. 467).

Language such as this would emerge only awkwardly in a schema based on *veritas* (truth) where the focus is not on the process but on the end result. Newman's language is more readily consonant with the contemporary notion of the academy and the guidelines of academic freedom. Such a supple and confident use of the word *knowledge* provides the necessary *elbowroom* for university endeavors, a phrase indeed that Newman in other situations calls upon.[19]

Mention must be made of Discourse Nine, which describes the Church's role in a Catholic university, although the leitmotif remains knowledge; the "Duties of the Church Towards Knowledge" is the discourse's title. Having earlier argued that the completeness of academic inquiry requires theology's contribution, Newman here addresses the de facto tendency of human inquiry on rationalistic principles alone "to measure and proportion [revelation] by an earthly standard . . . to tune it, as it were, to a different key, and to reset its harmonies" (*Idea*, p. 217). Lest the university become a rival of the Church in theological matters, the Church consequently "breathes her own pure and unearthly spirit into it . . . and watches over its teaching . . . and superintends its action" (*Idea*, p. 216). The Church, then, has an active role to play.

It is so typical of Newman to consider matters in their existential propensities—for example, his constant references to sinful beings such as we are—that he is sensitive to the myopias of "reason alone" in matters of revelation. The methodology of physical science urges a private-judgment view of revelation and that of literature a natural explanation of the human condition. While these contentions are argued with greater nuance and with allowable exceptions in part two of *Idea*, they frame the contention of Discourse Nine that revelation is safeguarded by an agency greater than reason alone, which is the Holy Spirit acting through the Church. It would be strange to find Newman speaking in *Idea* on this matter differently than in his other major works, for example, *An Essay on the Development of Christian Doctrine*, where the Church is the God-given teacher of the revelation in Christ.[20]

On the other hand, the question remains as to how the Church is to superintend the functioning of the university, granting that for Newman it indeed enjoys this role. Everything he mentions about freedom of inquiry, necessary elbowroom, and giving error sufficient rope must also be taken into account, and indeed in a dialectical fashion do inquiry and authority, "Athens and Rome," come together in his scheme. One must reread the fifth chapter of Newman's *Apologia*, perhaps the most subtle of his writings, to sense the conflict between the "restless intellect" and the weight of Church authority, and his dialectical, almost paradoxical, contention that they are *sustained* by conflict with each other. Furthermore, one must recall that he dropped his original Fifth Discourse from the 1859 edition, not because he agreed with Pope Pius IX's position that Catholic doctrine conditions every discipline to be taught in the university—he noted that his "idea" expressed there was otherwise—but because of tact, that is, that oft-noted "principle of reserve" in his writings. Lest that interpretation seem contrived, note this letter of 1868 to the person who succeeded him as university rector: "It is *essential* that the Church should have a living presence and control in the action of the University. But still, till the Bishops leave the University to itself, till the University governs itself, till it is able to act as a free being, it will be but a sickly child" (*LD*, XXIV, p. 46).[21]

Leaving, for the moment, Newman's thinking on the first thesis I framed at the outset, let me turn to my second thesis, namely, the question of process *versus* content in the educational process, the content aspect having been recently focused upon by William Bennett. In Newman's essay on "Christianity and Letters," the key question is posed: "How best to strengthen, refine, and enrich the intellectual powers"? (*Idea*, p. 263). The question brings together what I have been terming the material and formal aspects of knowledge, that is, what *subjects* beget the genuine *habit* of mental cultivation? Although Newman's ready answer regarding subject matter in this essay is the Classics because their track record in so doing has been proven, it remained true for him that other subjects could provide that selfsame exactness and suppleness of mind if they were properly taught. In the essay "Discipline of Mind," Newman mentions various subjects that can work.

> Consider what a trial of acuteness, caution, and exactness, it is to master, and still more to prove, a number of definitions. Again, what an exercise in logic is classification, what an exercise in logical precision it is to understand and enunciate the proof of any of the more difficult propositions of Euclid. . . . And so of any other science,—chemistry, or comparative anatomy, or natural history; it does not matter what it is, if it be really studied and mastered. (*Idea*, pp. 501–2)

The pedagogical process of educating students is more important than academic content itself in Newman's scheme, and for achieving the aim of an university it is key. His full analysis is lodged in the extended discussion of the "professorial system" in *Historical Sketches* where it is distinguished from the "college system." By the latter he means the structured residential life of the university (the realm of the administrators, the deans, the governing polity). The distinction is examined throughout these little-known writings. It is "Athens" compared to "Rome," it is individuality compared to structure, it is freedom compared to law, and it is influence compared to system. I shall return to the distinction below in view of its dialectical interplay, but first a few remarks on the professorial system itself.

Though many things are needed to constitute a university in its fullness, in essence, however, a university "is a place for the communication and circulation of thought, by means of personal intercourse" (*HS*, III, p. 6). While one may learn from books, "the air, the life which makes it live in us, you must catch all these from those in whom it lives already" (*HS*, III, p. 9). It is the ability of the professors, which Newman simply calls personal influence, that essentially achieves the aim of the university.

> It is the place where the professor becomes eloquent, and is a missionary and a preacher, displaying his science in its most complete and most winning form, pouring it forth with the zeal of enthusiasm, and lighting up his own love of it in the breasts of his hearers. . . . It is a seat of wisdom, . . . an Alma Mater of the rising generation. (*HS*, III, p. 16)

How would Newman's ideal professor teach? We catch a glimpse in his essay "Elementary Subjects" in which he demonstrates how he himself would teach Greek or Latin to an undergraduate. Readers of Newman understandably jump these pages with their forbidding sections of Greek and Latin texts, yet one would perceive here how the professor prods and pushes the student to accuracy of judgment and to integration of new insight with what is previously known: "The mist clears up . . . and the rays of light fall back upon their centres. It is this haziness of intellectual vision which is the malady [of the current age]" (*Idea*, p. 333).[22]

The Bennett debate, lately assumed by his successor at NEH, Lynne Cheney, focused on the content of the core curriculum, which in fact meant the Western cultural heritage.[23] It equated exposure to that content with genuine liberal education. While Newman is indeed bullish about much of the same material, he opts instead for the pedagogical process over the content as the effective cause of genuine education. Indeed, in Newman's vocabulary, one might even say that curricular content is a "structure" compared to the "personal influence" of the professor, and of that distinction he noted pungently: "With influence there is life, without it there is none. . . . An academical system without personal influence of teachers upon pupils, is an arctic winter; it will create an ice-bound, petrified, cast-iron University, and nothing else" (*HS*, III, p. 74). Admittedly, in this text Newman was viewing academic residences as the structure, yet his idea holds for structured credit distributions if considered only in themselves. The act of teaching is primary in the aim of a university to educate students, and what is taught is somewhat secondary to it. Thus would I situate Newman's observations on a much later debate.

The recent *Apostolic Constitution on Catholic Universities*, on its very first page, defines a Catholic university's aim as existentially uniting two seemingly antithetical orders: "The search for truth and the certainty of already knowing the font of truth."[24] The theme of *truth* is so central to what follows that earlier drafts of the document coopted the university into the Church's own evangelizing mission, an incorporation that if strongly pushed would have troubling consequences for academic freedom and for legitimate institutional independence.[25]

Under the press of many interventions, and notably those by American university presidents, the final document softens the connection with the Church's teaching mission. It describes the university as making "an important contribution" to it and being "in harmony" with it.[26] Whereas the earlier drafts depicted a juridic bond to the local ordinary, the final document speaks only of "close personal and pastoral relationships . . . between University and Church authorities."[27] Universities, however, established by the Holy See, or by an episcopal conference, or by a local ordinary are obligated to incorporate into their statutes the eleven articles of norms of the papal document. All other institutions are invited to internalize these norms as far as possible.

My concern, in the main, is with the ideology of the document. It proceeds on a philosophical and pastoral analysis of *truth*, not *knowledge* as Newman chose. It speaks of the formation and transmittal of a Christian culture, but this task is continually to be clarified *in lumine revelationis.*[28] The pope's extended analysis of Christian culture allows the impression that if one substituted *ecclesia* for *universitas*, one was reading *Gaudium et Spes* of Vatican Council II. Pope John Paul II is not to be faulted for so construing the topic, for he is a pastor and not a provost. But from such an orientation certain assertions logically follow, as, for example, the four essential characteristics of a university qua Catholic: *inspiratio Christiana* of individuals and institution; reflection *in lumine fidei*; *fidelitas* to the Christian message as interpreted by the magisterium; *diakonia* to the People of God and to the human family.[29] Within this context other items do not so easily fit and are certainly not mentioned: the possibility of errors in the struggle for truth, that research may seem to clash with received doctrines, that a Catholic scholar might dissent from noninfallible authoritative magisterium.[30] In a certain respect, the document is a harmonious analysis of the expected harmony between faith and reason, a fundamentally Catholic principle to be sure and worthy of a university to fathom. Yet a university must seek such harmonies through academic struggle and debate, whereas a pastor may assert it readily as a formal and final cause, again to speak Thomistically.

The arena of academic freedom presents the major potential difficulty for American Catholic colleges and universities in light of the pope's recent *Apostolic Constitution*. The history of a particular phrase illustrates this point. A group of American Catholic university presidents met in 1967 at Land O'Lakes, Wisconsin, in preparation for a Vatican-sponsored international meeting the following year. Their "Land O'Lakes" document reads: "To perform its teaching and research functions effectively the Catholic university must have a true autonomy and academic freedom in the face of authority of whatever kind, lay or clerical, external to the academic community itself."[31] They further say that "Catholicism is perceptibly present and effectively operative" in a Catholic university. They recognized the tension by affirming both thoughts!

An international meeting of Catholic administrators (Rome, 1972) delineated the four essential characteristics of a Catholic university, which the Pope's recent *Apostolic Constitution* reiterated, but they noted that "the legitimate and necessary autonomy of the university requires that an intervention by ecclesiastical authority should respect the statutes and regulations of the institution as well as accepted academic procedures,"[32] which procedures have definite meanings in the American context of academic freedom. The Pope's *Apostolic Constitution* mentions necessary institutional autonomy, "so long as the rights of the individual person and of the community are preserved within the confines of the truth and the common good." This same phrase delimits the definition of academic freedom given in the footnote, and the phrase is vague enough—like its canon law cousin, *salvatis salvandi*—to mean almost anything. Some paragraphs further, the pope says that although bishops do not enter directly into the internal governance of the university, they "should be seen not as external agents but as participants" in the university's life.[33] The reference to the Land O'Lakes presidents seems evident; their phrase is fully gone.

How implementable is the pope's vision of a Catholic university in an American context of academic freedom? This question demands more extended treatment than possible here, but I would note the cautions of the American Canon Law Society regarding canons 807–814, which pertain to Catholic universities, given that the *Apostolic Constitution* on universities was written in light of those canons. The American canonical commentators write:

> The Catholic institutions in the United States, in order to satisfy the nature and purpose of higher education, follow the distinctive American pattern. At the same time they remain completely free to conduct instructional and research programs in the light of Catholic faith and with the interaction of all academic disciplines. This pattern differs so greatly in style of academic governance and in cultural and social dimensions from the European system of higher education that it is seriously questionable whether the canons are indeed applicable in the United States.[34]

There is undoubtedly a tension in Catholic academic settings, posed by canon law and the pope's *Apostolic Constitution*, on the one hand, and, on the other hand, by the "secular canons" on academic freedom to which American Catholic universities seek to comply for professional accreditation purposes. As with all legitimate tensions, it should never become a matter of the hegemony of one pole. It rather becomes an ongoing and never-fully-worked-out balancing of the legitimate interests of each pole, for there are values in each of them. But such balancing will involve struggle and momentary clash and prudential judgments by university president and local bishop alike.

I conclude with Newman concerning the dynamics of struggle in situations of tension. It is well known that to solve difficulties Newman tended to describe competing forces, giving each force its full and just due. As mentioned above, the *Apologia*'s fifth chapter describes the ever recurring conflict between human inquiry (in religious matters) and the constraints of Church authority, citing the need for both and, moreover, the desirability for the conflict itself.[35] Again, the Church's three offices (the devotional, the theological, and the juridic), of their nature, tend to clash, yet each is sustained in its integrity by the tendencies and claims of the other two offices. Newman describes the conflicts between the three Church offices in the 1877 Preface to his reedition of the *Prophetical Office*, a marvelous piece of subtle writing. Newman's 1859 essay "On Consulting the Faithful in Matters of Doctrine" argues for the role of the laity in witnessing to revelation, which role was meant to complement other sources of revelation, for example, episcopal magisterium; the essay outlines the conflicts between laity and bishop during the fourth century. In these three pieces of writing, Newman was describing a process of dialectics that I have examined elsewhere in greater detail.[36] There was no other way for Newman to depict the complex realities of the tension than in this dialectical picture, and the dialectical process itself was not the means to the solution but the very solution itself.

Newman's dialectical penchant also operates in his vision of the university. There is, as we have seen, a collision of knowledge with knowledge, in which genuine insight may initially lurk within a wider error. The university, moreover, is a composite of inquiry and received tradition, of freedom and structure, of professor and administrator. In *Historical Sketches* he focused on the competing and at times clashing aims of university and residential college, and his answer was not to make an easy harmony of them but to describe their counterbalancing contributions.

> A University embodies the principal of progress, and a College that of stability; the one is the sail, and the other the ballast; each is insufficient in itself for the pursuit, extension, and inculcation of knowledge; each is useful to the other. . . . The University being the element of advance, will fail in making good its ground as it goes; the College, from its Conservative tendencies, will be sure to go back, because it does not go forward. (*HS*, III, pp. 228–29)

Unlike contemporary college catalogs, Newman does not give detailed answers to how the university achieves its aims. He rather describes a dialectical process, assuming the benevolent will of the entire university community to engage one another with a civility of discourse "and in a neighbourly way."[37]

Were there nothing else of viability in Newman's university "idea," this last encouragement is surely such for our campus environments.

Notes

1. *John Henry Newman: Autobiographical Writings*, ed. Henry Tristram (New York: Sheed and Ward, 1956).
2. Pope John Paul II, *Ex Corde Ecclesiae* (Vatican City, Rome: Libreria Editrice Vaticana); William Bennett, *To Reclaim A Legacy* (NEH: November 1984). Bennett's general thesis is continued by his successor at NEH, Lynne V. Cheney, in *50 Hours: A Core Curriculum for College Students* (NEH: October 1989) and *Tyrannical Machines: A Report on Educational Practices Gone Wrong and Our Best Hopes for Setting Them Right* (NEH: November 1990).
3. See *The Letters and Diaries of John Henry Newman*, ed. Charles Stephen Dessain et al., vol. XIV, p. 257, n. 2.
4. *AW*, pp. 280–83, see *LD*, XIV, p. 315, which masks the later hesitations.
5. They were delivered on May 10, 17, 24, 31, and June 7, 1852, each being published a week after delivery by a Dublin publisher. Newman clearly intended an eventual "library edition"; see *LD*, XV, p. 83.
6. They were actually published on February 2, 1853, but backdated to the dedication of November 21, 1852, and thereafter they were known as the 1852 edition of Newman's *Idea of a University*. Page references hereafter to *Idea* are to the uniform edition unless noted otherwise.
7. Newman deleted the fifth discourse so as not to offend papal sensibilities. In the papal Brief of March 20, 1854, concerning the University, "Pio Nono" stated that Catholic doctrine was to be intrinsic to the lectures in all the subjects. Newman notes in *AW*, p. 323, that his discourses, and especially the fifth, were based "on a different idea."
8. See *Letters and Diaries, John Henry Newman: Autobiographical Writings*, and *My Campaign in Ireland*, papers of Newman posthumously and privately printed by the Birmingham Oratory in 1896 (Aberdeen: A. King, 1896).
9. John Henry Newman, *Historical Sketches*, vol. III, uniform ed. (London: Longmans, Green, 1891).
10. Opposition to the Oxford reform was led by pamphleteers from Edinburgh who argued for utilitarian studies. See *Idea*, pp. 2, 153. Some years later they also championed the ideals of the newly founded University of London *pace* Oxford's espousal of liberal arts and theology. In the expurgated fifth discourse, Newman refers to the *Edinburgh Review* of February 1826. See Ian Ker's edition of John Henry Newman, *The Idea of a University* (Oxford: Clarendon Press, 1976), p. 420.
11. See *Idea*, pp. 113, 121, 125 (especially), 134, 151.
12. Bernard Lonergan, *Insight: A Study of Human Understanding* (New York: Harper and Row, 1978). In Lonergan's *A Second Collection* (ed. W. Ryan and B. Tyrrell [Philadelphia: Westminster, 1974]), he acknowledges Newman's influence; see pp. 38, 263.
13. Such Thomistic distinctions can be useful in understanding Newman's ideas,

but Newman himself was not a Thomist in either his expressions or his conceptualizations.

14. In his expurgated fifth discourse, Newman described how science itself can be called a philosophy, provided "it is knowledge which has undergone a process of intellectual digestion. It is the grasp of many things brought together in one." See Ker (ed.), *Idea*, p. 423.

15. For an analysis of first principles in Newman's thinking and for the pertinent references, see Edward Jeremy Miller, *John Henry Newman on the Idea of Church* (Shepherdstown, W.Va.: Patmos Press, 1987), pp. 9–20.

16. See also *Idea*, p. 134.

17. See also the analogy with an infant, *Idea*, p. 332.

18. See *Idea*, pp. 76ff.

19. *Idea*, p. 476, reads: "Great minds need elbow-room, not indeed in the domain of faith, but of thought. And so indeed do lesser minds, and all minds." Another palmary text is in his "Letter to Pusey": "Life has the same right to decay, as it has to wax strong. This is specially the case with great ideas. You may stifle them; or you may refuse them elbow-room; or again, you may torment them with your continual meddling; or you may let them have free course and range, and be content, instead of anticipating their excesses, to expose and restrain those excesses after they have occurred," John Henry Newman, *Certain Difficulties Felt by Anglicans in Catholic Teaching*, vol. II (London: Longmans, Green, 1898), p. 79.

20. On the matter of university appointments to the Catholic University Dublin, Newman was opposed to the hiring of non-Catholics; see *LD*, XVI, p. 203.

21. When Archbishop Manning attempted to establish his own Catholic university at Kensington in 1873, Newman refused the invitation to cooperate, knowing the venture would be overly controlled and would lack academic freedom.

22. Also see the preceding pages.

23. Bennett, *To Reclaim a Legacy*, pp. 10–11. Admittedly, William Bennett's report is also concerned with how the humanities are taught, but there is little description of the process *à la Newman*; rather, it is an attack on the misuse of the humanities for ideological purposes; see p. 16.

24. *Ex Corde Ecclesiae*, (Vatican City, Rome: Libreria Editrice Vaticana), official English translation, no. 1.

25. The "Proposed Schema" of 15 April 1985, nos. 17, 19, asserts that a Catholic university "takes on an ecclesial function." For background to the final document see Alice Gallin, "On the Road: Toward a Definition of a Catholic University," *The Jurist* 48 (1988): pp. 536–58.

26. *Ex Corde Ecclesiae*, no. 49.

27. *Ex Corde Ecclesiae*, no. 28.

28. *Ex Corde Ecclesiae*, nos. 3, 5, 13, 46, 49.

29. *Ex Corde Ecclesiae*, no. 13. These characteristics reiterate the document *The Catholic University in the Modern World* from the second international congress of Catholic university delegates, Rome, November 1972.

30. The literature on whether dissent from authoritative noninfallible magisterium is possible has become vast, especially because of the birth control issue sur-

rounding Pope Paul IV's *Humanae Vitae.* See also *Lumen Gentium* of Vatican II (no. 25) and commentaries upon it. On June 26, 1990, the Congregation for the Doctrine of the Faith issued the "Instruction on the Ecclesial Vocation of the Theologian," which decidedly limits the possibilities of dissent; see nos. 25–31. The *Report of the Catholic Theological Society of America Committee on the Profession of Faith and the Oath of Fidelity* (1990) argues for greater latitude in possibilities of dissent.

31. Printed in Neil McCluskey, *The Catholic University: A Modern Appraisal* (Notre Dame, Ind.: Notre Dame Press, 1970), pp. 336–41.
32. In McCluskey, *The Catholic University: A Modern Appraisal*, no. 58.
33. *Ex Corde Ecclesiae*, nos. 12, 28.
34. *The Code of Canon Law: A Text and Commentary*, commissioned by the Canon Law Society of America, ed. James A. Coriden et al. (New York: Paulist Press, 1985), p. 571.
35. See the fine analysis by Ian T. Ker in his *John Henry Newman: A Biography* (New York: Oxford University Press, 1990), pp. 549ff.
36. For an analysis of the dialectics in Newman's ecclesiology, see Edward Jeremy Miller, *Newman on the Idea of Church*, chap. 4. For Newman's 1859 essay, see *On Consulting the Faithful in Matters of Doctrine*, ed. John Coulson (London: Geoffrey Chapman, 1961).
37. See *Idea*, p. 465.

Part 4

Commitment

8

The Grammar of the Heart: Newman on Faith and Imagination

M. Jamie Ferreira

"Heart speaks to heart"—*cor ad cor loquitur*. Newman's well-known motto is obviously a gracious and rich one. There are, however, some nonobvious riches in it that I want to explore, and they relate to Newman's understanding of the role of imagination in the transition (or *conversion*) to faith.

Two of Newman's most important axioms about the *heart* are found in his *Grammar of Assent*; he writes there that grounds for believing should touch our hearts, and that the "heart is commonly reached . . . through the imagination" (*GA*, pp. 425, 92).[1] The expectation generated by those axioms is that, for Newman, all significant believing, including religious believing, would be deeply anchored in, dependent on, and mediated through imagination—and if we look deeply enough, we shall find that expectation to be fulfilled explicitly. Newman emphasizes the role of imagination in belief—sometimes obsessively—and presents it as both necessary and legitimate; I propose that we can learn something of importance about religious faith, especially about transitions, or conversions, to religious faith, if we attend to how he does this.

I will focus on two themes: (1) I will consider how Newman's reliance on the category of *critical threshold* in religious certitude reveals his decisive commitment to the importance of imagination, and (2) I will consider how this commitment to imagination in achieving religious certitude is expressed in terms of a *reorienting vision*. In both cases I will argue implicitly that his descriptions of illative reasoning are in effect descriptions of what he calls the "trained imagination" (*GA*, p. 315).[2] Before exploring these themes in detail, let me briefly suggest how Newman's close tie between the heart and imagination is relevant to both of them.

First, with respect to *critical threshold*, I want to argue that Newman's view of the "subtle" method of reasoning in concrete cases expresses an appreciation of imagination because the way in which we come to religious certitude is through the achievement of a critical threshold—and that critical threshold is constituted by an imaginative shift in perspective. Newman contrasts imagination with "pure intellect" (*GA*, p. 139) in a way that suggests that imagination is, for him, a "holistic" activity. Like the biblical notion of heart, to which he explicitly refers in speaking of the "right or renewed heart" (*US*, pp. 203, 234),[3] the subtle method of reasoning is a complex, holistic, interpenetration of intellect, emotions, and will. Both the subtle method of reasoning and the "right heart" fall on the side of imagination. The achievement of the critical threshold of certainty is mediated through the heart and is thus imaginative in its method as well as in its result.

Second, his close tie between the heart and imagination indirectly suggests another feature of imagination—namely, its relation to *vision*. Newman's references to the biblical relation between a right heart and the discernment of truth are made clearer when he explicitly emphasizes the biblical claim that "the pure in heart shall see God."[4] In that beatitude the heart is a metaphorical organ of vision—the "pure" heart refers to the single-mindedly devoted center of our personality (emotions, intellect, and will), and what it achieves is a *vision*, a new way of seeing. I want to suggest in what follows that the transition to faith, for Newman, is a kind of imaginative re-visioning or reorientation. That is, I propose that the transition is constituted by coming to see the world and self under a new description—and that such re-visioning is an activity of imaginative extension and imaginative synthesis. To make the transition to faith is to "see" God, and to see God is to re-vision—imaginatively—the world and the self.

These, you can see, are both *descriptive* concerns—about how Newman sees the imagination at work. He also has a *prescriptive* concern: imagination not only functions in religious belief, but it does so in ways that can be evaluated as epistemologically legitimate. Newman himself hints at this when, in listing a variety of "logical methods," he calls one of them the "Logic of Imagination" (*TP*, I, p. 94).[5] To speak of a "logic" of imagination is clearly to contrast it with emotionally based beliefs. Newman's predilection for the category of "grammar" is thus relevant not only to assent but also to imagination. What is important about this category of "logic" is that, like the category of grammar, it suggests that the activity of imagination is contoured rather than arbitrary, that it is public rather than uncriticizably private.[6] His appeal to imagination, then, specifically excludes indiscriminate wishful thinking or what he calls "make-belief" (*GA*, p. 82).[7] There is, for Newman, a logic or grammar of religious awareness and belief, as of any significant awareness or belief, and he tells us *both* that it is a grammar of the heart and that the grammar of the heart is a grammar of imagination. In the following three sections, I consider Newman's evaluation of imagination and then its role in faith-transitions in terms of critical threshold and reorienting vision.

I. The Double-edged Evaluation of Imagination

Newman's concern with imagination is, at times, obsessive. For example, within the space of twenty-four pages in the *Grammar* (pp. 117–40), he uses the word "imagination" (or "imaginative") twenty-one times (in addition to references to "image"); elsewhere he uses it eight times in the space of eight pages (pp. 75–82). But to determine Newman's *evaluation* of imagination, we do need, as I hinted earlier, to look *deeply* because Newman (like many others before and after him) was ambivalent toward imagination. An appreciation of the dual-edged potential of imagination is found throughout his work: "The imagination," he writes, "is a wonderful faculty in the cause of truth, but it often subserves the purposes of error" (*TP*, I, p. 152). This evaluation reveals his rejection of both the rationalist denigration of imagination and the sentimental romanticization of imagination. By far the greatest number of explicit comments on imagination highlight its negative potential: the *Oxford University Sermons*, for example, generally bear a very negative tone.[8] Indeed, the theme that the imagination is "the great enemy to faith" (*TP*, I, p. 47) is reinforced throughout his work. He expresses the negative potential in terms of two kinds of limit. First, as one would expect in the rejection of an over-romanticized notion of imagination, he recognizes the danger of wish-fulfillment, illusion, fantasy—the illegitimate overextension of imagination. But what is rather more unexpected is that he also warns of the danger of using imagination as the limiting standard for determining what is possible: he warns against the illegitimate restrictive straitjacket of imagination. He constantly repeats that conceivability or imaginability is too limited a test for what is possible; he claims over and over again that it is the shock to imagination, not the offense to reason, that keeps us from embracing many warranted ideas.

The theme that it is imagination that tethers us in our search for truth is found not only in the theological papers of 1857[9] but also in the suggestion in the *Apologia Pro Vita Sua* that the "stain" (*Apo.*, p. 101) of imagination can hinder reason's conclusions,[10] as well as in the *Idea of a University* where he notes how the conclusions of science are devastating, "not because it really shocks our reason as improbable, but because it startles our imagination as strange" (*Idea*, pp. 300–301);[11] the "terrible influence" of imagination results from its being "bewildered" in the face of what is strange (*Idea*, p. 302). This destructive influence—the way in which it "usurps" reason (*GA*, p. 81)—is a variation on the theme that imagination can generate irrational nonevidential doubts.[12] Moreover, it can motivate emotions that can distort the apprehension of the truth (for example, as in reading Strauss's *Life of Christ*).[13] For these reasons imagination needs to be controlled by reason.[14]

In addition to the explicit negative evaluations, however, we do find explicit positive assessments of imagination, illustrating his claim that imagination is "a wonderful faculty in the cause of truth." At the very least he clearly affirms its practical influence in motivating emotions that can reinforce our certainty (*GA*, pp. 77, 82–83, 89). Even more fundamental is his understanding of the necessity of imagination in supplying objects for our assent (*GA*, p. 89). His emphasis on the importance of "real" apprehension is precisely an emphasis on imagination: imagination is necessary if we are to "realize" things (*GA*, p. 79)—that is, imagination is necessary to make things concrete. The supreme positive evaluation of imagination is suggested in his claim that the love of God is "founded on faith, not on reason—that is, in other words on an imagination" (*Phil.N.*, II, p. 121).[15]

But in the end, whether or not explicit negative comments outnumber explicit positive comments, a commitment to both the necessity and the legitimacy of imagination is integral, as Newman's readers have increasingly come to appreciate, not only to his view of "real" *apprehension* but also to his understanding of the process of illative or informal reasoning in general. In fact, the roles of imagination that I want to highlight (namely, imaginative extension and synthesis) are at work in real apprehension, but here I want to focus on how they operate in reasoning—to help us appreciate why Newman can describe the actual processes of informal reasoning that lead to assent and certitude in the same ways that he describes the activity of the "trained imagination." We shall see as well how Newman anticipates the contemporary discussion of imagination "not as the image-making faculty, but rather as the paradigmatic (pattern-making and pattern-recognizing) faculty."[16]

II. Certitude and Imagination

We find perhaps the most striking appreciation of both the necessity and legitimacy of imagination in his well-known but rather novel claim that certitude "does not come under the reasoning faculty; but under the imagination" (*TP*, I, p. 126). Newman's account of certitude in the papers preparatory to the *Grammar* contains a number of crucial elements that all point directly to the role of imagination—that is, they lead one to expect this, perhaps otherwise surprising, association between certitude and imagination. The features of certitude that he highlights and that lead up to his conclusion that certitude is under the rubric of imagination are the following: first, it is a "recognition" rather than a "passive admission of a conclusion" (*TP*, I, p. 126; this is why it "elevates . . . into a higher order of thought"); second, "certitude does not admit of more or less [that is, there are no degrees]" (*TP*, I, p. 124). In this section I want to explore how his emphasis on these two features carries in its train an appreciation of imagination, and I want to consider in particular how the implied category of critical threshold bears on his account of the transition or conversion to faith.

1. Transcending Dualisms

Newman's suggestion early in his writings that certitude is a "recognition"[17] is extended in the *Grammar*'s claim that it is an "active recognition": "Certitude is not a passive impression made upon the mind from without, by argumentative compulsion . . . it is an active recognition of propositions as true" (*GA*, pp. 344–45). It is not a mere acceptance, but an active "*certifying*" of a conclusion, giving it a "*certificate*" (*TP*, I, p. 126)—yet it is still a "recognition." Certitude is not a rational conclusion forced on us by the evidence, but neither is it something we can simply will by fiat. The will, he says clearly, "cannot create <force> certainty" (*TP*, I, p. 15).[18] The achievement of certitude, then, is something that is at the same time active and yet, as he says often, a "perception."[19] Newman is thereby suggesting that certitude transcends any dichotomy between active and passive, between will and reason: it is *both* active *and* a recognition, *both* bestowed *and* called forth as a demand.[20] In this respect Newman's characterization of certitude calls to mind Iris Murdoch's suggestion that imagination is that by which dualisms between active and passive, will and reason, are transcended.[21] The transcending of such dualisms is distinctive of imagination precisely because it is a distinctive activity of imagination to hold opposite elements in tension. Samuel Taylor Coleridge's definition of imagination also makes this clear: in "the act of thinking," he says, "there are evidently two powers at work, which relatively to each other are active and passive; and this is not possible without an intermediate faculty, which is at once both active and passive. In philosophical language, we must denominate this intermediate faculty in all its degrees and determinations, the IMAGINATION."[22] It is not at all surprising, then, that Newman's emphasis on certitude as an "active recognition" immediately precedes his conclusion that certitude is under the imagination.[23]

2. Critical Thresholds

The second feature of certitude as Newman presents it, leading up to the conclusion that certitude is under the imagination, is that it has no degrees: "Certitude does not admit of more or less—but is a state of mind, definite and complete, admitting only of being and not-being" (*TP*, I, p. 124). This is by far, I think, Newman's most striking contribution to any discussion of certitude (and ultimately to any account of religious conversion). Through it Newman makes certitude what I have many times called a "threshold" concept, a concept that is not applicable at all until it is simply and totally applicable—in short, it is an all-or-nothing concept. A threshold concept refers to a state or condition that is not expressed gradually or by degrees. For example, explosive material gets hotter and hotter by degrees, but it does not explode gradually; it does not explode at all until it reaches a critical threshold. To use one of Newman's own examples, water gets hotter and hotter, but it does not boil until it reaches a critical threshold.[24] Newman's point is that something (for example, heat) is registered all the while, but there is a qualitative change at a critical threshold, and that change is decisive since any increases after that threshold are superfluous.

Imagination and qualitative transitions. What is the relevance of imagination to the critical threshold of certitude? Consider more closely Newman's descriptions of how the certitude necessary to religion (*GA*, p. 220) is reached through the "subtle" (*GA*, pp. 288, 303, 317) method of reasoning appropriate to concrete cases. He introduces this subtle method, which he says is the "real and necessary method" of reasoning in concrete cases, by comparing it to the way a portrait exhibits the detailed filling-in of a mere sketch (*GA*, p. 288). This fleshing-out of a sketch is obviously an imaginative activity, but Newman's comparison represents more than his appreciation of the role of imagination in making things concrete, or *concretizing* (as happens in "real apprehension"). What is more important here is that it introduces an *extending and synthesizing activity* of imagination that effects a *qualitative* shift.[25]

That becomes clear when Newman elaborates what goes on in the filling-in of the sketch (the "real and necessary method" of reasoning in concrete cases) through his description of the "principle of concrete reasoning," which "is parallel to the method of proof which is the foundation of modern mathematical science" (*GA*, p. 320). That the method both is imaginative and involves a qualitative shift is suggested in his use of the imaginative mathematical notions of "limits" and "sums" in explaining this principle.

Consider first the category of a limit in his famous metaphor of a polygon expanding within a circle to illustrate the "principle of concrete reasoning": "We know that a regular polygon, inscribed in a circle, its sides being continually diminished, tends to become that circle, as its limit; but it vanishes before it has coincided with the circle, so that its tendency to be the circle, though ever nearer fulfillment, never in fact gets beyond a tendency (*GA*, p. 320). This metaphor of a polygon inscribed in a circle exemplifies an asymptotic approach to a limit that involves an imaginative extension. It is only through imagination that we can be said to grasp what is "as if" coinciding with the circle without getting "beyond a tendency" to do so. Newman is referring to this same imaginative function when he speaks early on in the Oxford University sermons of the "reaching forward of the mind" in implicit reasoning (*US*, pp. 224, 249, 275); it is also what he means by the element of "anticipation" in concrete reasoning (*GA*, p. 299). The very idea of a polygon tending to "become" a circle "as its limit" thus implies the achievement, through imaginative extension, of a qualitative transition (from polygon to circle) via a critical threshold.

This imaginative extension in the method of concrete reasoning is high-lighted when he observes that

> the conclusion in a real or concrete question is *foreseen* and predicted rather than actually attained; *foreseen* in the number and direction of accumulated premises, which all converge to it, and as the result of their combination, *approach it more nearly than any assignable difference*, yet do not touch it logically (though only not touching it), on account of the delicate and implicit character of at least part of the reasonings on which it depends. (*GA*, p. 321; emphasis added)

Our *foreseeings* approach the result "more nearly than any assignable difference." Insofar as there is no "assignable difference," there is a qualitative shift. The hypothetical or imaginative concept of limit thus implies imaginative extension by which a qualitative shift is achieved on reaching a critical threshold.

Such imaginative extension is also operative at times as imaginative *synthesis*: it is at work when we recognize evidence "only as a body, and not in its constituent parts" (*GA*, p. 292) or when "we grasp the full tale of premisses and the conclusion, *per modum unius*,—by a sort of instinctive perception" (*GA*, p. 301). Such imaginative synthesis is at work in the general process in which "probable reasons [are] viewed *in their convergence and combination*" (*GA*, p. 327; emphasis added).

Indeed, Newman brings to our attention the peculiarly imaginative activity of what psychologists call "configurational," as opposed to "linear," thinking:

> It is by the strength, variety, or multiplicity of premisses . . . by objections overcome, by adverse theories neutralized, by difficulties gradually clearing up, by exceptions proving the rule, by un-looked-for correlations found with received truths, . . . by all these ways, and many others, it is that the practised and experienced mind is able to make a sure divination that a conclusion is inevitable, of which his lines of reasoning do not actually put him in possession. (*GA*, p. 321)

This "practised and experienced mind" is, we shall see, what Newman only pages earlier in the *Grammar* refers to as the "trained imagination" (*GA*, p. 315).

The process is, he concludes, one of "summation and coalescence of the evidence into a proof, which I have compared to the running into a limit, in the case of mathematical ratios" (*GA*, p. 325). The references to the mathematical concept of a limit are supplemented by reference to the mathematical concept of a sum; he writes,

> To this conclusion he comes . . . not by any possible verbal enumeration of all the considerations, minute but abundant, delicate but effective, which unite to bring him to it; but by a *mental comprehension of the whole case, and a discernment of its upshot*, sometimes after much deliberation, but, it may be, by a clear and rapid act of the intellect, *always, however, by an unwritten summing-up, something like the summation of the terms, plus and minus* of an algebraical series. (*GA*, p. 291–92; emphasis added)

Thus, the imaginative or hypothetical concepts of limit and sum express the imaginative extension and synthesis by which a qualitative shift is achieved on reaching a critical threshold.

The "principle of concrete reasoning," which is parallel to the mathematical method of proof via limits and sums, is, in effect, that "real ratiocination and present imagination" give "methodical processes of inference" a "sense beyond their letter" and "while acting through them, reaches to conclusions beyond and above them" (*GA*, p. 316). Such a principle is precisely that by which, in Newman's own words, we "feel the true force" of a nondemonstrative argument (*GA*, p. 314), and it is striking that Newman's explanation of just how we come to feel the "force" of such argument refers quite explicitly to the "trained imagination" (*GA*, p. 315).

Critical thresholds and the ladder of imagination. Now I want to consider briefly the relation between imagination and critical thresholds from another perspective. In his sensitive study, *Imagination and Religion*, which focuses on Newman, John Coulson suggests that Newman's metaphor of a polygon inscribed in a circle is really just another idiom for Kierkegaard's idea of a *leap* of faith[26]—but it can be misleading to speak of Newman's concept of reaching certitude as a leap insofar as the concept of leap seems to many to imply simple unmitigated discontinuity. The term *leap* impresses on us the qualitative character of the achievement, but it obscures the continuity involved, and the continuity is as crucial to Newman's thought as the discontinuity.

One of the distinctive features of a critical threshold is that there is continuity at the same time as there is discontinuity. The transition achieved in reaching certitude is a qualitative transition: it is an all-or-nothing kind of movement. Although it is not a quantitative cumulation by degrees, it is nevertheless anchored in what preceded it. Evidence, like heat, can be registered during a process, even though the qualitative transition only occurs after the critical threshold is reached. A qualitative transition need not be simply radically discontinuous with what precedes it.

I think Newman's own lengthy description in the *Apologia* of his process of reaching religious certitude illustrates the importance of the element of continuity. And it relates interestingly to one kind of criticism of him that he reports there. He tells us that "a gifted and deeply earnest lady" described his conduct as he sought to reach certitude as follows:

> All my fears and disquiets were speedily renewed by seeing the most daring of our leaders [Newman] . . . suddenly stop short and declare he would go on no further. He did not, however, take the leap at once, but quietly sat down on the top of the fence with his feet hanging towards the road, as if he meant to take his time about it, and let himself down easily. (*Apo.*, p. 170)

As I read this, it emphasizes the element of continuity in Newman's critical threshold of conversion: it was not a dramatic *leap over* a fence but, rather, the use of the fence to make what is nevertheless a radical or qualitative transition.

Putting together both that passage and the crucial category of critical threshold, I suggest that the metaphor most appropriate for Newman's idea of how we reach certitude, the parallel to the polygon-circle image, is not a leap but rather a *ladder*. A ladder effects a qualitative transition while it obviates in some sense the very need for a leap. A ladder is a particularly apt metaphor for a transition that is both discontinuous and continuous at the same time. Although a ladder can be used to effect a horizontal bridge between parallel and qualitatively similar domains, the distinctive character of a ladder includes the vertical dimension, one that suggests a creative and qualitative achievement lacking to a mere horizontal bridge. But while a ladder can be seen as facilitating a transition to a qualitatively different domain, it does so without requiring the absolute discontinuity of a simple leap across a gap, for a ladder necessarily maintains continuity in an important way (that is, it requires and touches the ground throughout the process of transition). Thus, a ladder provides a very useful metaphor for a transition understood as a qualitative ascent that nevertheless allows for continuity in the face of discontinuity; that is, it provides a very useful metaphor for a transition understood as a critical threshold.

Any metaphor issues in an imaginative reconceptualization by imaginatively holding two perspectives in tension, but there is, in addition, an intriguing historical connection between the imagination and the particular metaphor of ladder. St. Bonaventure, like many others, presents imagination as a rung on the ladder of the mind's powers in the ascent to God.[27] Imagination is a transitional mediator between the senses and reason, or between the senses and the higher powers of the soul. But in his discussion of the soul's ascent to God, Bonaventure also explicitly brings in the biblical image of Jacob's dream in which Jacob saw a ladder connecting earth and heaven.[28] Thus, insofar as imagination mediates between the earth of the senses and the heaven of reason, it too is a ladder by which we can make a spiritual ascent. Insofar as continuity and discontinuity (and activity and passivity) are maintained in tension in the transforming shift of perspective that constitutes certitude, imagination is necessary to maintain that tension, and the ladder of imagination is a particularly apt metaphor for Newman's view of the critical threshold transition involved in achieving certainty.

III. Conversion and Reorienting Vision

What I have been claiming thus far is that the transition to religious certitude via a critical threshold is an imaginative activity, both because it transcends a dualism between active and passive (or will and reason) and because it is a qualitative shift constituted by an imaginative extension and synthesis. In particular, I have argued that Newman's image of the polygon expanding within a circle is a fruitful metaphor for a critical threshold transition, and the concept of critical threshold implies an imaginative achievement—a qualitative shift in perspective. The qualitative imaginative shift occurs (through imaginative extension and synthesis) when we come to see that the conclusion (though not logically complete) is "as good as proved." The conclusion, he says, "*is* proved *interpretative*" (*sic*, *GA*, p. 323)—not compelled, but interpreted—and it is the "trained imagination" that can see all that is embodied and implied in what is nevertheless an incomplete proof according to demonstrative standards. We can actually pick out two qualitative shifts that occur in reaching religious certitude— the coalescing of evidence into a "proof" and the assent to the conclusion (certifying, ratifying it, treating it as unconditional). Although, strictly speaking, the achievement of informal inference (the process in which the "trained imagination" can see the evidence coalesce into a "proof") is not the same as the achievement of assent, the image of the polygon in the circle can represent both informal inference and assent, or certitude, insofar as Newman says that the pages on informal inference "illustrate the intellectual process by which we pass from conditional inference to unconditional assent" (*GA*, p. 329). That is, since the reasoning process informing each is the same, we can treat them equivalently and speak of one critical threshold.[29]

Here I want to parallel that threshold of religious certitude with the conversion experience and suggest that in the transition or conversion to faith a coalescence of evidence, through imaginative extension and synthesis, generates a new *seeing*. I want to highlight how, for Newman, conversion can be seen as a case of *reorienting imaginative re-visioning*.

Newman speaks in the *Apologia* of his initial conversion at the age of sixteen: "This beginning of divine faith in me," he says, was a time when a "great change of thought took place in me" (*Apo.*, p. 16). This is clearly not a volitionalist account of conversion—not conversion by an act of willpower. He goes on to speak of his own turning to Rome as a conversion many times in the *Apologia*.[30] What precisely does he see the critical threshold of conversion to consist in? Is it a "great change of thought"? Is it an intellectualist alternative to a volitionalist account?

Newman writes in the *Grammar* of "the change which so often takes place in what is called religious conversion" as a new understanding (*GA*, p. 80)—to the one converted, Scripture is a "new book." That this new understanding is a new way of *seeing* is made clear when he suggests that the story of Job's conversion is a striking example of his very point. The "change in the character of [Job's] apprehension" after his trial is, he quotes Job, that "with the hearing of the ear I have heard Thee, but now *mine eye seeth Thee*." Job came to see God, the world, and himself differently. This reinforces the way Newman had early on spoken of religious apprehension as a "master vision" that can be obscured (*US*, p. 322) and of God's impression on us as the "vision of an object" (*US*, p. 330). If religious apprehension is a master vision, the transition to it is a re-visioning of world and self. Supporting the language of vision in respect to religious conversion is the fact that such vision is also at work in his account of real concrete reasoning. His description of how we discern "the true force of an argument," which is attributed to the "trained imagination," is explained in terms of two explicitly visual analogues. "To feel the force of an argument like this," he writes (that is, a nondemonstrative or concrete argument), "the series of deductions . . . if they are to be realized, must distil like dew into our minds, and form themselves spontaneously there" (*GA*, p. 314). This distillation (or coalescence) is elaborated in terms of two examples of an "exercise of sight," each making a different point.

The first example is as follows: these deductions "are analogous to the knowledge which we at length attain of the details of a landscape, after we have selected the right stand-point, and have learned to accommodate the pupil of our eye to the varying focus necessary for seeing them" (*GA*, p. 315). Note here that even if we select the standpoint and try to focus, the seeing comes in a sense of itself: it is not the direct result of an act of willpower. But the nonvolitional character of the seeing is made even clearer when, giving a second analogy, he writes of what one today calls a "gestalt-shift":

> Or they may be compared to a landscape as drawn by the pencil . . . in which by the skill of the artist, amid the bold outlines of trees and rocks, when the eye has learned to take in their reverse aspects, the forms or faces of historical personages are discernible, which we catch and lose again, and then recover, and which some who look on with us are never able to catch at all. (*GA*, p. 315)

He concludes that "our mode of dealing" with such concrete, probabilistic arguments is "analogous to such an exercise of sight" (*GA*, p. 315).

Here he says explicitly that the "trained imagination sees" in the words of the argument what the "mere barren intellect" cannot (*GA*, p. 315). "We often hear," he writes, "of some great lawyer, judge or advocate, who is able in perplexed cases, when common minds see nothing but a hopeless heap of facts, foreign or contrary to each other, to detect the principle which rightly interprets the riddle, and, to the admiration of all hearers, converts a chaos into an orderly and luminous whole" (*GA*, p. 372). He thus refers to the imaginative activity of forming and recognizing patterns. The trained imagination can detect the cosmos in the apparent chaos; it can come to see the faces in the trees, or it can come to see as convex what first looked concave.

Thus, conversion for Newman is neither intellectualist nor volitionalist, but just as certitude is an "active recognition" that transcends such a dualism, so too conversion is an "active recognition" that transcends such a dualism. Like certitude, conversion is under the imagination. His own deliberate use of visual analogues to explain the processes by which we come to feel the force of a concrete argument reinforces an understanding of conversion as such a transforming shift in perspective— a gestalt-shift—through an imaginative re-visioning which reorients us in practical ways.

Conversion, in this view, is, I suggest, a responsible activity of seeing things differently rather than either a brute decision or an ineffable happening. While some people agree that the faith-transition, or conversion, is not a brute decision, they often do not explore the kind of human activity involved; they appeal to grace or ineffable happenings as if grace and human activity were mutually exclusive. I propose that Newman was not limited by that false dichotomy but was able to see the religious transition as *our* activity, however grace-enabled, but an activity that is an act neither of pure intellect nor of willpower. Rather, like certitude, it is under the imagination—in particular, it is an imaginative re-visioning.

Thus, in his century Newman proclaimed an appreciation of imagination that anticipated what contemporary thinkers have been reminding us of in recent years. In Iris Murdoch's words, "to reach [what is real] we need strength and refinement of imagination"; she echoes Newman's evaluation of an imaginative "reaching out" toward the real when she suggests that "to be a human being is to know more than one can prove, to conceive of a reality which 'goes beyond the facts' in these familiar and natural ways."[31]

Notes

1. John Henry Newman, *An Essay in Aid of a Grammar of Assent* (Westminster, Md.: Christian Classics, 1973). The pagination is identical to the standard (Longmans) edition.
2. Though I am in significant and extensive agreement with Robert Holyer's fine essay ("Religious Certainty and the Imagination: An Interpretation of J. H. Newman," *The Thomist* 50 [July 1986]: pp. 395–416), I am arguing, *pace* Holyer, that Newman quite explicitly draws the relevant connections between imagination and certainty in the *Grammar*, and I am elaborating how the role of imagination in the appraisal of arguments involves more than the generation of emotional conviction.
3. *Newman's University Sermons: Fifteen Sermons Preached before the University of Oxford, 1826–43*, with introductory essays by D. M. Mackinnon and J. D. Holmes (London: S.P.C.K. 1970).
4. For example, he makes reference to this beatitude in *US*, p. 198.
5. *The Theological Papers of John Henry Newman on Faith and Certainty*, ed. Hugo M. de Achaval and J. Derek Holmes (Oxford: Clarendon Press, 1976).
6. Mark Johnson addresses the way in which imagination is "non-rule-governed": it appears "irrational" ("there does not appear to be a *logic of creativity*") because there is no "definite pattern, algorithm, or inferential structure for creative reasoning" (*The Body in the Mind: The Bodily Basis of Meaning, Imagination and Reason* [Chicago: University of Chicago Press, 1987], p. 166). Newman's position expresses a tension between seeing imagination as "irrational" and seeing its influence (far from "irrational") through "direct impressions, by the testimony of facts and events, by history, by description" (*GA*, p. 92).
7. See *US*, p. 231: "We cannot make facts. All our wishing cannot change them."
8. *US*, pp. 122, 124, 132, 149, 284.
9. *TP*, I, pp. 47, 115.
10. John Henry Newman, *Apologia Pro Vita Sua*, ed. David DeLaura (New York: W. W. Norton, 1968).
11. John Henry Newman, *The Idea of a University*, ed. Martin J. Svaglic (New York: Holt, Rinehart and Winston, 1960).
12. For example, he attributes to the power of imagination "the wild unhealthy state of mind which says 'Perhaps there is poison in my breakfast, poison in my dinner'—or 'perhaps if I go out walking, I shall break my leg'," *The Philosophical Notebook*, vol. II, ed. Edward Sillem (Louvain: Nauwelaerts Publishing House, 1969), p. 195; *GA*, pp. 198, 202–3.
13. *TP*, I, p. 46; *GA*, p. 213.
14. *GA*, pp. 121, 220; *Apo.*, p. 100.
15. Newman repeats at the conclusion of the paragraph the same equation: love is based "on faith, on an imagination."
16. See Garrett Green's fine work, *Imagining God: Theology and the Religious Imagination* (San Francisco: Harper and Row, 1989), p. 94.
17. *TP*, I, pp. 14, 31, 126.
18. The angled brackets indicate Newman's alternative readings; see *TP*, I, ix

(editor). Note that an image in real assent is contrasted with an "abstraction" by the fact that the latter can be "made at will" (*GA*, p. 87).

19. Newman uses the word "perception" often, and it is clear that neither perception nor image is necessarily "visual" for him.

20. It is an active recognition "such as it is the duty of each individual to exercise at the bidding of reason, and when reason forbids, to withhold" (*GA*, p. 345).

21. Iris Murdoch, "The Darkness of Practical Reason," *Encounter* 27 (July 1966).

22. Samuel Taylor Coleridge, *Biographia Literaria* (1817), Everyman's Library Edition (London: J. M. Dent and Sons, c. 1906), chap. VII, p. 60. The integrating or mediating function of imagination to which Coleridge repeatedly calls attention is able to be understood precisely in terms of the activity of holding in tension.

23. His contrast between imagination and reason is not dualistic, for he admits that "sense, logic, authority, testimony, belong to the process" and constrain the conclusion (even though the conclusion is "beyond them and independent of them" insofar as it is not compelled by them [*TP*, I, p. 126]).

24. *The Letters and Diaries of John Henry Newman*, ed. Charles Stephen Dessain et al., vol. XXVII (November 27, 1874), pp. 161–62; I discuss this in more detail in *Scepticism and Reasonable Doubt: The British Naturalist Tradition in Wilkins, Hume, Reid, and Newman* (Oxford: Clarendon Press, 1986), especially pp. 186–88.

25. I would argue that these functions are at the bottom of the "putting-in-relation," which constitutes "real apprehension" as well.

26. Coulson writes: "The difference between Newman and Kierkegaard may well amount to no more than that between retrospective and prospective ways of looking at the same fact: it is spoken of as a 'leap' *before*, and is conceived as a polygon expanding into a circle after" (*Religion and Imagination: 'in aid of a grammar of assent'* [Oxford: Clarendon Press, 1981], p. 71).

27. *The Works of Bonaventure*, trans. José de Vinck, vol. l, *Mystical Opuscula* (Paterson, N.J.: St. Anthony Guild Press, 1960), *The Journey of the Mind to God*, chap. 1, sec. 6, p. 11.

28. Bonaventure, *Journey*, chap. 1, sec. 9, p. 13.

29. The qualitative transition occurring at that critical threshold is not, strictly speaking, the transition between inference and assent. The same inferential process underlies both; the informal reasoning coincides. The gap between the circle and the polygon that we bridge imaginatively, in a qualitative transition, is the gap between logical completeness (demonstration) and the informal inference that it is "as good as proved." The difference between such an inferential conclusion and an assent to it lies in whether we treat the conclusion in and of itself or treat it in its dependence on the process of reasoning. Assent results not from more reasoning or some leap of faith: it is the result of seeing a "proof" in the reasoning, of interpreting, anticipating, and projecting what is already there—not adding something external to it. It is the recognition that now the conclusion can be seen independently of the evidence.

30. *Apo.*, pp. 153, 157, 184.

31. Murdoch, "The Darkness of Practical Reason," p. 49.

9

The Living Mind:
Newman on Assent and Dissent

GERARD MAGILL

> Catholic Christendom . . . presents a continuous picture of Authority and Private Judgment alternately advancing and retreating as the ebb and flow of the tide.
>
> —Newman, *Apologia Pro Vita Sua*

Introduction

Public and private dissent has become a significant feature in religion today among theologians and laity alike. In recent decades, morality seems to have had the lion's share of dissent, causing a strident reaction from Church officials. John Henry Newman was no stranger to the realities of dissent and episcopal scrutiny, both as an Anglican and as a Catholic: in this regard the role of moral conscience was of paramount importance. Most noticeably, his anxiety about the personal integrity and the theological legitimacy of dissent from Anglicanism led to his conversion in 1845 and inspired his *Apologia* in 1864 in which he publicly defended the change of his religious opinions.[1] Moreover, a natural flair for controversy permeated his life, a personal characteristic that he clearly recognized in a very private letter to Emily Bowles, dated May 1863: "The only reason why I do not *enjoy* the happiness of being out of conflict is, because I feel to myself I could do much in it" (*LD*, XX, p. 445; Newman's emphasis).[2]

Although Newman rarely discussed dissent, in reality it accompanied his lifelong inquiry into religious assent. He associated assent, and therefore also dissent, with the *living mind*, a dynamism of perception that engaged a personal mode of reasoning and a mental alertness to the plurality of historical circumstances. In this essay I argue that Newman implemented his view of assent as an appeal to the living mind in his understanding of conscience to justify theological dissent, even from legitimate ecclesial authority. I sketch a systematic account of the relation between assent and dissent, notwithstanding the inconsistencies that arise from the occasional nature of his writings. To do so, I explain that he metaphorically bridged the chasm, so to speak, between assent and dissent by three interlocking spans, conscience, theology, and authority (denoting an interaction rather than a dialectic because no overarching synthesis appears in his thought). I begin by analyzing his religious epistemology of assent (section I) which he implements in his explanation of conscience (section II). Those two topics provide the context for examining his approach to theology (section III), which, in turn, illumines his respect for authority (section IV) and his justification of dissent (section V).

To evaluate Newman's contribution today, I will compare his argument with a recent official teaching from the Catholic Church on assent and dissent, the "Instruction on the Ecclesial Vocation of the Theologian."[3] In that document the "sense of faith," which characterizes the living mind of the Church, is closely associated with the "Magisterium of the Church's Pastors" and is contrasted explicitly to what is called "a supreme magisterium of conscience."[4] Newman offers, I suggest, a more nuanced view of authority and conscience in terms of relating assent and dissent.

I. Assent

Newman explained, "Assent is . . . unconditional" (*GA*, p. 259),[5] an absolute affirmation of truth that can be elicited in matters of faith and morals. He argued that we can reach certainty even when the particular conclusion cannot be demonstrated strictly by the available evidence or proven by logical reasoning. To warrant assent he appealed to personal reasoning. This mode of reasoning functions through a congruence of arguments, interpreted as a whole and assimilated by the individual to justify the conclusion. This occurs, for example, when spouses examine their reasons for marriage: there comes a point when the various arguments (none of which may be persuasive in itself) converge, being interpreted by the partners in a holistic way that justifies the decision to marry. Newman referred to that mode of *personal reasoning* as *"informal inference,"*[6] and it was as important for his view of theology as it was for his theory of assent. He illustrated the process of informal inference in a letter, dated July 1864, to a regular correspondent, Canon Walker: "A cable which is made up of a number of separate threads, each feeble, yet together sufficient as an iron rod. . . . [This] represents a moral demonstration . . . which *rationally demanded* to be considered sufficient for certitude" (*LD*, XXI: p. 146; Newman's emphasis).

In 1870 he presented the clearest explanation of his argument in the *Grammar of Assent*, defining assent as a "perception of the legitimate conclusion in and through the premisses" (*GA*, pp. 301–2). Rational justification of assent was mandatory even though its unconditional nature meant that the proposition was true in itself.[7] To describe the process of reasoning that warrants assent, he used a metaphor from education, "the living mind" (*GA*, p. 360), or "living personal reasoning" (*GA*, p. 300). The 1870 metaphor of "the living mind" is reminiscent of his earlier metaphor for sound education: in his sixth discourse on university education (1852), he referred to the "enlargement of mind" (*Idea*, p. 125),[8] which he had previously described in a sermon preached as an Anglican vicar at St. Mary's in 1840 as "living knowledge" (*US*, p. 287).[9] This parallel reveals an important affinity between his philosophy of education and his religious epistemology.

Two significant features of assent result from the metaphor of the living mind (informal inference). First, assent entails "an active recognition of propositions as true" (*GA*, pp. 344–45). This mode of reasoning entails reaching forward to insights in a personal fashion by affirming truth (assent) that may not be perceived by others. It recalls the argument in his Dublin university discourses of educating "the intellect to reason well in all matters, to reach out towards truth, and to grasp it" (*Idea*, p. 126). In addition, assent (affirming the conclusion as true) organizes and illumines other knowledge: "When the conclusion is assumed as a hypothesis, it throws light upon a multitude of collateral facts, accounting for them, and uniting them together in one whole" (*GA*, p. 323). A significant corollary of this process is that the possibility of error is diminished when assent meaningfully accounts for previously known truths. Again, this explanation of assent parallels his view of education in which "enlargement or illumination" (*Idea*, p. 126) requires "a comparison of ideas one with another, . . . and a systematizing of them" (*Idea*, p. 134): this meant "reducing to order and meaning" (*Idea*, p. 134). The verification of assent therefore entails interpretation by illumining other knowledge, that is, by accounting for and uniting together known truths into a new systematic synthesis. This insight was the epistemological basis both of his philosophy of education in the *Idea* and of his argument on assent in the *Grammar*.

In sum, Newman's assent is neither a logical conclusion nor a whimsical guess but has these basic features. First, it is the personal reasoning of informal inference (recalling his metaphor, "the living mind") that justifies assent. Second, assent transcends particular arguments as an active recognition of truth. Third, assent entails interpretation, beforehand in the congruence of inferences, and afterwards in the synthesis it brings to previous knowledge. Using this theory of informal inference to warrant assent, Newman traversed the apparent chasm between religious assent and legitimate dissent by metaphorically building a bridge with three interlocking spans—conscience, theology, and authority—each of which I now examine.

II. Conscience

Unfortunately, the similarity between assent and conscience has been obfuscated by the classical argument from conscience to the existence of God in Newman's thought. For example, from Newman's unpublished paper on the "Proof of Theism" (1859), Adrian Boekraad and Henry Tristram emphasized Newman's claim that "there is a God, because there is a moral obligation" (*Proof*, p. 103).[10] But when Newman discussed conscience in 1870, he openly declared: "I assume the presence of God in conscience" (*GA*, p. 417).[11] This approach to God's existence sheds light on his famous distinction between conscience as "a judgment of the reason and a magisterial dictate" (*GA*, p. 105).[12] That is, his argument from the sense of moral sanction to the notion of a Supreme Judge should not be construed as a proof: "I am not proposing here to prove the Being of a God" (*GA*, p. 104).[13] Because Newman understood conscience as a religious but nonetheless reasonable judgment, he was able to draw a crucial parallel between assent and conscience: "A mind thus carefully formed upon the basis of its natural conscience, . . . has a living hold on truths . . . is able to pronounce by anticipation, what it takes a long argument to prove . . . interprets what it sees around it" (*GA*, p. 117).

Here, the three crucial features of assent are applied to conscience. First, the "living hold on truths" recalls his educational metaphor for eliciting assent, "the living mind." Second, discerning truth "by anticipation" points to the active recognition of propositions as true that is required for assent. Third, the mind that "interprets what it sees around it" encapsulates the interpretative process of assent. This threefold parallel, which has escaped the attention of Newman commentators, indicates that he applied his theory of assent to conscience. Such a connection can be traced as early as 1831 to one of his sermons for the University of Oxford, preached at St. Mary's. There he explained that "an educated conscience, . . . seems to detect moral truth" (*US*, p. 66) by a reasoning process that he later associated with informal inference.[14]

Newman also attributed a communal character to the judgments of conscience. In 1859 he published in the *Rambler* his article "On Consulting the Faithful in Matters of Doctrine" in which he argued that the "Consent of the faithful" was a "consensus" that should be regarded as "a sort of instinct, a *phronema* deep in the bosom of the mystical body of Christ" (*Cons.*, p. 73), and he described this as the "conscience of the Church."[15] He was referring to the historical judgments of conscience made by the believing community as a whole, the term *phronema* expressing the communal character of personal reasoning. He later referred to the individual form of that type of personal reasoning when recalling Aristotle's practical moral reasoning (*phronesis*) to illustrate informal inference: "It is . . . with the controlling principle in inferences that I am comparing *phronesis*" (*GA*, p. 356).

Unlike Aristotle, Newman used practical reasoning (informal inference), which he called "right judgment in ratiocination" (*GA*, p. 342), to justify assent. Only two months after publishing the *Grammar*, Newman explained that he did not use practical "in opposition to speculative" but "to assert that probable arguments may lead to a conclusion which is not only safe to act upon, but is to be embraced as true" (*LD*, XXV: p. 114).[16] This is a crucial distinction for understanding the meaning of dissent in the Catholic Church today: for example, the recent Catholic *Instruction* claims that the obligation to follow conscience cannot legitimate dissent because conscience illumines only the practical judgment.[17] In contrast, Newman applied his theory of assent to conscience, and he prescribed consulting the conscience of the faithful precisely to ascertain truth for doctrinal pronouncements. Hence, his use of *phronema* to describe the conscience of the Church anticipated his later theory of assent: both were engaged in discerning truth.

But that raises an anomaly because Newman also claimed that consulting the faithful did not refer to judgment: "Their judgment on the question of definition is not asked; but the matter of fact, viz. their belief, *is* sought for, as a testimony to that apostolic tradition" (*Cons.*, pp. 54–55; Newman's emphasis). Perhaps this ambivalence illustrates Newman as controversialist, the textual ambiguity being a cloak for a daring argument that would predictably provoke an outcry. My association of "consulting" with conscience as judgment (like assent) is supported in his subsequent argument: he openly referred to "the consent of the faithful . . . being [a] . . . *judgment*" (*Cons.*, p. 67; Newman's emphasis). Both the textual evidence in his article and its coherence with his broader view of conscience suggest that consulting the faithful referred to the judgments of conscience.

Newman's view of conscience, then, included not only an epistemological dimension but also a theological dimension. He argued that consultation should precede doctrinal definition[18] because the assents of the faithful as judgments of conscience are a theological source of truth: "The *fidelium sensus* and *consensus* is a branch of evidence which it is natural or necessary for the Church to regard and consult, before she proceeds to any definition" (*Cons.*, p. 55; Newman's emphasis). In sum, the striking parallel between the three features of assent and conscience indicate that Newman applied his theory of assent to conscience. And those judgments of conscience bear a theological dimension that is central to his argument for consulting the faithful.

III. Theology

Recently, Avery Dulles has claimed that theology played only a modest role in Newman's article "On Consulting the Faithful."[19] But he fails to appreciate the importance of theology for Newman's argument on the consent of the faithful (as the conscience of the Church). The need for theology appears clearly in Newman's letter of June 1867 to Canon Walker, a professor at St. Edmund's College, Ware, in which he discussed the issue of theological condemnation in the *Syllabus of Errors* (1864): "For myself I think the securus judicat orbis terrarum, is the real rule and interpretation of the words of the Church, i.e. the sensus theologorum primarily, then consensus fidelium next" (*LD*, XXIII, p. 254).

Here Newman used an Augustinian phrase, which he translated as "the Christian commonwealth judges without misgiving" (*LD*, XXIV, p. 354), to express confidence in the historical judgments of the believing community for formulating doctrine.[20] In another letter, dated October 1869, to Magdalene Helbert, an Anglican drawn to Catholicism, Newman emphasized the importance of theological interpretation, anticipating the debate on infallibility in the First Vatican Council:

> How shall we know that the coming Council is a true Council—but by the after assent and acceptance of it on the part of that Catholic organization. . . . How can we *interpret* the decisions of that Council, how the Pope's decisions in any age, except by the Schola Theologorum, the great Catholic school of divines dispersed all over the earth? (*LD*, XXIV, p. 355; emphasis added)

Moreover, he argued in his "Letter to the Duke of Norfolk" (1874) that "the *Schola Theologorum* is competent to determine . . . the exact interpretation" (*Diff.*, II, p. 176) of papal and synodal utterances. Newman's emphasis upon the theological interpretation of doctrine was a nuanced articulation of his earlier principle for interpreting Scripture: we must "endeavour to look beneath the veil of the literal text" (*PS*, II, p. 162).[21] The role of theological interpretation, he argued, belongs to the entire community of faith. Similarly, the recent Catholic *Instruction* explains that the "sense of faith" belongs to the whole people of God, yielding "a universal consent in matters of faith and morals."[22] However, Newman articulated how the sense of faith functions by implementing his theory of assent in conscience as a theological undertaking: "To a mind thus carefully formed upon the basis of its natural conscience, . . . the theology of a religious imagination . . . has a living hold on truths . . . is able to pronounce by anticipation, . . . it interprets what it sees" (*GA*, p. 117).

In this fuller version of the citation that I mentioned earlier to indicate the shared characteristics of conscience and assent, the "living hold of truth" (in the judgments of conscience as assent) is clearly the remit of theology. Further, the theological "imagination" is synonymous with his educational metaphor "the living mind," each indicating the importance of the living mind in his thought. The collective judgment of theologians, therefore, operates just like the collective conscience of the community, that is, by using the personal reason of informal inference. In this regard Walter Jost and David Hammond have shown that theology provides the richest store of Newman's discussion of method.[23] Likewise, I am arguing that Newman adopted the same use of reason (informal inference) for his theological method as he did for assent and conscience. Informal inference was the basis for his religious epistemology of assent, which he implemented in his view of conscience: it was this mode of reasoning that led him to award a central place to theology in his 1877 preface to *The Via Media*: "Theology is the fundamental and regulating principle of the whole Church system" (*VM*, I, p. xlvii).

The context of this remark dealt with the three offices of the Church: the priestly, the prophetic, and the regal, referring to the domains of worship, teaching, and governance. Newman gave priority to theology because of its interpretative method, that is, discerning truth through informal inference. Hence, the search for religious truth, not obedience to ecclesial authority, guides theology: "Truth is the guiding principle of theology and theological inquiries" (*VM*, I, p. xli). Furthermore, Newman was wary of relying upon deductive logic alone in theology because, he warned in 1863, "the consistent need not be truth" (*TP*, I, p. 114). The upshot of his connection between assent, conscience, and theology was that the consent of the faithful (the communal assent and conscience of the Church) was perceived as a theological process. To safeguard theological interpretation, he promoted theology in the university, defending its freedom of inquiry.[24]

The university, Newman argued, is the place "in which the intellect may safely range and speculate, sure to find its equal in some antagonist activity, and its judge in the tribunal of truth. . . . It is a seat of wisdom, a light of the world, a minister of the faith" (HS, III, p. 16). Theology is at home in the university because it adopts the same method of reasoning (informal inference) as Newman celebrated in his philosophy of education: "The process of enlightenment or enlargement of mind" (Idea, p. 130) in the university functions primarily by "reducing to order and meaning" (Idea, p. 134), which I have shown anticipated his later argument of convergence in the theory of assent.[25]

Newman's defense of freedom in theology was counter-cultural in an increasingly ultramontanist Church. In an appendix to the Apologia, he wrote: "The freedom of Schools, indeed, is one of those rights of reason, . . . this implies not to moral questions only, but to dogmatic also" (Apo., p. 447). Such an appraisal of theological freedom as a right of reason was echoed a century later in the Second Vatican Council's (1962–65) appeal to reason to justify the right of religious freedom.[26] Emulating the great medieval schools of theology, Newman associated academic freedom with personal courage: "It is manifest how a mode of proceeding, such as this, tends not only to the liberty, but to the courage, of the individual theologian or controversialist" (Apo., p. 239).[27] Further, academic freedom clearly included professional teaching: in a lecture at his Dublin university in 1854, he promoted "the ancient method, of oral instruction . . . the personal influence of a master, and the humble initiation of a disciple" (HS, III, p. 8). Academic freedom, then, protects the integrity of teaching positions at university and promotes freedom of intellectual inquiry.

In sum, for Newman the interpretative function of theology, using informal inference, could flourish in the university only when academic freedom was protected. Inquiry in theology and inquiry of conscience are closely connected because each uses the same mode of reasoning to justify assent. To appreciate how Newman linked dissent with assent I now examine the rapport between conscience, theology, and the third span of his bridge, so to speak, the authority of the Church.

IV. Authority

At the end of the *Apologia*, Newman balanced academic freedom in theology, as one of the rights of reason, with the right of ecclesial authority to intervene in theological controversy. Occasions may arise, he explained, when a theologian is "just one of those persons whom the competent authority ought to silence; and, though the case may not fall within the subject-matter in which that authority is infallible, . . . it is clearly the duty of authority to act vigorously in the case" (*Apo.*, p. 232).[28] Unfortunately, Newman did not offer any criteriology for implementing such discipline. But by extending authority to noninfallible teaching, he clarified the terrain for discussing theological dissent. Then, as now, the possibility of dissent is discussed in relation to authoritative but noninfallible Church teachings.

The Second Vatican Council explained that beyond the "ex cathedra" infallibility of the Pope in matters of faith and morality, the ordinary magisterium of bishops has authentic teaching authority whose force can be discerned by three criteria: the character of the documents, the frequency of proposing the doctrine, and the manner in which the doctrine is formulated.[29] There is, then, a "hierarchy of truths" that varies in relation to the foundation of faith in Catholic teaching.[30] Hence, the debate on dissent today focuses not upon the freedom of conscience but on the authority of the ordinary magisterium in general[31] and of the Congregation for the Doctrine of the Faith in particular.[32]

Newman justified the intervention of bishops in theological controversy on account of their Apostolic Office. Even as an Anglican in 1830, he defended this principle when writing to another Anglican vicar, Simeon Lloyd Pope: "A system of Church government was *actually established* by the Apostles, and is thus the *legitimate* enforcement of Christian truth" (*LD*, II, p. 265; Newman's emphasis). But just as theological freedom has limits, episcopal authority also must be restrained. That is why in his argument for consulting the faithful, theology and authority work together: "Each constituent portion of the Church has its proper functions, and no portion can safely be neglected" (*Cons.*, p. 103). The crux of the matter, then as now, is whether theology is independent of, though cooperative with, the hierarchy; or is theology delegated by, and derivative from, the bishops?[33] The recent Catholic *Instruction* on the vocation of the theologian also has acknowledged a reciprocity between theology and the magisterium, recognizing that each must enrich the other and accepting that the magisterium's authority only is intelligible in relation to the truth of doctrine.[34] Newman's vision for theology centered upon the interpretative pursuit of truth would be at home here.

However, Newman was appalled at the tyranny against theology by Catholic authorities in his own day. He recognized the right of Church authority to intervene in theological disputes, but he berated the abuse of that power. In his Dublin university lectures in 1854, he warned his audience of a "wrong Conservatism" among clerics, due to "an over-attachment to the ecclesiastical establishment" (*HS*, III, p. 132). He was sensitive especially to the suspicion of his article "On Consulting the Faithful" in 1859 that incurred a Vatican inquiry after he was reported to Rome by Bishop Brown of Newport. Following that inquiry, Newman began to record an expanding web of conservatism and suspicion that stifled theological freedom. Obliquely referring to the Vatican inquiry of his own work in the *Apologia*, he complained that when authority oppressed the theologian, "the freedom of his intellect might truly be said to be beaten out of him" (*Apo.*, p. 239). Four years later, in August 1868, writing to Henry Wilberforce, one of his oldest friends since Oriel, his discouragement was obvious: "Every word I publish will be malevolently scrutinized, and every expression which can possibly be perverted sent straight to Rome, . . . I shall be fighting *under the lash*, which does not tend to produce vigorous efforts in the battle or to inspire either courage or presence of mind" (*LD*, XXIV, p. 120; Newman's emphasis). Not surprisingly, two years later in the *Grammar*, when explaining the theory of assent, he called upon reason "to emancipate us from the capricious *ipse dixit* of authority" (*GA*, p. 262; Newman's emphasis).

Yet Newman also was astute politically. In his argument for consulting the faithful, he had no interest in fomenting disquiet among the laity.[35] Quite the contrary was the case because he adopted a submissive attitude toward episcopal oppression. He confided to Emily Bowles in May 1863, referring to the Vatican's inquiry of his work: "As what was said to me was very indirect and required no answer, I kept silence and the whole matter was hushed up" (*LD*, XX, p. 447). This silence applied not only to the Church authorities in Rome but also to his theological writing: "The cause of my not writing from 1859 to 1864 was my failure with the *Rambler*. I thought I had got into a scrap and it became me to be silent" (*AW*, p. 272).[36] But his submissiveness did not betoken intellectual diffidence: rather, it was a theological strategy to cope with an intractable situation. In July 1861 he wrote to Sir John Acton, a former associate with the *Rambler*, explaining that he was afraid of "the loss of union among ourselves, and the injury of great interests" (*LD*, XX, p. 5).[37] Newman was determined to maintain Church union and to minimize harm.[38]

Obedience and patience became the instruments of his theological tactics. Writing in January 1863 to William Monsell, a convert and friend in the Irish government who was fearful of the ecclesiastical restriction of religious freedom, Newman described his approach for handling Propaganda's suspicion of theological inquiry: "All this will be overruled; it may lead to much temporary mischief but it will be overruled. And we do not make things better by disobedience. We may be able indeed to complicate matters, and to delay the necessary reforms; but our part is obedience. If we are but patient, all will come right" (*LD*, XX, p. 391).

His commitment to obedience also is evident in a letter to his ordinary, Bishop Ullathorne. Even though Newman considered it imprudent to define the anticipated doctrine of infallibility ("no impending danger is to be averted, but a great difficulty is to be created"), he vowed submission if the doctrine should arise: "If it is God's will that the Pope's infallibility should be defined . . . I shall feel I have to bow my head to His adorable, inscrutable Providence" (*LD*, XXV, pp. 18–19). Newman again appealed to patience in April 1871 when he responded to Alfred Plummer's correspondence that had contained Döllinger's argument against papal infallibility. In it Newman disagreed with Döllinger's views but supported him in his plight by appealing to patience: "Let us be patient, let us have faith, and a new Pope, and a re-assembled Council may trim the boat" (*LD*, XXV, p. 310). Patience was necessary because theological change occurs slowly over a long period of time, for Newman a basic principle of doctrinal development.

Rather than construing his submissiveness to authority merely as personal compromise or intellectual diffidence, there is sufficient textual evidence to recognize a strategy for putting political expedience at the service of theological truth. Newman, therefore, adopted a prudential approach in obedience and patience that illustrated an underlying principle in his works: "The principle of Economy is this; that out of various courses, . . . that ought to be taken which is most expedient and most suitable at the time for the object in hand" (*Apo.*, p. 441).[39]

In short, by obedience Newman attempted to avoid provoking ecclesial authority in order to maintain the principle of unity among believers. By patience he attempted to minimize harm in the community in order to support the principle of charity. He recognized the right of authority to intervene in theological disputes, but he berated the abuse of this power: freedom of conscience and theological interpretation are restricted by authority but not suffocated. For Newman theological freedom and episcopal authority were legitimate and necessary, each restraining the other. Both Ian Ker, in his biography on Newman, and John T. Forde, in a theological analysis of Newman's thought, have argued that Newman maintained a keen balance between theology and authority.[40] I have traced the systematic foundation underlying this balance by relating theology to conscience and to authority in Newman's thought. It is this threefold interaction between conscience, theology, and authority, like three interlocking spans on a bridge, that provides the crucial connection between assent and dissent.

V. Dissent

To appreciate Newman's complete view on the ecclesial vocation of the theologian as enacting an appeal to the living mind (using informal inference), it is necessary to trace the moments both of private dissent and of public dissent in his own life. First, private dissent was quite explicit in his response as an Anglican to his bishops after publishing Tract 90 in February 1841, in which he examined whether the doctrine of the ancient Church was contained in the Thirty-Nine Articles:[41] "I yielded to the Bishops in outward act, viz. in not defending the Tract, . . . not only did I not assent inwardly to any condemnation of it, but I opposed myself to the proposition of a condemnation on the party of authority" (*Apo.*, p. 416).

His private dissent was directed against the opposition of the Anglican bishops to his tract. This type of private dissent is common in the Catholic Church today. For example, artificial contraception is condemned by the Catholic bishops because of an inseparable bond between sexual union and procreation in marriage.[42] Yet contraception is used frequently by Catholic spouses, often justified in their consciences by a convergence of arguments, akin to Newman's mode of informal inference.

In this regard, Newman's argument for consulting the faithful provides two important theological insights. First, his argument promotes interpreting the assents of the faithful as the conscience of the Church. On this point Newman was aware that the active recognition of truth in assent implies that others may not recognize the conclusion that is warranted by informal inference in conscience. This suggests a reason why most Catholic bishops do not formally accept or approve the experiential judgment of the laity to use artificial contraception: insofar as informal inference depends upon concrete experiences, the diverse experiences of celibate bishops and married laity create different contexts for discerning truth that elicits justified assent.

Second, Newman's argument promotes a subtle theology of doctrinal development. I have shown that when assent is justified it should illumine other knowledge. Arguably, then, assent (in the consciences of spouses) to the use of artificial contraception as the means of enhancing personal relations in marriage can illumine and safeguard a more basic Catholic doctrine, that is, the importance of personal relations in marriage as the generative context for future procreation. In other words, the interaction between conscience and theology as espoused by Newman creates a horizon of interpretation that inspires doctrinal development (in this case, on artificial contraception).

Newman's own experience of private dissent, then, supplies a spur to episcopal authority today to continue dialogue with the faithful and theologians alike. Private dissent, however, was not the only type of dissent to which he acceded. Legitimate public dissent can also be traced in his life. Of course, Newman rejected any dissent from infallible teaching. Hence, in his preface to the third edition of the *Via Media* in 1877 he explained: "The Catholic Church is ever more precise in her enunciation of doctrine, and allows no liberty of dissent from her decisions, (for on such objective matters she speaks with the authority of infallibility)" (*VM*, I, p. lxxv).[43] Nonetheless, in the same preface he implied that public dissent from noninfallible teaching was possible: "It is the worst charity, . . . not to speak out, not to suffer to be spoken out, all that there is to say. Such speaking out is . . . the triumph of religion, . . . but it is not always so" (*VM*, I, pp. lvi–lvii).

The context of this citation is suggestive of his preference for obedience to authority when embroiled in theological controversy. Speaking out is not always wise, he explained, because "veracity, like other virtues, lies in a mean" (*VM*, 1, p. lix). Here is another illustration of his principle of economy or reserve. Language cannot adequately express truth, so it is legitimate to withhold truth or to set it out to advantage,[44] for example, by being submissive through obedience. Robin Selby has shown persuasively that Newman personalized this principle of reserve in his life, always tending toward moderation.[45] But his sketch of Newman's character is incomplete without adverting to theological courage, a virtue that Newman openly extolled, and one that led to the public dissent of leaving the Anglican Church in 1845, and to the less dramatic controversies pertaining to private dissent within the Church, first, Tract 90 in 1841, and then, "On Consulting the Faithful" in 1859.

For Newman the role of obedience in theology was limited. By combining his concern for moderation with his commitment to courage, he constrained the call to obedience with the freedom of conscience. In his "Letter to the Duke of Norfolk" (1874), he defended "the supremacy of Conscience" by excluding the possibility of giving "an absolute obedience" to the Pope (*Diff*, II, pp. 243). By implementing assent in his understanding of conscience, he had utmost confidence in the supremacy of conscience as the primary mental instrument for discerning religious truth. Therefore, obedience must answer first to conscience.[46] Newman's stance illumines the long-standing teaching in the Catholic Church that "the religious submission of the will and the intellect" ("obsequium religiosum") must be given to the authentic authority of the ordinary Magisterium of Bishops.[47] He appreciated, both as an Anglican and as a Catholic, the possibility and the legitimacy of theological dissent within a doctrinal Church. In doing so, he contributes to the debate today on justified dissent between theologians[48] and bishops.[49]

Conclusion

Newman's defense of the supremacy of conscience did not idolize "a supreme magisterium of conscience," a phrase that I referred to in the introduction of this essay. This phrase appears in the recent Catholic "Instruction on the Ecclesial Vocation of the Theologian" to repudiate an exaggerated view of conscience, one that Newman also refuted. But Newman also opposed another extreme position, the ultramontanist promotion of uncritical obedience to ecclesiastical authority. For Newman, the ecclesial vocation of the theologian must strike a balance between the two extremes of unbridled conscience and unrestricted authority. To resist such polarization, he established an interaction between conscience and authority by appealing to the living mind of theology. In that way he maintained a constructive tension between the conscience of the community (the "sense of faith") and the authority of the bishops (the "Magisterium of the Church's Pastors").

Unfortunately, when the recent Catholic *Instruction* discusses the indissoluble bond between the "sense of the faith" and the "Magisterium of the Church's Pastors," a straw figure is drawn in the assertion that "the opinions of the faithful cannot be purely and simply identified with the *sensus fidei*."[50] The contribution that Newman can make to understanding the "sense of faith" is to elucidate the basic issue at stake, not opinion but rather the reasoning and judgment of assent in conscience. From an epistemological perspective, he presented a personal mode of reasoning (informal inference) as a nuanced and supple way for discerning truth. Hence, the "sense of faith" arises from the conscience of the Church, from judgments rather than from opinions, that is, from warranted assents. From a theological perspective, these assents arise as interpretations of the entire community of believers. Therefore, both the authority of conscience (the "sense of faith") and the bishops' authority (the "Magisterium of the Church's Pastors") must be respected.

Newman's achievement, then, is to provide the theological means for maintaining an indissoluble bond between the faithful and the Bishops. His larger strategy mentally was to build a bridge with three interlocking spans (conscience, theology, authority) that enabled him to traverse the apparent chasm between assent and dissent. In a more particular way, he relied upon personal reason (represented by his educational metaphor "the living mind") in theology to retain a healthy tension first between conscience and authority, and thereby between assent and dissent. Theology can be described as the central span of his bridge, holding in tension the other spans of conscience and authority: it was this appeal to the living mind in theology that enabled him to make an epistemological connection between assent and dissent. However, if we accompany Newman on his mental journey, we must be cautious. Bridges are notorious places for suicide. To discover the ecclesial vocation of the theologian, Newman advises us to beware of speedy but deluding solutions.

Notes

1. John Henry Newman, *Apologia Pro Vita Sua* (1864), edited with an introduction and notes by M. J. Svaglic (Oxford: Clarendon Press, 1967).

2. *The Letters and Diaries of John Henry Newman*, ed. Charles Stephen Dessain et al. Ian Ker's biography offers many examples of Newman's powers of irony, sarcasm, and satire as a controversial writer (*John Henry Newman: A Biography* [Oxford: Clarendon Press, 1988], for example, p. 66).

3. "Instruction on the Ecclesial Vocation of the Theologian," *Origins* (July 5, 1990): pp. 118–26; noted as *Instruction*.

4. *Instruction*, nos. 4 and 38.

5. John Henry Newman, *An Essay in Aid of a Grammar of Assent* (1870), edited with introduction and notes by I. T. Ker (Oxford: Clarendon Press, 1985); page references are to Newman's final edition (1889).

6. Emphasis added; see chapter VIII, sec. 2, "Informal Inference," in *GA*, pp. 288–329.

7. M. J. Ferreira has presented an insightful philosophical account of Newman's distinction between conditional inference and unconditional assent in terms of dependence and independence from the inferences ("Newman on Belief-

Confidence, Proportionality and Probability," *The Heythrop Journal* XXVI [1985]: p. 167).

8. John Henry Newman, *The Idea of a University Defined and Illustrated* (published 1873), integrates the *Discourses on the Scope and Nature of University Education* (published 1853) with the *Lectures and Essays on University Subjects* (published 1859), edited, introduction, and notes by I. T. Ker (Oxford: Clarendon Press, 1976); page references are to Newman's final edition (1889).

9. *Newman's University Sermons: Fifteen Sermons Preached before the University of Oxford, 1826–43*, with introductory essays by D. M. Mackinnon and J. D. Holmes (London: S.P.C.K. 1970); page references are to the third edition (1873). Elsewhere I explain how Newman also uses this metaphor in catechesis ("Newman's View of Catechesis: Safeguarding Faith and Morals," *The Living Light* vol. 27, no. 2 [1991]: pp. 103–11).

10. Adrian J. Boekraad and Henry Tristram, *The Argument from Conscience to the Existence of God, According to J. H. Newman* (Louvain: editions Nauwelaerts, 1961), noted as *Proof*, pp. 74, 103. Chapter IV contains Newman's unpublished paper "Proof of Theism." One justification for their view appears in these words of Newman: "Such is the argument for the being of God which I should wish, if it were possible, to maintain. It has been my chosen proof of that fundamental doctrine for thirty years past" (*Proof*, p. 121).

11. I believe that it was through emphasizing the orientation of conscience to God that Arthur Calkins did not develop the implications of Newman's "hermeneutical principles" for conscience; see "John Henry Newman on Conscience and the Magisterium," *The Downside Review* LXXXVII (1969): pp. 358–69.

12. For a detailed analysis of these aspects of conscience in terms of the autonomy and theonomy of moral discernment, see Gerard Magill, "Imaginative Moral Discernment: Newman on the Tension between Reason and Religion," *The Heythrop Journal* XXXII (1991): pp. 493–510, at pp. 499–507. Surprisingly, there is no mention of the landmark work on Newman's view of conscience, Boekraad and Tristram, *The Argument from Conscience*, in S. A. Grave's *Conscience in Newman's Thought* (Oxford: Clarendon Press, 1989).

13. Further, in a theological paper written in preparation of the *Grammar*, Newman explained that he did not intend to draw out a proof for the existence of God (*The Theological Papers of John Henry Newman on Faith and Certainty*, ed. Hugo M. de Achaval and J. Derek Holmes, vol. I [Oxford: Clarendon, 1976], p. 139).

14. In his 1873 edition, a footnote described the reasoning of conscience as "an *implicit* act of reasoning" (*US*, p. 66; Newman's emphasis), a term that he later identified with informal inference: "Such a process of reasoning is more or less implicit" (*GA*, p. 292).

15. He expressed this in French, "cette conscience de l'Eglise" (John Henry Newman, *On Consulting the Faithful in Matters of Doctrine* [1859], edited with an introduction by John Coulson [London: Geoffrey Chapman, 1961], p. 73). Later, he again referred to this capacity of communal perception as "the ecclesiastical sense or *phronema*," from "A Letter Addressed to His Grace the Duke of Norfolk on Occasion of Mr. Gladstone's Recent Expostulation"

(1874, published 1875), in *Certain Difficulties Felt by Anglicans in Catholic Teaching*, vol. II (London: Longmans, Green, 1898), p. 313.

16. A letter dated April 1870 to Richard Holt Hutton, the literary editor of the *Spectator*.

17. *Instruction*, no. 38. The opposite view, that "the teaching office is dependent on the conscience of the faithful," was stated by some European theologians in "The Cologne Declaration," *Origins* (November 2, 1989): p. 634.

18. He argued that "the *fidelium sensus* and *consensus* is a branch of evidence which it is natural or necessary for the Church to regard and consult, before she proceeds to any definition" (*Cons.*, p. 55).

19. Avery Dulles, "The Threefold Office in Newman's Ecclesiology," in Ian Ker and Alan G. Hill, eds., *Newman After a Hundred Years* (Oxford: Clarendon Press, 1990), p. 382.

20. This phrase is also cited in his 1859 article (see *Cons.*, p. 78). The positive meaning that Newman accorded to this Augustinian phrase is manifest in the rule of Vincent of Lerins (died circa 450): "That is to be received as Apostolic which has been taught 'always, everywhere, and by all.' Catholicity, Antiquity, and consent of Fathers, is the proper evidence of the fidelity or Apostolicity of a professed tradition" (John Henry Newman, *The Via Media of the Anglican Church* [1837], edited with introduction and notes by H. D. Weidner [Oxford: Clarendon Press, 1990], p. 51). Page references are to Newman's 1889 edition of the *Via Media*, vol. I.

21. John Henry Newman, *Parochial and Plain Sermons*, 8 vols., from 1834 (London: Longmans, Green, 1891); also see *VM*, I, p. lvi.

22. *Instruction*, no. 4, referring to the "Dogmatic Constitution on the Church," no. 12, in Austin Flannery, ed., *Vatican II* (Wilmington: Scholarly Resources, 1975).

23. Walter Jost, *Rhetorical Thought in John Henry Newman* (Columbia: University of South Carolina Press, 1989), pp. 108–38; holding a view for Newman meant interpreting a concrete problem, based upon personal experience, and structured for comprehension (p. 111). David Hammond referred to this emphasis upon method as Newman's "hermeneutical theology" in "Imagination and Hermeneutical Theology: Newman's Contribution to Theological Method," *The Downside Review* 106 (1988): pp. 17–34.

24. Newman wrote, "Religious teaching itself affords us an illustration of our subject" (John Henry Newman, *Historical Sketches*, vol. III [London: Longmans, Green, 1891], p. 14).

25. Nicholas Lash has traced a development in Newman's theological method from using deductive to using inductive reasoning ("Was Newman a Theologian?" *The Heythrop Journal* XVII [1976]: pp. 322–25). Also, I have examined the influence of Newman's philosophy of education upon the development of his theological method ("Newman on Liberal Education and Moral Pluralism," *Scottish Journal of Theology*, vol. 45, no. 1 [1992]: pp. 45–64).

26. The "Declaration on Religious Liberty," no. 9, in Flannery, *Vatican II*.

27. Newman also stated in a letter, dated 1870, that relying upon the "Schola Theologorum" was a maxim upon which all depends; see *LD*, XXIV, pp. 354–55.

28. In his 1877 preface to the *Via Media*, Newman again asserted that "there was nothing wrong in censuring abrupt, [startling], unsettling, unverified disclosures" (*VM*, I, p. lv); the word [*startling*] appears in the standard edition (Longmans, Green, 1891), but not in Weidner's critical edition.

29. The "Dogmatic Constitution on the Church," no. 25, in Flannery, *Vatican II*, pp. 379–81, and the *Instruction*, nos. 15–17, 24. For the definition of infallibility at the First Vatican Council (1870), see H. Denzinger and A. Schönmetzer, eds., *Enchiridion Symbolorum* (Rome: Herder, 1967), no. 3074. More recently, the *Instruction* asserts that truths proposed in a definitive way "must be firmly accepted and held" (no. 23), referring to the text of the new profession of faith, "Profession of Faith and Oath of Fidelity," *AAS* 81 (1989), no. 15, and the new *Code of Canon Law*, canon 833.

30. The "Decree on Ecumenism," no. 11, in Flannery, *Vatican II*, p. 462, and "On the Interpretation of Dogmas," *Origins* (May 17, 1990): pp. 1–15 at no. III:3. The importance of this hierarchy of truths was a central part of the theologians' criticism of Church authority in "The Cologne Declaration," *Origins* (November 2, 1989): p. 633. Charles Curran has developed the distinction between infallible and noninfallible teachings by differentiating what is central and peripheral to the faith ("Public Dissent in the Church," *Origins* [July 31, 1986]: p. 181). For an overview of the relation between the Catholic Magisterium and the hierarchy of truths, see Stephen Happel and James J. Walter, *Conversion and Discipleship* (Philadelphia: Fortress Press, 1986), pp. 184–91.

31. For a succinct history of the term *ordinary magisterium*, see William W. May, "Catholic Moral Teaching and the Limits of Dissent," in *Vatican Authority and American Catholic Dissent*, ed. William W. May, (New York: Crossroads, 1987), pp. 87–90.

32. The *Instruction* claims that documents from this Congregation "expressly approved by the pope participate in the ordinary magisterium" (no. 17), which can withdraw "from a theologian who departs from the doctrine of the faith the canonical mission or the teaching mandate" (no. 37). This question centers upon "the degree of authority" with which a doctrine is taught; see "The Apostolic Constitution on Catholic Universities," *Origins* (October 4, 1990): no. 29, referring to the "Dogmatic Constitution on the Church," no. 25, in Flannery, *Vatican II*. A crucial issue in the controversy over the Vatican's withdrawal of the teaching mandate from the Catholic moral theologian Charles Curran was "the possibility of public theological dissent from some non-infallible hierarchical teachings," Charles Curran, "Public Dissent in the Church," *Origins* (July 13, 1986): p. 179.

33. Charles Curran argued that the requirement of a mandate in the new *Code of Canon Law*, canon 812, implies the latter view ("Public Dissent in the Church," p. 179). Newman, akin to Curran's view, espoused the former view.

34. See, *Instruction*, nos. 14, 40.

35. Newman's caution disarmed a whimsical remark made in 1867 by Monsignor George Talbot to Archbishop Manning: "Dr. Newman is the most dangerous man in England, and you will see that he will make use of the laity against

your Grace" (Wilfred Ward, *The Life of Cardinal Newman* [London: Long-mans, Green, 1913], vol. II, p. 147). Also, see Newman's letter to George Talbot written in August 1850 (*LD*, XIV, p. 35). In 1850 Monsignor Talbot, as papal chamberlain to Pius IX, had sought Newman's counsel about the state of the English Catholic Church.

36. *John Henry Newman: Autobiographical Writings*, ed. Henry Tristram (New York: Sheed and Ward, 1956).

37. Newman was referring to Richard Simpson's reaction to the bishops: "He will always be flicking his whip at Bishops, cutting them in tender places, throwing stones at sacred Congregations, and, as he rides along the high road, discharg-ing pea shooters at Cardinals who happen by bad luck to look out of window" (*LD*, XX, pp. 4–5), an approach that he later described as "ill sounding words on sacred and delicate subjects" (*LD*, XX, p. 391, to William Monsell, dated January 1863).

38. Although William Ribando made no reference to Newman's interpretative theology, he shrewdly noted that his teaching of truth was regulated by pastoral concerns ("Newman on Prophecy and Dissent," *The Catholic World* [January/February 1990]: p. 42). Similarly, Terence Merrigan called this Newman's "devotional sense" in "Newman the Theologian," *Louvain Studies* (Summer-Fall, 1990): p. 113.

39. Newman recovered the principle of economy from the early Alexandrian Church; see *The Arians of the Fourth Century*, 1833 (London: Longmans, Green, 1890), p. 65. Closely connected was his sacramental principle, which he learned from Bishop Butler (see *Apo.*, pp. 29–30). Together, these principles expressed his awareness of the importance and limitations of language and symbol (see *Apo.*, pp. 36–37).

40. Ian Ker has argued that for Newman truth is attained through the conflict of opposites (*John Henry Newman: A Biography*, pp. 553–54), and John Forde has examined how Newman theologically encountered these conflicts ("Danc-ing on the Tightrope: Newman's View of Theology," *Proceedings: The Catholic Theological Society of America* 40 [1985]: pp. 127–44).

41. John Henry Newman, "Remarks on Certain Passages in the Thirty-Nine Articles" (Tract 90), *Tracts for the Times*, vol. VI (London: Rivington, 1841). His Anglican biographer Sheridan Gilley described the difficulty of Newman's attempt in Tract 90 to prove that the Thirty-Nine Articles of Anglicanism could be read in a Catholic sense as an exercise that looked like squaring the circle (*Newman And His Age* [London: Darton, Longman and Todd, 1990], p. 198). As would be the case with his later article "On Consulting the Faithful" (1859), Newman proclaimed that he anticipated no reaction to his theological argument on the Thirty-Nine Articles in correspondence with Mrs. T. Mozley, March 1841, referred to by his Catholic biographer Ian Ker (*John Henry Newman: A Biography*, p. 218).

42. "Humanae Vitae" (Encyclical Letter of Pope Paul VI on the Regulation of Birth, July 25, 1968), in *Love and Sexuality*, ed. Odile M. Liebard (Wilmington, N.C.: A Consortium Book, 1978), nos. 12–14, pp. 336–38. F. Bak argued that Newman would have supported this papal teaching against artificial con-

traception ("Bernard Häring's Interpretation of Cardinal Newman's Treatise on Conscience," *Ephemerides Theologicae Lovaniensis* 49 [1973]: pp. 124–59). The serious flaw in this essay is that Bak attributed to Newman the view that theology can only legitimately influence the laity indirectly, that is, through their confessors (p. 148).

43. As an Anglican vicar in 1837, he discussed the concept of infallibility when he published his weekday parochial lectures on the prophetical office of the Church in the *Via Media*, and he explicitly defended the theology of an infallible Church in *An Essay on the Development of Christian Doctrine*, 1845 (Notre Dame, Ind.: University of Notre Dame Press, 1989); see the sections, "Doctrine of Infallibility Morally Considered," "Doctrine of Infallibility Politically Considered," "The Indefectibility of the Catholic Church," in his *Via Media*, vol. I, pp. 83–105, 106–27, 189–213, and the section, "An infallible Developing Authority to be expected" in *Dev.*, pp. 75–92; also see *Apologia* pp. 223–31, *LD*, XXIV, p. 92, dated June 1868; and *LD*, XXV, p. 277, dated January 1871.

44. Newman explained that the principle of economy was engaged in "withholding the truth" and the ancient "Disciplina Arcani" with "setting it out to advantage" (*Ari.*, p. 65).

45. Robin C. Selby, *The Principle of Reserve in the Writings of John Henry Cardinal Newman* (Oxford: Oxford University Press, 1975), pp. 99–101.

46. This view has been most clearly expressed by James Gaffney ("Newman as a Moralist," *The Catholic World* [January/February 1990]: p. 27).

47. *Instruction*, no. 23, referring to the "Dogmatic Constitution on the Church," no. 25, in Flannery, *Vatican II*. For the equivalent teaching in the First Vatican Council, see Denziger and Schönmetzer, no. 3008. Although "obsequium" is often translated as submission or obedience, the English version of the new *Code of Canon Law* uses the word "respect" (canon 752).

48. For example, Charles Curran enunciated six reasons to justify some public theological dissent: the distinction between infallible and noninfallible teachings, historical errors in papal teaching, epistemology, theology, ecclesiology, authority and truth ("Authority and Dissent in the Church," *Origins* [November 6, 1986]: p. 375). For a study on the distinction between private and public dissent, see Richard M. Gula, "The Right to Private and Public Dissent from Specific Pronouncements of the Ordinary Magisterium," *Eglise et théologie* 9 (1978): pp. 323–32. The most insightful collections of essays by theologians on authority and dissent in the Catholic tradition are: William W. May, ed., *Vatican Authority*; and Charles Curran and Richard McCormick, eds., *Readings in Moral Theology No. 6: Dissent in the Church* (New York: Paulist, 1988).

49. In a pastoral letter from the Catholic bishops of the United States, three norms are listed as conditions for legitimate theological dissent. Following the tradition of the Manuals in Moral Theology, the Bishops explained that the reasons for dissent had to be serious and well-founded, that the manner of dissent must not question the teaching authority of the Church, and that scandal should not be given ("Human Life in our Day," [the National Conference of Catholic Bishops, November 15, 1968], no. 49). Unfortunately, such

explicit criteriology for legitimate dissent is not discussed in Pope John Paul II's "Apostolic Constitution on Catholic Universities" (1990); nonetheless, the document recognizes that the Catholic university "possesses that institutional autonomy necessary to perform its functions effectively and guarantees its members academic freedom, so long as the rights of the individual person and of the community are preserved within the confines of the truth and the common good" (*Origins* [October 4, 1990]: pp. 266–75, at no. 12). For a recent episcopal explanation of the possibility of theological dissent, see Archbishop Quinn, "Observations on the Doctrinal Congregation's Instruction," *Origins* (September 6, 1990): p. 203.

50. *Instruction*, no. 35. On the relation between the "*sensus fidei*" and the "magisterium" of bishops, see the "Dogmatic Constitution on the Church," no. 12, in Flannery, *Vatican II*.

Part 5

Interpretation

10

Receiving Newman's Development of Christian Doctrine

C. J. T. Talar

> A literary work is not an object that stands by itself and that offers the same
> view to each reader in each period. . . . It is much more like an orchestration
> that strikes ever new resonances among its readers and that frees the text
> from the material of the words and brings it to a contemporary existence.
> —Jauss, *Toward an Aesthetic of Reception*

The *Rezeptionsästhetik* of H. R. Jauss is part of a larger movement within literary theory from a text-centered criticism to a greater concern with the activity of the reader.[1] Attention shifts from the work as "artifact"—the text in print—to the "aesthetic object"—reader realizations or "concretizations" of the text. A single artifact thus may result in many different aesthetic objects according to its many particular realizations among readers.[2] Jauss believes that this multiplicity of meanings, and the inevitable disagreements about meaning that arise, must be explained. He further observes that the most interesting disagreements are those that obtain between reader realizations belonging to different historical periods. Attending to the interaction over time between texts and their readers is productive of histories of reception: of individual works, of authors, of genres, and of normative periods (for example, romanticism).[3]

Central to Jauss's early work is the notion "horizon of expectations." While the term remains somewhat imprecise in Jauss's usage,[4] basically it refers to a set of assumptions and conventions in a given period that govern the practice of writers and readers. The assumptions would include those that are literary (about the nature of genre, for example) as well as nonliterary (about the "wide" horizon of the context of literature, assumptions about life). Insofar as the contemporary readers of a particular author read his or her work within a dominant horizon of expectations that is shared, the writer will be readily understood by contemporaries. When a work exceeds the expectations of contemporary readers, it will meet difficulties in interpretation and may even generate resistance. It is precisely these cases in which "aesthetic distance" is large that are of most interest to Jauss. For the text may be productive of readings that challenge the prevailing systems of literary and extraliterary norms, and if those readings gain sufficient adherents, a mutation of horizon may result. The original horizon may undergo elaboration, correction, or modification.[5]

Even in the case of a work that gains initial acceptance by its contemporaries, change in a horizon of expectations over time stemming from other sources may alter its reception for a later generation. Since a single work is conceived as embodying several different structures with different dominants and hierarchies of components, the way is open to a multiplicity of concretizations according to the theoretical context of reception. The work becomes an "unambiguous structure" only if perceived against the background of a particular tradition in relation to which the work is judged to conform or to deviate.[6]

For Jauss, then, the meaning of a text is a "convergence of the structure of the work and the structure of the interpretation, which is ever to be achieved anew."[7] In what follows, we shall be concerned with one particular work, John Henry Newman's *Essay on the Development of Christian Doctrine*, at two points of "convergence": its initial reception by contemporary readers and its turn-of-the-century reception in the context of the modernist crisis. To provide a point of focus, attention will center (though not exclusively) on French readers.

I. Initial Reception

When *An Essay on the Development of Christian Doctrine* was published in November 1845, it contained an "Advertisement" that set forth the modest aim of the work, quoted previous statements made by its author against the Church of Rome in order to retract them, and submitted the book to the judgment of that Church. That, coupled with a statement of its author's conversion to Catholicism, should have disarmed any Catholics inclined to fasten upon any of its shortcomings. Nonetheless, a month after its publication, James Hope wrote to Newman asking "how the Roman Catholics in general regard your book," adding, "My experience would lead me to think that many of them would be startled by it, and I look with anxiety for notices of it in that quarter." Newman replied promptly, informing him that Catholic reaction had thus far been favorable.[8]

Hope's anxieties were not idle. The discordant note, however, was sounded not by English Catholics but by an American, Orestes Brownson, himself a recent convert. In July 1846, in the first of a series of articles, he attacked Newman's book in strong language, denying the very existence of historical variations in doctrine and censuring it as "essentially anti-Catholic and Protestant."[9] The American reception of the *Essay* is of interest here chiefly for the anxiety it provoked in Newman. Soon after arriving in Rome, he learned that Brownson's initial criticisms of his book were known in Rome and that in some quarters it was deemed that he had carried the principle of development too far.[10] To J. D. Dalgairns he declared his concern for the exactness of the planned French translation, fearful lest an "incautious rendering of particular phrases . . . ruin everything."[11]

Thus, there was a range of responses providing a larger context for French reception of the *Essay on Development*: from the favorable reception accorded it by English Catholics, responding either to the "difficulty" that Newman was attempting to address or simply to the book's role as catalyst for conversions to Roman Catholicism; to the difficulties and objections it raised among Roman theologians; and further to the rather harsh criticism it sustained in some American circles. Given the relative lack of knowledge of English among Roman theologians, the French translation of the work and its French reception assumed importance.

Before the translation over which Newman had expressed concern to Dalgairns appeared, an unauthorized one was published in 1847 by L. d'Auvigny. Chadwick dryly comments, "Though this buccaneer edition proved the lively interest which the *Essay* had aroused in Catholic France, its translator did not possess the two qualities required to translate competently—he understood neither theology nor the English language."[12] The authorized translation by Jules Gondon did not appear until 1848,[13] a year that also saw a number of published reactions.

Neither Newman's book nor French responses to it appeared in a vacuum. Both the person of Newman and the Oxford Movement in which he had played so prominent a role were followed with interest in French Catholic circles. As Louis Allen has pointed out, both via personal contacts and via the French Catholic press information on the Tractarians was disseminated in France.[14] Newman himself had appeared in French periodicals in the course of his controversy with the Abbé J.-N. Jager in the mid-1830s[15] and in person on his journey to Rome following upon his conversion.

The first evaluation of the *Essay* in the Gondon translation appeared in *L'Univers* of January 9 and 20, 1848—appropriately enough, for *L'Univers* had been the most regular and most complete source of information on Anglican and Roman Catholic matters in England.[16] The author credited Newman's originality while stressing his connection with the Roman Catholic theological tradition, citing Vincent of Lerins, St. Gregory the Great, and Suarez.[17]

Following close upon these appreciations of Newman's book was an article by Mgr. Clément Villecourt, bishop of La Rochelle, which was published in *L'Ami de la religion*.[18] While also careful to establish connections between Newman and previous theologians, he is even more extravagant with his praise than were the *Univers* articles.

Shortly after Villecourt's encomium, an appreciation of a rather different sort surfaced in the review *La liberté de penser*. Its author, Emile Saisset, concluded his treatment of the *Essay* by noting that "whether [Rome] knows it or not, in absolving Dr. Pusey's disciple she is granting absolution to rationalism."[19] Saisset's evaluation is introduced into this recital of French Catholic reception of Newman partly to show that on French turf as well the *Essay* could be read in many ways but also because it evoked a defense from the Abbé Darboy, future archbishop of Paris. In it he carefully distinguished between rationalist and Catholic understandings of development, ranging Newman on the side of the latter.[20]

From the foregoing survey, brief as it is, it is apparent that the "artifacts" (the presence of translations makes it necessary to speak in the plural) of the *Essay on Development* were realized in a diversity of "aesthetic objects." Further, the presence of this diversity is reflective of the complexity inherent in the "horizon of expectations." Confessional and ideological diversity is complicated along national and cultural lines. In Jauss's theory the horizon of expectations provides an intersubjective framework for text reception. A given text, however innovative, is understood against a background, assimilated to a preunderstanding of the genre, to the forms and themes of already familiar works. "A literary work, even when it appears to be new . . . predisposes its audience to a very specific kind of reception by announcements, overt or covert signals, familiar characteristics, or implicit allusions."[21]

Against a background of scholastic theology the *Essay* was apparently difficult to classify.[22] Newman offered "development" as an "hypothesis"—

an alternative to "immutability," on the one hand, and "corruption," on the other. Taking his stand on historical terrain, thus distinguishing his work from the prevailing deductivist theology, he based his argument on several analogies—some derived from logic, others more organic in character. As Nicholas Lash has argued, structured into the work is not so much a theory of development but "in rudimentary form, the seeds of a number of such theories, the systematic elaboration of which might show that they are not mutually compatible."[23]

In French Catholic reception, there is a common tendency to assimilate Newman's *Essay on Development* to the familiar works of the tradition, referencing canonical theologians or even quoting them at some length. While the utility of this theory for controversy is celebrated, it is not explicated. The structure of Newman's argument is summarized; the structures of the *Essay* suggested in Lash's observation are not deeply probed.

Contingent upon the objectification of the horizon of expectation is the historical objectification of "aesthetic distance"—the disjuncture between the dominant convention, on the one hand, and the individual work, its formal structure and the concretizing interpretation, on the other. Where aesthetic distance is great, the work may throw into relief aspects of the historical consciousness that had heretofore remained largely unconscious. Through the question it poses, it may serve as an individual disruption of an answer that had become common knowledge.[24] Aesthetic distance is greatest in Brownson's reception. The Vincentian Canon is reaffirmed, any variation or historical development of doctrine thereby excluded, and a Church "withdrawn from the ordinary law of human systems and institutions by her supernatural origin, nature, character, and protection" defended against Newman.[25] Also motivating the attack was the use that the Unitarians of Boston were making of Newman's arguments to argue against Roman positions. This constitutes a reminder that Jauss's concept of horizon has a nonliterary component: while theological works are received within an immediate context of a disciplinary matrix, the latter is not independent of wider social contexts. Here this component can only be referenced rather than developed. French Catholic reception, by contrast, exhibited minimal disjuncture.

II. Reception During the Modernist Period

In the years following the *Essay on Development*'s initial reception in France, it continued to receive a modest amount of attention, though it could not be said to have had significant impact on French theology.[26]

Indeed, between 1870 and 1890 only a handful of "newmaniens" could be counted in France. Yet at the turn of the century that state of affairs would change dramatically. Additional works by Newman would be translated; articles and books commending and controverting Newman's positions mushroomed within a very short span until, with the condemnation of modernism, a cloud would once again descend upon the figure of the famous English convert.

How to explain this sudden revival of interest? The *Grammar* was still not translated, and the *Essay*'s depths still largely unprobed. From across the channel Wilfred Ward discerned specifically French causes for this unexpected revival. He felt that Auguste Sabatier's *Esquisse d'une philosophie de la religion* (1897) to a great extent accounted for it.[27]

Although Ward, at the end of his article, was careful to differentiate Newman from Sabatier in several crucial respects and sought to demonstrate the cardinal's superiority in dealing with matters of development, much of his analysis highlighted areas of "very close resemblance."[28] Quoting Sabatier's contention that "dogmas . . . have an inner life and develop continually by a kind of secret and irresistible growth," an "evolution" rendered possible by this "living power" and "absolutely necessary by the laws of history," he observed that these "are precisely the points emphasized in the introduction to Cardinal Newman's *Essay on the Development of Christian Doctrine*."[29] By emphasizing the evolutionary and organic aspects of Newman's thought in juxtaposing them to Sabatier's, Ward was reflecting a line of interpretation that Alfred Loisy had set forth in his 1898 article in the *Revue du clergé français*[30] (*RCF*) and would develop in *L'Evangile et l'église* (1902).

Antedating Loisy's RCF article was a critical review of Sabatier's *Esquisse*, published in *Le Correspondant* of 1897 by Mgr. Eudoxe-Irenée Mignot. While critiquing Sabatier's conception of development as an evolutionary naturalism and finding it reflective of a whole current of thought then influential in France, Mignot argued that development could be represented in terms not incompatible with the Christian idea. A laudatory reference to Newman signaled the proper alternative.[31]

Clearly influenced by this evolutionary current of thought, Loisy found Mignot's refutation of Sabatier "a bit insufficient."[32] In setting forth his own account of the cardinal's theory in the *RCF* he not only accentuated the organic and evolutionary side of Newman's approach but also sought to develop Newman on development. Newman was represented as being more interested in setting forth the notion of development than in determining its exact scope of application. Primarily a patristic scholar, Newman attempted to account for the fact of development within Christian history. Aware of the problems posed by historical criticism in the period since the *Essay*'s initial publication, Loisy expanded the range of development to encompass the Scriptures themselves. In this Loisy is conscious of having to go beyond Newman in grappling with the problem of how revelation itself enters into the developmental process.[33]

The problem was developed further in subsequent "Firmin" articles on the level of principle and in *L'Evangile et l'église* on that of historical application. While the latter work contains reassuring references to development by "deduction" and to "logical necessities," they are ultimately subordinate to the predominance of organic metaphors and a perspective that invokes life over logic. In this Loisy was consistent with his 1898 *RCF* article though one-sided in his emphasis where Newman's thought was concerned. While such organicist analogies can be found in the *Essay*, they are not the prime analogate or the leading idea.[34]

The attractiveness of this notion of evolution is evidenced by the testimony of some of those who were critical of Loisy's work. Abbé Hippolyte Gayraud, writing on *L'Evangile et l'église* shortly after the book's publication, showed himself receptive, in principle, to a conception of Christianity as "living" and a notion of development that is less logical and more organic. However, he remains anxious to preserve Christianity's substantial identity within that organic framework.[35]

To others, such as Charles Maignen, the notion of evolution was inherently corrosive of Christianity, and any concession to it was ultimately a concession to rationalism.[36] Any attempt to claim the mantle of Newman's authority for a theory of development was delegitimated by categorizing the *Essay on Development* as "the story of a soul in quest of truth" written while its author was "still Protestant."[37]

III. Outcomes of Modernist Reception

Between initial French reception of Newman's *Essay* and turn-of-the-century renderings of it, there obviously occurred a shift in the horizon of expectations. Through a combination of extraliterary factors (for example, what Lonergan has termed a shift in "cultures" from a "classicist" culture to one more historically oriented) and specifically theological factors (for example, the increasing impact of historical criticism on Catholic biblical scholarship or the publication of Sabatier's *Esquisse*), the context of reception underwent significant change. Something of the nature of that later horizon, both from the side of the neo-scholasticism dominant in Catholic theology and from that of the progressive perspectives that judged it inadequate, can be determined from *L'Evangile et l'église* itself. The latter represents one of Jauss's "ideal cases" that "evoke the reader's horizon of expectations, formed by a convention of genre, style, or form, only in order to destroy it step by step."[38] Blondel perceptively appreciated the similarity Loisy was able to invoke between Harnack's liberal Protestant *fixisme* and that of neo-scholasticism.[39] In attacking the first, Loisy sought to undermine the other in order to create a space for his own rendering of development.

In so doing, he reformulated the question Newman had posed and likewise its answer. Though disagreeing with Newman, Brownson accurately rendered the problem: "How to explain, in accordance with Christian truth, the variations or differences of doctrine and discipline which the Roman Catholic Church presents to-day, from the doctrine and discipline presented by the primitive Church."[40] For Loisy, at issue was not only the continuity between primitive Church and nineteenth century Catholicism but the continuity between the Gospel and the Church. At stake was not only development of doctrine, worship, and institution within the Church but development within revelation itself.

For Jauss, the historical conditions of question and answer set limits on the range of possible interpretations of a text. The possibility of multiple interpretations is a product of textual indeterminacy: the structures it embodies are capable of being constituted and interrelated in a number of ways, leading to varied historical realizations as aesthetic objects.[41] The presence of different conceptions of doctrinal development that are to be found in the *Essay*, neither fully elaborated nor systematically interrelated, together with the various types of analogies that give them expression, render it a relatively "open" text. As an "open" text, with a high degree of indeterminacy, it was capable of a realization in response to Loisy's question that emphasized its evolutionary and organicist aspects. To Maignen, on the other hand, for whom revelation was a "deposit," the existence of the problem addressed by Loisy was simply denied, the *Essay* devalued, and the exegete's effort judged as rationalist—echoing, interestingly, Saisset's earlier judgment of Newman. Loisy's reception of Newman, while welcomed in some quarters,[42] in others heightened an "aesthetic distance" with respect to the expectations of the dominant theology. The cautious receptivity of a Gayraud to organic conceptions of development would become increasingly impossible in a climate that reflected Brownson's conception of the supernatural character of the Church and its doctrine and that interpreted historical development as naturalistic when read in the context of the evolutionary strain of thought present in Sabatier. As the modernist crisis deepened, Newman's thought would be drawn into that distance.

Loisy's work represented one portion of a larger revival in France founded on Newman's teaching. B.-D. Dupuy has noted the existence of several different tendencies among French progressives. He distinguishes, first, the tendency represented by Loisy to emphasize the symbolism of Christian revelation, drawing Newman's thought into contact with that of Auguste Sabatier. A second tendency, finding its exemplar in Abbé Charles Denis, appealed to Newman's thought in support of the philosophy of Action. A third group gave prominence to the psychological, historical, and moral elements of Christianity dealt with by Newman, as an antidote to scholastic thought. Its most famous representative was Abbé Henri Bremond.[43]

While Loisy represents engagement with one of the primary questions of the modernist period—that of history, the history of dogmas and religious history—the latter two groups tended to focus on another—the process of intelligence (to use the Blondelian expression). Nonetheless, while the problem of the process of reason served as the principal focus of Bremond's attention, he was not disinterested in issues that engaged Loisy.[44] Since his work bears significantly on French reception of Newman's *Essay on Development*, a word must be said about it here.

In 1905 Bremond brought out the first of what would be a series of works on Newman: *Newman: Le développement du dogme chrétien*. It was not a reissue of an integral translation of the *Essay* but rather Bremond's presentation of Newman, combining material from the Oxford University sermon on development and the *Essay*, interposed with Bremond's analytical summaries. Bremond's book went into a third edition in less than a year, attesting to French interest in Newman. It was based, however, on the defective translation of d'Auvigny (thus realizing Newman's anxieties of some decades earlier). That, coupled with Bremond's own representation of Newman in the book's introduction, drew forth a severely critical response from Wilfred Ward. He noted the instance of an article by an Old Catholic containing "pages of the most highly stringent theological criticism," criticism based however on Bremond's unfaithful rendering of Newman rather than on Newman's true position.[45] The instance signaled by Ward was but symptomatic of Bremond's influence as an interpreter of Newman in France. Even where the response to Newman would be considerably less enthusiastic than Bremond's, as in the case of de Grandmaison, nonetheless Bremond's interpretation was accepted.[46]

Variety of reception, where Newman was concerned, among French progressives was replicated among French traditionalists. If de Grandmaison found Newman acceptable only within specified limits, others sought to assimilate him to the scholastic position. In 1905 J. Bainvel claimed that Newman's position on development did not differ significantly from that of Vincent of Lerins.[47] At the opposite extreme, George Tyrrell wrote the following year that he had heard that Mgr. Turinaz was insistent on Roman condemnation of the *Essay on Development*.[48]

While Newman's own work escaped condemnation, in post-*Lamentabili*, post-*Pascendi* Catholicism his thought became suspect to many. Little wonder, given Ward's comparison of Newman to Sabatier, while Loisy's own proximity to Sabatier's position would have further assimilated Newman's thought into that current.[49] And, significantly, Pierre Colin has argued that the model underlying *Pascendi* was importantly inspired by Sabatier's work in the philosophy of religion.[50] In that atmosphere, to be called a "Newmanist" in Vaticanese meant to be placed "on the downward slope to Modernism."[51] In French circles Newman's writings went into another period of eclipse.[52] Postmodernist reception of Newman is suggested in Janusz Sławinski's comment:

> The reader in whom the literary historian takes interest is not innocent and defenseless in his approach to the text: since he is already formed by his previous reading experiences, he knows how to read "properly," that is, according to the standards of a defined literary culture. Nor for that matter is the text "innocent" by the time it reaches the reader, but replete with meanings ascribed by earlier readings, locked up in explications and judgments, inscribed in classifications and axiological hierarchies. Inevitably, a text is read together with the remains of earlier, alien readings.[53]

In Jauss's terms, the *Essay on Development* was a "productive" text, one possessing the capacity to enter into different schemes of coordinates outside its original one. Likewise, both Loisy and Bremond represent "productive receptions" of the *Essay*, readings of considerable normative power.

In the end, Thomas Carlyle's observation made with respect to the reception of German literature in England might well be applied to the impact of Newman's work in France: "The history of its progress here would illuminate the progress of more important things; would again exemplify what obstacles a new spiritual object, with its mixture of truth and falsehood, has to encounter from unwise enemies; still more from unwise friends."[54]

Notes

1. Hans Robert Jauss, *Toward an Aesthetic of Reception*, trans. Timothy Bahti (Minneapolis: University of Minnesota, 1982), p. 21 (hereafter cited as *TAR*).
2. Here Jauss's theory reveals a particular indebtedness to the Prague Structuralists. See Felix Vodička, "The Concretization of the Literary Work," in Peter Steiner, ed., *The Prague School*, trans. John Burbank et al. (Austin: University of Texas, 1982).
3. Rien T. Segers, "An Interview with Hans Robert Jauss," *New Literary History* 11 (1979): pp. 89–90 (hereafter cited as *NLH*).
4. See Robert C. Holub, *Reception Theory* (London: Methuen, 1984), pp. 58ff.
5. *TAR*, pp. 22ff. Rita Schober, "Réception et historicité de la littérature," *Revue des sciences humaines* LX (1983): p. 10. In Jauss's later work, this "negating" aspect of texts in relation to prevailing expectations diminishes in prominence.
6. Steiner, p. 103. Claude de Grève, "Méthodologie de la réception comparée," *Oeuvres et Critiques* XI (1986): p. 165.
7. *NLH*, p. 84.
8. *The Letters and Diaries of John Henry Newman*, ed. Charles Stephen Dessain et al., vol. XI, pp. 75n. and 75–76. For particular reactions, see C. S. Dessain, "The Reception among Catholics of Newman's Doctrine of Development: Newman's Own Impressions," *Newman Studien*, vol. VI (Nuremberg: Glock and Lutz, 1964), pp. 180–81.
9. Brownson's series of articles, which originally appeared in *Brownson's Quarterly Review* between July 1846 and October 1848, are collected in *The Works of Orestes A. Brownson*, vol. XIV (Detroit: H. F. Brownson, 1906). The quoted portion may be found on page 5 of the latter. While Brownson later publicly owned that his criticism of Newman was based on a misunderstanding of the *Essay on Development*, he continued to disagree profoundly with Newman on issues concerning truth and logical certainty. See Daniel R. Barnes, "Brownson and Newman: The Controversy Re-examined," *Emerson Society Quarterly* 50 (1968) Supplement: pp. 9–20.
10. Roman difficulties with the *Essay on Development* are set forth in Owen Chadwick, *From Bossuet to Newman* (Cambridge: Cambridge University, 1957), chap. VIII.
11. Letter of November 15, 1846, *LD*, XI, p. 274.
12. Chadwick, *From Bossuet to Newman*, p. 175.
13. As *Histoire du développement de la doctrine chrétienne* (Paris: Sagnier et Bray, 1848). In the translator's forward, Gondon devoted several pages to pointing out errors in d'Auvigny's translation; see pp. vii–xv.
14. Allen notes a half dozen journals, plus instances of personal contacts; see Louis Allen, *John Henry Newman and the Abbé Jager* (London: Oxford University, 1975), pp. 1–3.
15. In addition to Allen, see Jean Stern, "La controverse de Newman avec l'Abbé Jager et la théorie du développement," *Newman Studien*, vol. VI.
16. It was *L'Univers* that had signaled the gross insufficiency of d'Auvigny's translation in the form of two articles on January 9 and 10, 1847, and a letter of Dalgairns on January 19.

17. *L'Univers*, January 9 and 20, 1848. Two further articles on the book appeared on June 5 and 9, 1849. The product of the same author, they noted that the book's importance made a more complete analysis of it obligatory and continued the high estimation of Newman: "The sixty pages which comprise the first chapter would suffice to place Mr. Newman in the rank of the premier thinkers of Europe."

18. *L'Ami de la religion*, t. 136 (February 24, 1848): pp. 461–67, and (March 7, 1848): pp. 549–52.

19. Emile Saisset, "De l'origine et de la formation du christianisme, à l'occasion du livre de M. Newman," *La liberté de penser* 1 (March 15, 1848): p. 357.

20. G. Darboy, "Comment y a-t-il progrès doctrinal dans le catholicisme?," *Le Correspondant* 23 (December 10, 1848): pp. 281–93. In 1852 Darboy devoted another article to Newman in *Le Correspondant*, this time dealing with three further French translations of his work. They included a number of Newman's Oxford University sermons, which Newman had been particularly desirious of having translated, deeming them important background for an adequate understanding of the *Essay on Development*.

21. *TAR*, p. 23.

22. See Darboy, p. 293; Villecourt, p. 550; *L'Univers*, June 5, 1849.

23. Nicholas Lash, *Newman on Development* (Shepherdstown, W. Va.: Patmos, 1975), p. 56. Lash explores Newman's analogies and the various conceptions of development they harbor in chap. 4. On the "essentially unsystematic character" of the *Essay*, see Ian Ker, *The Achievement of John Henry Newman* (Notre Dame, Ind.: University of Notre Dame, 1990), pp. 110–15.

24. Hans Robert Jauss, "Response to Paul de Man," in Lindsay Waters and Wład Godzich, eds., *Reading de Man Reading*, (Minneapolis: University of Minnesota, 1989), p. 204.

25. Brownson, *Works*, vol. XIV, pp. 11, 24, 25.

26. Dupuy cites works of Mgr. Goux (1858) and Abbé Perreyve (1865). B.-D. Dupuy, "L'influence de Newman sur la théologie catholique du développement dogmatique," *Newman Studien*, vol. VI, pp. 149, 164n.

27. Dupuy judges Ward as having been perceptive in this regard. B.-D. Dupuy, "Newman's Influence in France," in John Coulson and A. M. Allchin, eds., *The Rediscovery of Newman: An Oxford Symposium* (London: S.P.C.K., 1967), p. 154. French readers were apprised of Ward's judgments by L. Maisonneuve, "Newman et Sabatier," *Bulletin de littérature ecclésiastique (BLE)* 3 (1901): pp. 209–24.

28. Wilfred Ward, "Newman and Sabatier," *Fortnightly Review* 69 (1901): p. 812.

29. Ward, "Newman and Sabatier," p. 810.

30. Published pseudonymously as A. Firmin, "Le développement chrétien d'après le cardinal Newman," *RCF*, vol. XVII (1898): pp. 5–20.

31. E.-I. Mignot, "L'Evolutionnisme religieux," *Le Correspondant* 187 (1897): pp. 3–42. Reprinted in *L'Eglise et la critique* (Paris: Librairie Victor Lecoffre, 1910).

32. Loisy to von Hügel, June 21, 1897. Alfred Loisy, *Mémoires pour servir à l'histoire religieuse de notre temps*, t. I, (Paris: Emile Nourry, 1930), p. 438.

33. See "Le développement chrétien," p. 13. While judging it necessary to go beyond Newman in this regard, Loisy remained indebted to his predecessor: "What Newman provided with his ideas of the 'development' of dogma and an 'intuitive sense' at the foundation of morality and faith was a new model for understanding revelation" (Ronald Burke, "Was Loisy Newman's Modern Disciple?" in Mary Jo Weaver, ed., *Newman and the Modernists* [Lanham: University Press of America, 1985], p. 146).

34. See Paul Misner, "The 'Liberal' Legacy of Newman," in Weaver, p. 12.

35. "That the progress of Christianity must be compared to the germination of a seed or of a plant rather than to a deductive or geometric construction, is something evident which no one, I believe, could contest" (*L'Univers*, December 31, 1902). Gayraud continued his evaluation in subsequent issues of January 2, 4, 9, and 10, 1903, all of which appeared before Cardinal Richard's ordinance condemning the book.

36. Maignen wrote two series of articles critical of *L'Evangile et l'église* in *La Vérité française* (*VF*) February 4 through 9, 1903, and March 2, 4, 6, 7, 12, 14, 21, 1903. Previously he had written against the Firmin article on development, correctly identifying Loisy as the author. Those articles, which had originally appeared in the *VF* of July 3 and 10, 1899, were reprinted in Charles Maignen, *Nouveau catholicisme et nouveau clergé* (Paris: Victor Retaux, 1902).

37. *VF*, March 12, 1903.

38. *TAR*, pp. 23–24.

39. Gabriel Daly, "Newman and Modernism: A Theological Reflection," in Weaver, pp. 196–97.

40. Brownson, *Works*, vol. XIV, p. 5.

41. D. W. Fokkema and Elrud Kunne-Ibsch, *Theories of Literature in the Twentieh Century* (London: C. Hurst, 1977), pp. 146–47.

42. In a letter to Mgr. Mignot, August 27, 1899, Loisy noted a "favorable commentary" on his Newman article, which had appeared in the *Sillon*, "Lettres de Loisy à Mgr. Mignot," *BLE* (1966): p. 29.

43. Dupuy, "Newman's Influence in France," pp. 166–67. These three tendencies are elaborated in Jouett Powell, *Three Uses of Christian Discourse in John Henry Newman* (Missoula, Mont.: Scholars Press, 1975), pp. 18–22.

44. Jean Dagens and Maurice Nédoncelle, eds., *Entretiens sur Henri Bremond* (Paris: Mouton, 1967), pp. 66–68.

45. Wilfred Ward, "Newman Through French Spectacles," *The Tablet*, July 21, 1906. The writer in question was Michaud whose article appeared in the *Revue internationale de théologie* of 1905. Ward wrote again in *The Tablet* on August 11, 1906.

46. See Léonce de Grandmaison, "John Henry Newman considéré comme maitre," *Etudes* 109 (1906): pp. 721–50 and 110 (1907): pp. 39–69.

47. Lash, p. 150.

48. Tyrrell to Mrs. Ward, April 11, 1906, *Letters from a "Modernist"* (Shepherdstown, W. Va.: Patmos, 1981), p. 163.

49. See Gabriel Daly's comment: "It is not without significance that [Loisy] chose Harnack rather than Sabatier as his adversary in *L'Evangile et l'église*. His debt

to Sabatier was too great, and the similarity of his position to Sabatier's too marked, for him to achieve a convincing discrimination between them" (*Transcendence and Immanence* [Oxford: Clarendon Press, 1980], p. 66).

50. Pierre Colin, "Le Kantisme dans la crise moderniste," in *Le modernisme* (Paris: Beauchesne, 1980), pp. 23ff.

51. Paul Sabatier's comment, quoted in Gary Lease, "Newman: The Roman View," in Weaver, p. 181n.

52. J. F. Leddy cites a number of factors that he judged to account for that. See "Newman and his Critics: A Chapter in the History of Ideas," *Report of the Canadian Catholic Historical Association* (1942–43): pp. 36–38.

53. Janusz Sławinski, "Reading and Reader in the Literary Historical Process," *New Literary History* 19 (1988): p. 523.

54. Quoted in John Boening, "Some Recent Theories of Reception and Influence: Their Implications for the Study of International Literary Relations," in Béla Köpeczi et al., eds. *Proceedings of the 8th Congress of the International Literature Association*, vol. 2. (Stuttgart: Erich Bieber, 1980), p. 549.

11

Theological Inquiry in an Authoritarian Church: Newman and Modernism

LAWRENCE BARMANN

By posing the question of whether or not Newman was a modernist, one immediately assumes the responsibility of explaining what he means by the question. The question, obviously, does not ask whether or not Newman was part of that international group of men and women working in various intellectual and social fields between about 1890 and 1910 who, in 1907, were delineated by Pope Pius X as "modernists." Newman was dead by August 1890. And no one, as far as I know, has ever suggested that he was historically part of that group. I stress this point because Nicholas Lash has rather superciliously remarked that to pose the question of Newman being a modernist is to be anachronistic! This same writer has gone on to suggest that to pose the question in any form is both "meaning-less" and "in the last analysis lacking in intellectual seriousness."[1] I propose to show that in fact it is not. A second meaning which the question might have is whether or not Newman worked from principles or assumptions, and by methods, which were similar to those used by the modernists, and whether he arrived at conclusions analogous to or preliminarily anticipatory of theirs. The question in this sense has been discussed vigorously through-out the twentieth century. Although I shall not primarily focus on the question in this sense, I will examine it and discuss what has been said about it thus far. There is, however, a third sense in which the question about Newman and modernism might be posed. Is there now, and has there been, in the modern Church a specific kind of tension between some of its more intellectual members and the wielders of ecclesiastical authority, which in the decades between 1890 and 1910 reached the breaking point and caused the latter to label the former "modernists" and as such to condemn them, but which tension has its analogues both prior to and subsequent upon that period? And was Newman one of those analogues in this earlier period? To pose the question in this third sense, and to address it historically, is the chief purpose of this essay.

In first looking at the question in our second sense, whether or not Newman's principles, methods, and conclusions were analogous to those of the modernists, several points need to be made. Neither Alfred Loisy nor George Tyrrell, the two men most obviously condemned in 1907 by the antimodernist encyclical *Pascendi dominici gregis*, were either explicitly or implicitly Newman's disciples. Both, on the other hand, had read his major writings and found in them support and inspiration for their own theological and apologetical work. In October 1896 Baron Friedrich von Hügel suggested to Loisy that he read Newman, and at once the latter requested from the baron several of Newman's works, including the *Essay on Development* and the *Grammar of Assent*. Two months later Loisy told von Hügel that Newman seemed to him to be the most open theologian in the Church since Origen.[2] That Loisy compared Newman to Origen is significant on many levels. But it is most significant, perhaps, because Origen was the first formally to recognize the necessity for a serious theology of doctrinal development in working out his own theory of the continuity between the Old and New Testaments, and Newman was one of the few people to have dealt with that idea deeply since the third century. Loisy's own *L'Evangile et l'église*, of course, carried the idea into a new dimension altogether.

Both the *Essay on Development* and the *Grammar of Assent* had important and lasting influence on Tyrrell's thought as well, even though he too eventually reached conclusions beyond any in either book. By 1904 he recognized what for him were the inadequacies of the *Essay on Development* in its attempt "to work the static idea of a deposit and the dynamic idea of development into one system."[3] Of the *Grammar of Assent*, on the other hand, he remarked in 1906 that it had effected "a profound revolution in my way of thinking, in the year 1885, just when I had begun to feel the limits of scholasticism rather painfully." But it was not to be any specific conclusions of Newman's which Tyrrell ultimately was to value; it was to be the spirit in which Newman reached them.

> I have long feared [Tyrrell wrote] lest the enthusiastic Newmanism of Mr. Ward's school should make Newman what St. Thomas Aquinas has become, an obstacle to the very progress which he initiated; lest the letter, and *ipse dixit*, of Newman should slay his spirit. Hence I have tried to keep alive the sense of Newman's limitations and to arrest the process of petrification; for thus only will Newman's influence remain vital and progressive.[4]

And if one had to distill this spirit of Newman's into a single modus operandi, insofar as it affected his theology, I would say, and I think Tyrrell might concur, that it was Newman's consistent habit of thought which began with and always took seriously the human and real *experience* of both Christian and unbeliever. *Experience* for the scholastic mind, on the other hand, was either a metaphysical category or an a priori assumption. For Newman it never was.

Although Newman's influence on both Tyrrell and Loisy is undeniable, even if not completely definable, on von Hügel it was both earlier and more pervasive in his life, and ultimately more lasting. Raised in the Austrian embassies at Florence and then in Brussels, where his father was ambassador, Friedrich von Hügel never experienced the structures and socialization of formal education at any level, having always been tutored privately. At the age of seventeen, while undergoing a religious crisis in his adolescent life, the young baron first read one of Newman's books, *Loss and Gain*, which, he later observed, was the first work to make him "realize the intellectual might and grandeur of the Catholic position."[5] In the immediately ensuing years he read the *Apologia, Anglican Difficulties, Grammar of Assent*, and others of Newman's works, and when he first contacted Newman in 1874, he told him that these books "at different times and in different ways formed distinct epochs in my young intellectual and religious life. Such intellectual discipline as I have had, I owe it to your books."[6]

At the age of twenty-four, von Hügel spent a week in Birmingham in order to have several interviews with Newman. Significantly, the topics on which von Hügel wanted to pick Newman's brain included human certainty about God, scholastic philosophy, papal infallibility, and the papal temporal power. When Newman died fourteen years later, von Hügel wrote to Father Ryder and the Oratory Community to express his sympathy and to indicate how much he owed Newman personally, concluding that he talked Newman even oftener than he knew.[7] Newman's influence on individuals who would later be labeled modernist was, clearly, both broad and deep.

Hardly surprising, then, is the fact that contemporaries of the modernists recognized Newman's influence in some of their ideas and saw parallels with Newman in the way they were treated by Roman ecclesiastics. Almost from the beginning of Loisy's public difficulties with Catholic authorities, English observers of the conflict drew an analogy with Newman's writings and experience. Loisy published *L'Evangile et l'église* in November 1902, and within weeks Cardinal Richard, archbishop of Paris, had condemned it, and the effort to get Rome to do likewise was under way. In England von Hügel orchestrated a publicity campaign to plead for tolerance, if not acceptance, of Loisy's method and conclusions, and both the religious and secular press followed developments with unusual interest. In October 1903, as a result of the furor created over *L'Evangile et l'église*, Loisy published a further explication of his ideas in *Autour d'un petit livre* in which he explicitly claimed Newman as his guide in the theory of development.[8] A not untypical review article on the new book in a London weekly, *The Pilot*, remarked that Loisy's "main historical conclusion and his views—exactly the same as Newman's—on the relativity of dogmatic statements are certainly right, and ought to be almost truisms, yet I am afraid they will still find too many opponents."[9] Two months following the review, *The Pilot* published a lengthy article, written by an anonymous "Roman Catholic Correspondent," drawing parallels between Newman and Loisy, which infuriated von Hügel by its political gamesmanship. The article, while admitting that Newman's principles were alive in Loisy's work, argued that the former was not condemned by Rome and the latter probably would be, not because of any dissimilarity in their intellectual positions, but because of the difference in their attitudes.

> In the case of those undefined doctrines which exercise the thoughts of Catholics [said the *Pilot* writer], a man's valuation at Rome is dominately a matter of his motive and spirit rather than of his opinion. Let him have the reverential, cautious, obedient spirit of Newman, and he may write the letter to Ullathorne, or may criticise the proofs of Christ's divinity from miracles and prophecy. Let him have the spirit of insubordination, criticism, and irresponsibleness, let him scandalise the little ones, and lecture prelates, and, were he as accredited as a Galileo in science, or a Lamennais in politics, the likelihood is that he will be struck off the roll of the Church's official apologists.[10]

While one might admire the writer's rhetoric, one must also acknowledge the big-lie tactic which his remarks embodied. Insubordination, irresponsibleness, scandalizing little ones, and lecturing prelates were in no way characteristic of Loisy at any point in his career to 1903. But the unsubstantiated moral judgment made by the writer would become, nevertheless, the leitmotif of future ecclesiastical dealings with Loisy as he was increasingly marginalized within the Church. The canonical issue about Loisy's books became immediately moot, however, when on Christmas Day 1903 the Congregation of the Holy Office and Index published a decree condemning five of them, including *L'Evangile et l'église* and *Autour d'un petit livre*.

For the next four years Rome selectively built her case against the various modernists, and in the summer of 1907 issued the condemnations of their lives and works in *Lamentabili* and *Pascendi dominici gregis*. On the face of both documents, various of Newman's ideas, contained primarily in the *Essay on Development, On Consulting the Faithful in Matters of Doctrine*, and the *Grammar of Assent*, would *seem* to have been condemned implicitly, if not in explicit intention. Most of the modernists thought it so, and many antimodernists feared it might be so as well. Consequently, a public debate on whether or not Newman was condemned by the papal documents ensued.[11] The antimodernists in England, especially the Oratorians, the Benedictine Francis Aidan Gasquet (soon to be Cardinal Gasquet), and the diocesan theologian for Westminster, Canon James Moyes, argued in a merely extrinsic way that Newman was not condemned because the pope and his secretary of state said that he was not. After all, for one pope to make a man a cardinal and for his successor to declare the same man a heretic was not the Roman manner. The modernists, on the other hand, argued from a comparison based on a theological understanding of what Newman actually wrote with what the encyclical said was unacceptable ecclesiastically. And these latter concluded that Newman had indeed been condemned by the letter of the documents, even if not by the actual intention of their authors.

Wilfrid Ward, who had already been appointed Newman's official biographer and who knew Newman's works better, perhaps, than anyone at the time, was a friend of von Hügel and Tyrrell, and was familiar with Loisy's work as well. Ward was convinced that Newman had been condemned by *Pascendi* and wrote to Father John Norris of the Birmingham Oratory:

> Gasquet had ridiculed the idea that the Encyclical hit J.H.N., but as I told Norfolk three weeks ago it not only hits him but the analysis of modernism includes all on which his heart was set for 40 years and brands it as false and absurd. . . . we cannot defend him successfully without going in the teeth of the Encyclical, which brands also positions essential to his views. . . . I think the situation simply tragic.[12]

Two days after Ward wrote that letter, Norris placed a letter of his own in the London *Times* which said, "I am enabled to state on information received to-day from the highest authority that the 'genuine doctrine and spirit of Newman's Catholic teaching are not hit by the Encyclical, but the theories of many who wrongly seek refuge under a great name are obviously censured.' "[13] Apparently that was all Ward wanted, for he wrote to Norris the same day: " 'Deo Gratias.' I simply cannot express the relief I felt when I read your letter in the 'Times' and the words you quote."[14] Several weeks earlier Ward had suggested to von Hügel a plan for getting Church authorities publicly to discriminate between those condemned by *Pascendi* and ideas of Newman which seemed to many to be very like those of the condemned modernists. Von Hügel thought the idea a bad one because it would be agreeing to the destruction of men and ideas also important to the Church in order to save Newman. "Even at this moment they *may* shrink from publicly admitting that Newman was also aimed at," von Hügel told Ward, " . . . but I am certain they as little like J.H.N. as they like you or me."[15]

When Ward came to publish his *Life of Newman* in 1912, he wrestled with the idea of publishing a note on "Modernism" in which, once and for all, he would lay to rest the suspicion that Newman had been tainted by whatever it was that Pius X had condemned in *Pascendi*. Ward's position on Newman's relationship to the modernists had by this time become formulated in an analogy in which he very genuinely believed. Just as the genuine thought and intention of St. Augustine was not condemned in the proscription of the Augustinian-based writings of Cornelius Jansen by Popes Innocent X and Alexander VII in the seventeenth century, Ward argued, so the genuine thought and intention of Newman was not condemned in the proscription of so-called modernist writings which had used Newman's ideas and methods in the twentieth century. The Birmingham Oratorians felt that this conceded too much, while modernists like von Hügel felt it conceded too little, and in the end Ward omitted any mention of modernism in the biography altogether.[16]

This issue, however, would not go away. And although Ward did not deal with it in his biography of Newman, many reviewers of the book insisted on dealing with it once the biography was published. The most blunt, perhaps, of all the reviews appeared anonymously in *The Edinburgh Review*. This writer quoted passages from Tyrrell, Edouard LeRoy, and the Italian clerical authors of *The Programme of Modernism*, asserting that although Newman would have been horrified at these modernists' conclusions, he had in fact laid down the very principles which they logically drew out. "Although Newman was not a Modernist, but an exceedingly stiff conservative," says the writer, "he did introduce into the Roman Church a very dangerous and essentially alien habit of thought which has since developed into Modernism. . . . One side of his religion was based on principles which, when logically drawn out, must lead away from Catholicism in the direction of an individualist religion of experience, and a substitution of history for dogma which makes all truth relative and all values fluid."[17] Whether or not one agrees with that assessment of Newman, one must admit that it sets in bold relief the real issues at stake in the

Newman-modernist controversy, and it honestly juxtaposes the Roman Catholic theological structure as it presented itself to the world at the turn of this century with those Roman Catholics who in one way or another were challenging the rigidity and narrowness of that structure.

The challenge of the *Edinburgh Review* writer was taken up at once by the English Jesuit journalist Father Sydney Smith who wrote at length in the Jesuit periodical *The Month*. While Smith ostensibly dealt with the *Edinburgh* writer's arguments point by point, he did so on the basis of an unarticulated assumption which became the standard Roman Catholic platform in this matter down to our own day. And that assumption is that what Newman *really* meant, when he spoke of such things as evidence and belief or of conscience and authority, was exactly what the scholastic expositors of official Roman Catholic doctrine in the nineteenth century meant by those terms. Anyone, for instance, who knows of Newman's lifelong relationship with the agnostic William Froude, of the many lengthy and carefully thought-out letters he wrote to Froude, and of the importance of Froude's experience to Newman's argument in the *Grammar of Assent*, knows that Smith's assumption is a false one. Smith concluded his article, apparently aware that the intrinsic cogency of his argument was inadequate, by quoting Pius X's defense of Newman against the modernists, and by asserting that the *Edinburgh* writer was "ill-qualified to judge on such a question."[18] In other words, authority, not reason and evidence, was to settle the question of Newman's relationship to modernism.

The elaboration of and response to the question of whether Newman was a modernist in our second sense, from the publication of Ward's biography down to our own day, has been full and circuitous. Even to mention the most important twists and turns in the argument over the past eighty years would require a book, and there is no time now to do more than mention several of the most recent articles on this point.

Until about thirty years ago modernist scholarship was in a wasteland, with only Alec Vidler's *The Modernist Movement in the Roman Church* of 1934 standing between general Roman Catholic rejection of the modern- ists and non-Catholic general indifference toward them. Since the Second Vatican Council, however, interest in the modernists for their own sake and interest in their relationship to Newman has revived. In 1971 Doctor B. M. G. Reardon of the University of Newcastle upon Tyne published an article on "Newman and the Catholic Modernist Movement" in which he suggested that although Newman would have been appalled at the conclusions of Loisy, Tyrrell, and others; still, Newman's approach to faith, his sense of the relationship of doctrine to life, and above all, his understanding of the necessity of a theory of doctrinal development, all at one or another point touch ideas and theories developed by and condemned in the modernists.[19]

Gabriel Daly dealt with the question of Newman and modernism in a theological reflection which served as an epilogical conclusion to a group of papers delivered in 1983 at the American Academy of Religion convention, and which were published as a book in 1985 under the title *Newman and the Modernists*. Daly says there that what unites Newman methodologically with the modernists was his non-scholastic approach to theological questions, his anti-rationalism, and his use of conscience as a trans-logical means for reaching religious truth. The exclusive theological paradigm of scholastic thought insisted on by Rome left both Newman and the modernists, as non-scholastic thinkers, without any negotiable theological referent and thus condemnable. The greater part of Daly's article is concerned with comparing and contrasting Newman's approach to doctrinal development with Loisy's and placing them both in their larger philosophico-theological context. Daly also deals briefly with Newman's influence on Tyrrell and von Hügel, seeing it as vague and somewhat problematic, and concludes that Newman's influence on the generation of modernists was ultimately more general than specific.[20]

Most recently, the question of whether Newman was a modernist in our second sense has been posed by John Coulson in a paper given at the International Newman Conference held in Birmingham in 1983 and revised and published in 1990. After voicing the usual Roman Catholic putdown of "modernists" in general, Coulson concludes that Tyrrell, von Hügel, and Newman did, after all, have a lot in common. One wonders, of course, just which modernists Coulson had in mind when he accuses them generally of excessive rationalism and despair. Coulson finds that Newman was ultimately not a modernist because he understood the limits of reason and logic in theology and the role of mystery in religion.[21] Those realizations, however, were also essential elements in the thought of both von Hügel and Tyrrell, and it was Tyrrell's chief accusation against scholastic theology, and against the authorities who imposed it as normative for Catholic doctrinal interpretation, that this theology was overly rationalistic and excluded the real dimensions of mystery. Tyrrell's article on "The Relation of Theology to Devotion," an article delated to Cardinal Vaughan as suspect and resulting in excessive prior-censorship of everything Tyrrell wrote thereafter as a Jesuit, embodies precisely this idea. And this article both Tyrrell and von Hügel considered to be perhaps the most important thing the former ever wrote, and the embodiment of the key idea of his entire life's effort![22] That Coulson should find the heart of Tyrrell's most characteristic writing, and what von Hügel called the chief aim of his own "poor life's work generally,"[23] to be the very thing that supposedly saved Newman from modernism is, to say the least, fascinating!

In the present climate of discussion, a knowledgeable and honest critic can admit that some of the intellectual paths pursued by Newman were paths pursued in a later generation by those called modernists, and often they pursued them in similar ways. History and human experience, for instance, were important to both in theological discussion, even though both might understand history, whether as a theory or a method, in sometimes dissimilar ways. However, many of the conclusions drawn by modernists at the beginning of this century went beyond anything with which Newman would have been comfortable a generation earlier. If, then, the question of whether or not Newman was a modernist in our second sense of sharing principles, methods, and conclusions with the historical modernists has been much discussed in the twentieth century; the question in our third sense has hardly been discussed at all. The question in this third sense is actually about ecclesiastical authority rather than about Newman and any specific modernists. Has the authority structure in the modern Church been a consistent stumbling block, an unnecessary stumbling block, to a steady stream of the Church's most intelligent, creative, and, yes, committed members—members like John Henry Newman, George Tyrrell and Friedrich von Hügel, Pierre Teilhard de Chardin, and now Hans Küng, Charles Curran, and Leonardo Boff? And if it has been such a stumbling block, why? This question about authority is intimately related to any question about Newman and the modernists, and it is this authority issue which deserves attention now.

John Henry Newman was neither a professional philosopher or theologian, nor was he a historian. He was, rather, a humanistically educated intellectual who knew philosophy, theology, and history, and who used these in strikingly personal literary productions of an apologetic nature. He was a highly idiosyncratic thinker whose personal history affected every page he wrote. Much the same can be said of both von Hügel and Tyrrell. Moreover, all three took their religion seriously, precisely in the sense of making religion the integrative existential factor of their own reality as continuously thinking and morally growing persons; and all three ran up against analogous problems and checks within the Roman Catholic Church because of their adult stance vis-à-vis religious authority. It is this confrontation with ecclesiastical authority, so historically different in the cases of all three, and yet so basically similar, that perhaps most strongly links

Newman with modernists like von Hügel and Tyrrell. The modernism systematized and defined in Pius X's encyclical never existed historically. At best the modernism of *Pascendi* is a gross caricature of the thought of many different writers, run together, pushed out of shape, and taken out of context. And at worst it is an attribution of vicious and arrogant motives to men who never held them. A modernist, then, is not someone who fits the pope's procrustean bed, but someone who has simply moved beyond the pope's purview. To be intellectually and morally alive to the inherent relativity of *all* human truth is to be a modernist.

The authority issue is not about whether there is a legitimate authority structure in the Church nor whether the pope legitimately focuses that authority. These are facts, both historically and theologically. Rather, the question is about the limits of such authority and the manner in which it is expressed. In the preface to the third edition of the *Lectures on the Prophetical Office of the Church*, written when Newman was seventy-six, and written incidentally seven years after the Vatican Council, he there makes the analogy of Christ's offices of prophet, priest, and king having their human counterparts in the Church's life of teaching, sacred ministry, and ruling. He insists that these offices belong to the Church, not just the pope, even though in their exercise the pope can act in the name of the Church. There are some problems, I believe, in arguing from this preface to New-man's general meaning, because he seems to use the words *Church* and *Christianity* interchangeably, and because he calls Christianity an *idea* rather in the vague and imprecise sense in which he uses the term *idea* in the *Essay on Development*. Nevertheless, he makes the point that though Christianity, or perhaps the Church, is "a philosophy, a political power, and a religious rite," it is so all at once and simultaneously. He pointed out that the three roles developed to full flowering only successively, however, and over centuries, with liturgical worship developing first, then a theology, and finally a political structure centered in Rome. Now this is a not insignificant observation. Moreover, Newman goes on to assert that of the three roles,

> theology is the fundamental and regulating principle of the whole Church System. It is commensurate with Revelation, and Revelation is the initial and essential idea of Christianity. It is the subject matter, the formal cause, the expression, of the Prophetical Office, and as being such, has created both the Regal Office and the Sacerdotal. And it has in a certain sense a power of jurisdiction over those offices, as being its own creations, theologians being ever in request and in employment in keeping within bounds both the political and popular elements in the Church's constitution,—elements which are far more congenial than itself to the human mind, are far more liable to excess

and corruption, and are ever struggling to liberate themselves from those restraints which are in truth necessary for their well-being.[24]

That is an extraordinary claim for the role of theology within the Church in light of the past one hundred and fifty years of Vatican policy. And even though Newman also says in the preface that sometimes theology must give way to the political expediency of Church authorities for the sake of peace and unity; still, the thrust of what he is saying is that theological development within the Church is the normative interpreter for the whole system, even for the role of authority. Ordinarily, says Newman, theological development must be able to work itself out over long periods of time, through the dialogue of disagreement within various schools of thought, and freely, without political interference or any threat from ecclesiastical authority.

Now the issue of papal infallibility was just such a theological matter to be debated, circled, and reflected on over time. There was no urgency in 1870 to define as dogma that the pope was infallible; at least there was no urgency striking at the heart of Catholic belief. Consequently, from the moment the idea of having the Vatican Council define papal infallibility was announced to the world Newman opposed it. "When has definition of doctrine de fide been a luxury of devotion," Newman wrote to his bishop, "and not a stern painful necessity? Why should an aggressive insolent faction be allowed to 'make the heart of the just to mourn, whom the Lord hath not made sorrowful'?"[25] And to David Moriarty, bishop of Kerry, Newman wrote: "Where is the Arius or Nestorius, whose heresy makes it imperative for the Holy Church to speak? What has M. Veuillot, or the Civiltà not to answer for, if a secret unbelief is creeping over the hearts of our brethren, at the rumor of an event which I trust will never be realized!"[26] But the event *was* realized, in July 1870, and Newman accepted it, carefully separating himself from Ignatz von Döllinger who maintained that to define papal infallibility as revealed dogma was essentially to alter the very constitution of the Church.[27] Newman always insisted that he personally had no difficulty about papal infallibility, but that he opposed the manner in which its definition was undertaken, and he feared how factions within the Church would interpret its meaning after the definition. Newman believed the Roman Catholic Church to be the genuine, contemporary embodiment of Christianity; and, if that Church in council declared the pope infallible, he would accept it. He also made clear that he would oppose that definition up to the very moment it happened, and afterwards he did everything within his power to contain its interpretation.[28] So it is that the reader of the *Letter to the Duke of Norfolk* finds no triumphalist paean to an inspired pope, but rather a minimalist interpretation of what papal infallibility might mean in practice. And as Professor Edward Kelly has shown in his Birmingham address of 1983, now published in the 1990 *Newman Studien*, for Newman this problematic meaning is ultimately determined by "the general Catholic intelligence."[29]

How, one might justly ask, had it happened that the political function in the Church came to usurp the theological function to such an extent as actually to force the ecclesial definition as dogma of that political function's own ultimate and absolute supremacy within the Church system? Catholic theology in the nineteenth century spoke commonly of the infallibility of the Church, and few argued against focusing that infallibility generally in the papacy. But to make the pope's personal infallibility a revealed dogma, without first ascertaining what infallibility might mean in itself and historically, and how a fallible person could also be infallible, was to court serious problems.

The risk was taken, however, and it was taken for political and very human reasons, not for theological reasons nor for reasons connected with protecting the faith from an imminent threat. The papacy's involvement in secular politics, in fact the pope as monarch of a petty state, was of such long standing and so complex that any widespread political upheaval in Europe was bound to affect the papacy quite as much as any secular state. The French Revolution changed monarchical Europe forever, and of all the monarchs who had to come to terms with this reality, the popes of the nineteenth century seemed least able.[30] At the beginning of the nineteenth century, the papacy was at its lowest level in international prestige since, perhaps, the tenth century. At the century's beginning Napoleon I had kidnapped one pope, and by mid-century Napoleon III's army alone stood between Italian revolutionaries and another pope. This was the price demanded for playing politics with secular practitioners of that art, but it was a game which churchmen had consistently been unable to resist since the fourth century. Moreover, in the course of the eighteenth century the Church had lost the intellect of Europe as well, and the Church's response to this situation in the nineteenth century was in actual practice, though not in theory, to equate a decadent scholasticism with revelation and to demand assent to its teaching.[31] In the search for what might be meant by *truth*, the European intellectual world had moved far beyond St. Thomas Aquinas's *adequatio intellectus cum re*; the official articulators of Roman Catholic belief had not. The theology of the Roman schools became the norm for orthodoxy throughout the Catholic world, and Roman theology came to be dominated often from the 1850s by single Jesuit professors at the Roman College or Gregorian University, and by their entourages. Father John Baptist Franzelin, for instance, was the chief touchstone for orthodoxy under Pius IX, as was Father Camillo Mazzella under Leo XIII, and Father Louis Billot under Pius X.[32] All three were made cardinals by their respective papal patrons. But for infallible popes to reduce the ongoing theological search for the truth of Christianity to the scholastic adumbrations of a single luminary of the Roman College, or even to the school of his followers, makes a mockery of Newman's idea of the authentic role of theology in ecclesial life, and reduces that life to mere obedience to papal authority. Such obedience, perhaps, and the infallible monarch who demanded it, were considered by some to compensate for the loss of the papal states and for the loss of a leading role in European intellectual life. For others they were seen as a tragedy and a burden almost beyond bearing. On July 17, 1870, the pope was proclaimed infallible; on September 20 Italian soldiers entered Rome; and on October 2 the City was proclaimed the capital of the secular Italian state. "It suggests the thought," Newman remarked, "that to be at once infallible in religion and a despot in temporals is perhaps too great for mortal men."[33]

If one studies the First Vatican Council with the controlled detachment of a historian, rather than with the enthusiasm of a partisan, one grasps the key to understanding the authority issue in the modern Church. When Pius IX took over the papal monarchy from Gregory XVI in 1846, he took over the most backward state in Europe and a Church not taken seriously by the intellectual world around it. His first two years were spent in dallying with ideas of reform, both political and ecclesiastical, and with building relationships with reformers. Although Pius IX at first supported some liberal acts, he never supported liberal ideas. Consequently, when he was driven from Rome in 1848 by revolutionaries, upon his return in 1850 he set his face unflinchingly toward reaction and marched straight ahead for thirty years. Pope Pius IX was determined to be taken seriously by the European world and, despite his well-known smile and charm, was inflexible in pursuing his goal. His bull *Ineffabilis Deus* of December 8, 1854, can be seen as a dry run for the *Pastor Aeternus* of July 18, 1870.[34] Although no pope in history had ever defined a dogma of faith without urgent necessity or without the Church in council, Pius IX had declared as a dogma of Christianity Mary's Immaculate Conception.[35] And if he in fact *did* so, and if it was accepted by the hierarchy and faithful of the Catholic world, then, of course, he must also be *able* to do so. *Ab esse ad posse valet elatio.* Consequently, in Roman logic this ability to define dogma on one's own must itself be a dogma!

When the Vatican Council was formally called, the issue of papal infallibility was not explicitly on the agenda. The idea had been floated from Rome several years earlier, but the outcry from German bishops and others caused a quick and quiet retreat.[36] In fact, it was not really clear to most bishops in December 1869 just why they had gathered in Rome. But in March 1870 the *schema* on papal infallibility was suddenly sprung on the council fathers, and though it was not debated until June, it at once split the group into majority and minority factions. The former wanted the definition as an unconditional expression of loyalty to the much harassed "Pio Nono," and the latter were frightened by what in practice such a definition might portend. Few council members dealt with the issue on the basis of history and theology. But one who did was the Dominican Cardinal Guidi, a theological light of the Minerva, archbishop of Bologna, and until the council a favorite of the pope. In mid-June on the council floor he delivered a speech more important, perhaps, than any others on the issue, and one which momentarily rallied the minority. Guidi's opening sentence pointed out that for the first fourteen hundred years of Christianity the very idea of a separate and personal infallibility of the pope was wholly unknown. He argued that defining dogma was the work of the church, not the pope, and that to hold otherwise would require an inspired pope. He argued from St. Thomas, he argued from Bellarmine, and he even argued from the Jesuit Perrone who had once found Newman's ideas bewildering, that "in defining dogmas popes have never acted alone, nor have they ever alone condemned something as heretical." Guidi wanted the *schema* amended to indicate that the pope's infallibility was not of his person but only of his acts. And if those acts do not depend on the approval of the episcopate, the pope, nevertheless, cannot act independently of the episcopate. Papal infallibility, Guidi argued, merely means that the pope teaches the Church's traditional doctrine, and every definition of that doctrine must be preceded by serious examination of such doctrine in the Church's tradition, and the normal means for ascertaining the truth of that tradition is to consult the bishops who are the natural witnesses to the faith of their people. The speech created a furor on the council floor, and Cardinal Manning was reported to have remarked that Guidi was out of his mind. Pius IX sent for Guidi at once, rebuked him for his "heresy and ingratitude," and threatened to force him to make a public profession of faith.[37] Such were the conditions under which papal infallibility became a required dogma of belief for Roman Catholics.

The problems bequeathed to the Catholic Church by the Vatican Council in the nineteenth century have been felt in every generation for the past century and more. The chief problem, consistently, has been that any thinker falling under the displeasure of a pope or his congregations has no recourse against the implicit infallibility in which the Vatican shrouds its own theological, moral, and even disciplinary positions. The Vatican is always right, always the norm in these matters, and not just when a formal determination of divine revelation is concerned. For many, perhaps most, of those who came to be called modernists, this issue of the rights of the intellect in the Church vis-à-vis the role and limits of authority in the Church was paramount. George Tyrrell wrestled with the problem in the practical conduct of his own clerical life, and was excommunicated for his efforts. Baron von Hügel wrestled with the issue mostly on the theoretical level in his writings, while living quietly and unaggressively; and, not unlike Newman, he remained under a cloud of suspicion to Roman eyes until his death. In the long introductory section of his major book, *The Mystical Element of Religion*, von Hügel dealt with Newman's trilogy of ecclesial functions. He placed them in a broader context than Newman had, and he focused them in religion rather than in the Church. But while he was working on this book, von Hügel wrote and delivered a lecture which deals directly and profoundly with this issue of ecclesial authority alone. On the evening of January 28, 1904, von Hügel addressed in London a small gathering of Anglican clerics on the topic of "Official Authority and Living Religion." As the title suggests, he was dealing with the role of ecclesial authority vis-à-vis those members of the Church body whose religion was really the defining framework of their lives, not the average, more or less passive, Church member. He contrasted the roles of the Church authority speaking in the name of the organization with that of the individual struggling, thinking, loving Church member. Although the roles of the two are practically contradictory in von Hügel's scheme of things; he showed, nevertheless, how the negative role of authority was necessary for the authentic and full growth of the believer within the Church structure. But then came a word of caution about "profound dangers and difficulties" attendant upon all official authority, and the warning that there are largely forgotten "laws and limits of its efficacious exercise." Official organization and authority in the Church, according to von Hügel, must always be seen as only a part, a necessary part, yes, but still only a part of what is a dynamic whole, and ultimately a life. Another necessary part of that whole and that life is the explanatory and investigative work of the serious theologian, or thinker, or mystic. Moreover, said von Hügel, official organization and authority must always be recognized as only a means, a necessary means but means, nevertheless, and not ends—and means for life, not for death. He ended those observations by applying some conclusions from the biblical criticism of his day to the two limitations he had placed on authority in the Church. First, he showed how present Church structure and authority derive only indirectly from the historical Jesus and his disciples, and thus have a merely human dimension. Second, he showed that if one takes Jesus' humanity seriously, one has to accept that intellectual growth and ongoing syntheses were a part of it since these are essential to all true human nature. And if this is so, von Hügel argued, then "it is truly impossible that theologians, or indeed Church authority generally, should have an inerrancy higher, or more extensive in degree or kind, than our Lord's; or, rather, that He should be less infallible than they."[38]

The balanced, precise, and reverent ideas of Newman and von Hügel on the legitimate role of authority in the Church have mostly been ignored by those who wield authority in Rome. Following the modernist condemnations in 1907, the most creative Catholic thinkers were intimidated, and Catholic scholarship lost two generations of fruitful productivity for the Church. Men like Henri de Lubac, for writing *Surnaturel*, and John Courtney Murray, for his publications on church-state relations, were treated like enemies of Christianity and forbidden to publish; while heresy hunters like Mgr. Joseph Clifford Fenton and expositors of traditional Thomism like Father Reginald Garrigou-Lagrange were promoted and honored. Then, unexpectedly, came the portly patriarch of Venice who, as Pope John XXIII, called for throwing open the Church's windows to fresh air and new light, and who did just that by summoning the Second Vatican Council. And from that gathering came documents which helped to balance the imbalance of the First Vatican Council, and documents which implicitly exonerated men like Newman and von Hügel, Murray and de Lubac, and also Tyrrell and Loisy.

But documents are dead things, and only living interpretations determine their meaning in any given time. Since the election in 1978 of Pope John Paul II, the collegial model for Church life promulgated by the Second Vatican Council has fallen into abeyance, as the old authoritarian model of Pius IX and Pius X reasserts itself. The past decade, for instance, has seen the systematic destruction by Rome of national episcopal conferences which were in any way progressive and which dared to construe their roles as more than mere Vatican altar boys, first in Holland, and now in Brazil. But perhaps the most significant indication in the present pontificate of just how far apart are official Rome and Newman's ideas on the Church's constitution is the publication earlier this year of the Vatican *Instruction on the Ecclesial Vocation of the Theologian*.[39] Despite a few passages of conciliatory rhetoric and a few chummy references to our common search for truth, this document evidences no sense of a trilogy of components and functions within the Church as Newman and von Hügel suggested. Rather, one finds there simply an authority function called the *magisterium* which, we are told, has a special "divine assistance" allowing it to control all other elements in the Church. This *magisterium* is not only infallible in interpreting revelation, but it is equivalently such when making pronouncements on non-revealed matters connected with faith, on moral matters normative for the consciences of believers, on teachings which could help to better understand revelation, and finally even on matters of discipline. In fact, dissent from Vatican positions on all matters theological or disciplinary, not merely matters of divine revelation, is explicitly forbidden; and to make this point, of course, is why the *Instruction* was issued. Not only is this universal *magisterium* normative and definitive when exercised by the pope, but also when exercised by his curial congregations. Although this *Instruction* calls the *magisterium* a constitutive element of Christ's Church, nowhere in the document is there any indication that there are any other constitutive elements. When priests, laity, theologians, indeed the hierarchy, are mentioned, it is only to assert that their legitimacy is in subordination to and in dependence upon this papal *magisterium*. The *magisterium*'s purpose is said to be vigilant maintenance of the faithful in the truth of God. Nowhere does this document explain how this human *magisterium* itself arrives at such truth; rather, the identification of *magisterium* and truth is simply assumed. In fact, the entire document makes sense only if one assumes a divinely inspired pope and curia. While Rome has always denied it, this has been the necessary, though unspoken, assumption of papal extremists since 1870, and this assumption has been a macabre presence in Catholic life for the past century through the imposition of loyalty oaths and the fostering of papal cults. Newman's opposition to the definition of papal infallibility was prescient in his own day, and prophetic in ours. In this recent Vatican *Instruction*, the ordinary human means for arriving at truth are never required for the pope and his congregations, only for theologians and the faithful. And the proposed harmonious working together between theologians and *magisterium* is possible only within the perimeters and on the pre-laid track of Vatican policy. Such a stance and practice has become possible precisely because of the definition of personal papal infallibility. Although infallibility enthusiasts have always insisted that popes would never use the definition to enforce their personal theological and disciplinary prejudices, in fact they always have. Cardinal Joseph Ratzinger's papally approved *Instruction* is just such a case in point. So, too, and even more recently, is the Vatican's refusal to allow Fribourg University to bestow an honorary doctor's degree on Milwaukee's Archbishop Rembert Weakland who had dared to extend Christ's love and compassion to those harassed by pro-life activists. A timid bystander who also loves the Church might wonder what has happened, in Ratzinger's and John Paul II's scheme of things, to the legitimate role of the world's bishops and theologians, or the believing laity for that matter, now that the Church's constitutive functions have been reduced to Peter's successors and their Roman congregations!

Early in 1870 the bishop of Kerry wrote to Newman to say that "if ever this definition [of papal infallibility] comes you will have contributed much towards it. Your treatise on development has given the key." Newman responded that "it has been my fate to have my book attacked by various persons, praised by none—till at last it is used against me." He added that he did not think "that infallibility follows on Supremacy—yet I hold the principle of development."[40] Newman never took a strong public stand against papal infallibility, his only public stand at all being the minimalist interpretation of the doctrine in his *Letter to the Duke of Norfolk*. But his whole Catholic life had been, perhaps, less fruitful than it might have been because of that infallible fog which covers every Roman position and those who claim to speak in the pope's name. Seven years before the Vatical Council, Newman confided to his *Journal*:

> O how forlorn and dreary has been my course since I have been a Catholic! . . . since I have been a Catholic, I seem to myself to have had nothing but failure, personally. . . . so far from being thought engaged in any good work, I am simply discouraged and regarded suspiciously by the governing powers as doing an actual harm.[41]

Without ever acknowledging that the Vatican ways of proceeding and of dealing with intellectuals within the Church should be challenged and contained, Newman bowed his head and endured. This was his way in most things once he became a Catholic, but there is no evidence that it was necessarily either good for him or for the Church. In 1911 Wilfrid Ward sent to Baron von Hügel the manuscript Introduction to the former's forthcoming biography of Newman, asking for comments and criticism. Among other remarks, von Hügel observed:

> I cannot but feel, more strongly than formerly and doubtless quite finally, one, to my mind quite grave, peculiarity and defect of the Cardinal's temper of mind and position. His, apparently absolute, determination never to allow— at least *to allow others*—*any* public protestation, *any* act or declaration contrary to current central Roman policy, cannot, simply, be pressed, or imposed as normative upon us all. For, taken thus, it would stamp *Our Lord* Himself, as a deplorable rebel; would condemn *St. Paul* at Antioch as intolerable; and censure many a great saint of God since then. And certainly this way of taking things can hardly be said to have done much good or to have averted much harm.[42]

Von Hügel wrote that letter four years after the Vatican had issued *Lamentabili* and *Pascendi*, and he knew whereof he spoke.

This entire collection's theme has been about Newman's intellectual ethos, and I would suggest that Newman's relationship to what has been called "modernism" is an important aspect of that ethos. Clearly, Newman was not one of the people designated by the term in its historical sense, since he was dead before the historical modernists began to make their contributions to the Church. However, many modernists found inspiration in Newman's life and writings; and some took the problems with which he had wrestled and sometimes took his methodological approaches to them as well, and often reached conclusions beyond most of those in which he had eventually rested. But it was Newman's effort to understand the faith in his own day and within his own time's terms which is his strongest link with the historical modernists, and that which links him, too, with de Lubac, Teilhard de Chardin, Murray, Küng, Boff, and Weakland. These are venturers, the risk takers, in the name of Catholic truth and life. The consistent reaction to their efforts over the past century on the part of Vatican authorities has been repression and condemnation. One does not find before the nineteenth-century popes who issued encyclicals and magisterial instructions every few months on every topic under the sun and intended as frameworks for all legitimate theological discussions among Catholics. Such practice has preempted the authentic theological development within the Church which Newman envisioned, and has created a more or less continual crisis of authority for some of the best and brightest in Catholic intellectual life.

In his wonderful essay on "Ultramontanism" written in 1863, Lord Acton remarked that "the defence of a thesis is far easier than the discovery of truth."[43] In conclusion, let me say, with a certain temerity, that I hope that I have not only defended a thesis here, but perhaps have uncovered a little truth as well. And, to quote Acton once again: "If the Past has been an obstacle and a burden, knowledge of the Past is the safest and the surest emancipation."

Notes

1. Nicholas Lash, *Newman on Development. The Search for an Explanation in History* (London: Sheed and Ward, 1975), pp. 149–50.
2. Alfred Loisy, *Mémoires pour servir a l'histoire religieuse de notre temps*, vol. I [1857–1900] (Paris: Emile Nourry Editeurs, 1930), pp. 415 and 426. "Je lis toujours Newman avec intérêt. Ce doit être le théologien le plus ouvert qui ait existé dans la sainte Eglise depuis Origène" (p. 426).
3. George Tyrrell to Friedrich von Hügel, February 19, 1905, in M. C. Petre, *Autobiography and Life of George Tyrrell*, vol. II (London: Edward Arnold, 1912), p. 220. See also George Tyrrell to Wilfrid Ward, January 4, 1904, in Maisie Ward, *Insurrection versus Resurrection* (London: Sheed and Ward, 1937), p. 167: "I have very carefully studied J.H.N.'s Sermon on Theological Developments; and have no doubts whatever that he held the pre-scholastic and patristic idea of the *permanence* of revelation in the minds of the faithful; and never quite twigged the school-theory of a mere formula of a long-past revelation as the subject matter of theology. He puts theology on all-fours with natural science in its relation to its subject matter. It formulates certain subjective immanent *impressions* of *ideas* exactly analogous to sense impressions, which are realities of experience by which notions and experience can be criticised. *In principle* (with one or two unimportant modifications) this is *liberal* theology. It cannot (and this is what I do not think you see clearly enough) combine with this impossible school-theology which ties us to the categories and thought-forms of the last twenty centuries. If Catholicism is to live, the school-theology must go."
4. George Tyrrell to M. Raoul Gout, May 26, 1906, in Petre, *Autobiography and Life*, vol. II, p. 209.
5. Friedrich von Hügel to Henry Ignatius Dudley Ryder, August 18, 1890, in Lawrence Barmann, *Baron Friedrich von Hügel and the Modernist Crisis in England* (Cambridge: Cambridge University Press, 1972), p. 5.
6. Friedrich von Hügel to John Henry Newman, December 13, 1874, in Barmann, *Baron Friedrich von Hügel*, pp. 5–6.
7. Friedrich von Hügel to Henry Ignatius Dudley Ryder, August 18, 1890, in Barmann, *Baron Friedrich von Hügel*, p. 6.
8. Alfred Loisy, *Autour d'un Petit Livre*, 2d edition (Paris: Alphonse Picard et Fils, 1903), p. 7.
9. *The Pilot*, vol. VIII, no. 188, October 24, 1903, p. 398.
10. *The Pilot*, vol. VIII, no. 196, December 19, 1903, p. 598. Von Hügel noted in his diary that he wrote a "hot letter" to D. C. Lathbury, editor of *The*

Pilot, protesting the unfairness of the writer's criticism of Loisy (*Diaries*, 23 December 1903). The baron's manuscript *Diaries*, forty-three volumes, for the years 1877–79, 1884–1900, 1902–24, are in the manuscript collection at St. Andrews University Library, Scotland.

11. For a discussion of this issue, see Barmann, *Baron Friedrich von Hügel*, pp. 204–6.

12. Wilfrid Ward to John Norris, November 2, 1907, in Edward E. Kelly, "Newman, Wilfrid Ward, and the Modernist Crisis," *Thought* XLII (Winter 1973): p. 515.

13. *The Times*, no. 38,481 (November 4, 1907): p. 10. Two days earlier W. J. Williams, a Roman Catholic student of Newman's thought and a friend of Tyrrell, had published a letter in *The Times* (no. 38,480 [November 2, 1907]: p. 10) stating that *Pascendi* had condemned Newman and that most English Catholics really thought so as well. He was insultingly attacked by Gasquet (*The Times*, no. 38,482 [November 5, 1907]: p. 8) who said that the Catholic religion did not rest on Newman or any other great name, but solely on the authority of the pope! Then Gasquet and Norris both jumped on Williams again (*The Times*, no. 38,484 [November 7, 1907]: p. 4), saying that no genuine Catholic really thought Newman was condemned in the first place. Perhaps the last laugh was had, however, by an anonymous Catholic graduate of Oxford who wrote (*The Times*, no. 38,488 [November 12, 1907]: p. 12): "Dr. Gasquet and others when speaking of authority forget that such a term can only properly be used of an *ex cathedra* definition of the pope. We are now face to face with an insidious attempt to turn a mere Encyclical letter into an infallible utterance. To clear modernists of disloyalty it should be pointed out that this is to go beyond the definition of the Vatican Council and to come perilously near heresy itself. When the Curia learns that infallibility extends solely to matters of faith and morals, but not to the philosophy, science, or history used in the formulation of dogma, there will be peace. Meanwhile, an ever-growing majority of Catholics will continue to work against a tyranny which condemns an eminent priest to the most terrible of punishments [George Tyrrell had just been excommunicated for publishing articles attacking *Pascendi*] merely for expressing the liberty which the Church has left open to all. As the mere criticism of a non-infallible document is now adjudged to be worthy of excommunication we know what childish temper the curia means to employ against those who disagree with its medieval science and philosophy."

14. Wilfrid Ward to John Norris, November 4, 1907, in Maisie Ward, *Insurrection*, p. 269.

15. Friedrich von Hügel to Wilfrid Ward, October 18, 1907, in Barmann, *Baron Friedrich von Hügel*, p. 205.

16. Wilfrid Ward to Friedrich Von Hügel, November 20, 1911, MS 3154 (St. Andrews University Library, Scotland).

17. "Cardinal Newman," *The Edinburgh Review*, vol. CCXV, no. CCCCXL (April 1912): pp. 288–89. This entire article of twenty-eight pages is full of intelligent, outsider insight into both Newman and the ultramontanist Roman Catholic system.

18. Sydney F. Smith, "Newman's Relation to Modernism," *The Month*, vol. CXX, no. 577 (July 1912): p. 15.

19. B. M. G. Reardon, "Newman and the Catholic Modernist Movement," *The Church Quarterly*, vol. 4, no. 1 (July 1971): pp. 50–60.

20. Gabriel Daly, "Newman and Modernism: A Theological Reflection," *Newman and the Modernists*, ed. Mary Jo Weaver (Lanham, Md.: University Press of America, 1985), pp. 185–207.

21. John Coulson, "Was Newman a Modernist?," *John Henry Newman and Modernism*, ed. Arthur Hilary Jenkins (Sigmaringendorf: Regio-Verlag Glock und Lutz, 1990), pp. 74–84.

22. George Tyrrell, S.J., "The Relation of Theology to Devotion," *The Month*, vol. XCIV (November 1899): pp. 461–73. See also Friedrich von Hügel to George E. Newsom, September 7, 1909, in *Baron Friedrich von Hügel: Selected Letters*, edited with a memoir by Bernard Holland (London: J. M. Dent and Sons, 1928), p. 166: "As for things for you to read, of or about Fr. Tyrrell, . . . I would point out that, among all his published papers, there is nothing to which he himself (in numerous confidential conversations) attached greater importance than 'Theology and Devotion' . . . and 'From God or from Men?' . . . Indeed, he used to say that in the first of these he found, looking back, the root and substance of all he had striven and suffered for."

23. Friedrich von Hügel to George Tyrrell, October 8, 1899, in Holland, *Selected Letters*, p. 77.

24. John Henry Cardinal Newman, *The Via Media of the Anglican Church*, vol. I (London: Longmans, Green, 1897), pp. xlvii–xlviii.

25. John Henry Newman to William Bernard Ullathorne, January 28, 1870, in *The Letters and Diaries of John Henry Newman*, ed. Charles Stephen Dessain et al., vol. XXV, pp. 18–19.

26. John Henry Newman to David Moriarity, January 28, 1870, *LD*, XXV, p. 17.

27. Ignatz von Döllinger, *Declarations and Letters on the Vatican Decrees, 1869–1887*, authorized translation (Edinburgh: T. and T. Clark, 1891), pp. 1–32. See also John Henry Newman to Alfred Plummer, January 15, 1871, in *LD*, XXV, p. 269: "As to Dr. Döllinger and others, the case is quite tragic. I wish he could see, as I do, that as little as possible has really been passed at the Council. I do not deny that the *proceedings* constitute a grave scandal—but as time goes on, the power of God will be recognized as having said to the proud waves 'Hitherto shall ye go and no further.'"

28. "If it be God's will that some definition in favour of the Pope's infallibility is passed, I then shall at once submit—but up to that very moment I shall pray most heartily and earnestly against it. Any how, I cannot bear to think of the tyrannousness and cruelty of its advocates, for tyrannousness and cruelty it will be, though it is successful" (John Henry Newman to David Moriarity, March 20, 1870, in *LD*, XXV, p. 57).

29. Edward Kelly, "Newman, Ward, and Modernism: Problems with Infallible Dogmatic Truth," *John Henry Newman and Modernism*, ed. A. H. Jenkins, pp. 173–74. See also John Henry Newman to Alfred Plummer, March 12, 1871, in *LD*, XXV, pp. 300–301: "I deeply grieve about Döllinger. . . . Of course

there are propositions which the Church could not impose on us—as that God was not good—but I marvel that he should so set his judgement against so very vague a definition as that which passed the Council—In the first place it says that the Pope has the Church's infallibility, but that infallibility has never been defined or explained—then it says that the Pope is infallible, when he speaks ex cathedra, but what ex cathedra is has never been defined. Nor can it be said that this is special pleading, because the definition would not have passed unless it had been so vague—and it is an acknowledged principle of the Church that 'Odiosa restringenda sunt,' as the wording of a law. The Ultras aimed at far more, and were disappointed because they could not get more. Even Gallicans say that *under certain circumstances* the Pope is infallible. Of course I do not defend the *way* in which it was passed, but other Councils were worse."

30. For an account of the papacy and the French Revolution, see Owen Chadwick, *The Popes and European Revolution* (Oxford: The Clarendon Press, 1981).

31. See George Tyrrell, *Medievalism: A Reply to Cardinal Mercier* (London: Longmans, Green, 1908).

32. Johann Baptist Franzelin was born at Aldein in the Tyrol on April 15, 1816, and died at Rome on December 11, 1886. He entered the Society of Jesus in 1834, and began his teaching career at the Roman College in 1850. In 1876 he was created a cardinal by Pope Pius IX. Franzelin's *Tractatus de Divina Traditione et Scriptura* (Rome: Typis S. C. De Propag. Fide, 1870) is considered his most influential work, and in it he attacks (p. 104) Newman's essay *On Consulting the Faithful in Matters of Doctrine*. Camillo Mazzela was born at Vitulano in Italy on February 10, 1833, and died at Rome on March 26, 1900. He was ordained a priest for his native diocese in 1855, and entered the Society of Jesus two years later. In 1867 he was sent to the United States to teach Jesuit seminarians at Georgetown University, and then at Woodstock College in Maryland. In 1878 Pope Leo XIII recalled him to Rome to teach at the Gregorian University, where he spearheaded the Pope's Thomistic revival. In 1886 Leo XIII created him a cardinal deacon; in 1896 a cardinal priest; and in 1897 a cardinal bishop—the first Jesuit on whom the dignity of cardinal bishop was bestowed. Louis Billot was born at Moselle in France on January 12, 1846, and died near Rome on December 18, 1931. He was ordained a priest in 1869, and entered the Society of Jesus in the same year. He, too, was called to Rome by Leo XIII to help in the Pope's promotion of Thomism. Billot was created a cardinal by Pope Pius X in 1911. Those familiar with Billot's work recognized in *Pascendi* ideas and formulas from his writings which gave rise initially to the belief, later disproved, that he had been the primary drafter of the encyclical.

33. Wilfrid Ward, *The Life of John Henry Cardinal Newman*, vol. II (London: Longman's, Green, 1913), p. 380.

34. "The Bull convening the Council was issued with its definite objects stated, dogma being only slightly mentioned as among those objects, but not a word about the Pope's infallibility. . . . Then suddenly, just as they are meeting it is let out that the Pope's infallibility is the great subject of definition, and the

Civiltà and other well informed prints say that it is to be carried by acclamation! Then Archbishop Manning tells (I believe) Mr. Odo Russell, that, unless the opposition can cut the throats of 500 bishops, the definition certainly will be carried; and moreover, that *it has long been intended*! Long intended, and yet kept secret! Is this the way the faithful ever were treated before? is this in any sort of sense going by Tradition? On hearing this, my memory went back to an old saying, imputed to Monsignore Talbot, that, what made the definition of the Immaculate Conception so desirable and important was that it opened the way to the definition of the Pope's Infallibility. Is it wonderful that we should all be shocked?" (John Henry Newman to Robert Whitty, S.J., April, 12, 1870, in *LD*, XXV, p. 94).

35. Unlike the *Pastor Aeternus*, however, the *Ineffabilis Deus* had been carefully and long prepared. In the same letter to Whitty quoted above, Newman says: "Consider how carefully the Immaculate Conception was worked out. These two words have been analyzed, examined in their parts, and then carefully explained;—the declarations and the intentions of Fathers, Popes, and ecclesiastical writers on the point have been clearly made out. It was this process that brought Catholic Schools into union about it, while it secured the accuracy of each. Each had its own extreme points eliminated, and they became one, because the truth to which they converged was one. But now what is done as regards the seriously practical doctrine at present in discussion [papal infallibility]? What we require, first of all, and it is a work of years, is a careful consideration of the acts of Councils, the deeds of Popes, the Bullarium. We need to try the doctrine by facts, to see what it may mean, what it cannot mean, what it must mean. We must try its future working by the past. And we need that this should be done in the face of day, in course, in quiet, in various schools and centres of thought, in controversy. This is a work of years. This is the true way in which those who differ sift out the truth. On the other hand, what do we actually see? Suddenly one or two works made to order. . . . Is this the way to gain a blessing on a most momentous undertaking?"

36. Emiliana P. Noether, "Vatican Council I: Its Political and Religious Setting," *The Journal of Modern History* 40, no. 2 (June 1968): pp. 228–32.

37. Quirinus, *Letter from Rome on the Council*, authorized translation from *Allegmeine Zeitung* (London: Rivingtons, 1870), pp. 674–78. "Lady Howard last night said that both Dr. Amherst and Dr. Clifford told her, that *Quirinus* is the most accurate witness of what took place at the Council" (John Henry Newman to Ambrose St. John, January 17, 1871, in *LD*, XXV, p. 270). See also Roger Aubert, *Le Pontificat de Pie IX* (Paris: Bloud et Gay, 1952), pp. 352–54. Interestingly, Edward Sheridan Purcell (*Life of Cardinal Manning, Archbishop of Westminster*, vol. II [New York: Macmillan, 1896]) does not mention the remark attributed by Quirinus to Manning, but on the whole Guidi issue merely quotes a letter from Odo Russell to Manning: "The loss of Cardinal Guidi has been a severe blow" (p. 444).

38. Baron Friedrich von Hügel, "Official Authority and Living Religion," *Essays and Addresses on the Philosophy of Religion*, 2d series (London: J. M. Dent and Sons, 1926), pp. 3–23. See also Lawrence Barmann, "Von Hügel's Idea of

Ecclesiastical Authority," *The American Ecclesiastical Review* 168, no. 4 (April 1974): pp. 268–82.

39. This document over the signature of Joseph Cardinal Ratzinger, Prefect to the Congregation for the Doctrine of Faith, was approved by Pope John Paul II on May 24, 1990 and was made public on June 26, 1990. The text of the *Instruction* used for this essay is the approved English version printed in the *National Catholic Reporter* 26, no. 35 (July 13, 1990): pp. 11–14. A historian of ecclesiastical documents might note the similarities of tone, intent, and logic of this document with the *Joint Pastoral Letter on the Church and Liberal Catholicism* issued over the signatures of Herbert Cardinal Vaughan, archbishop of Westminster, and the bishops of England and Wales in 1900. The latter document was not composed by the English bishops at all, nor even composed in England. Mgr. (soon to be cardinal) Merry del Val proposed to Vaughan that the "pastoral" be drafted and approved in Rome to make certain that Tyrrell and other English "liberals" were properly hit. The document was drafted by two Jesuits in Rome, approved by both the Jesuit General, Luis Martin, and Pope Leo XIII, before being sent to England to be published there under the signatures of the English and Welsh hierarchy. After its publication in England, it was then publicly approved and commended by the Pope! See David G. Schultenover, "Rome and the English Bishops' Joint Pastoral: Implications for the Historiography of the Modernist Period," *Historiography and Modernism*, ed. Ronald Burke, Gary Lease, and George Gilmore (Mobile: Spring Hill College, 1985), pp. 8–29. Just as the *Joint Pastoral*, through the metaphor of "Divine Teacher," equates the general will of the papacy and its congregations with God's inerrant will; so Cardinal Ratzinger's *Instruction*, through the metaphor of the "Magisterium," does likewise. For the text of the *Joint Pastoral*, see *The Tablet* (January 5, 1901): pp. 8–12, and (January 12, 1901): pp. 50–52. Commenting on the *Joint Pastoral*, Tyrrell wrote to von Hügel: "And then there is the 'Divine Teacher' fallacy: Christ or God; Peter or Christ; the Pope is Peter *ergo* he is, we dare not say God: but a Divine Teacher. There is not an attempt even at qualifying or limiting the Pope's delegated power. In Heaven's name, one asks, why does not he work miracles & raise the dead? Why is he not exposed on the altars for worship? Is he really present in the Blessed Sacrament? Yet these are the legitimate developments of the exegesis & principles of the Joint Pastoral which Leo XIII has blessed and approved. And there is not a man among us with sufficient freedom or authority to raise a protest against this rabid nonsense, this very drunkenness of absolutism! It seems like a horrible dream. If these things are true then all Newman has written is false. Of course W. Ward says the bishops have only failed in their analysis of facts. But a false analysis when it is acted on and approved officially becomes a false doctrine & rule; just as a false analysis of true art if accepted & imposed as a rule becomes productive of false art" (George Tyrrell to Friedrich von Hügel, February 20, 1901, British Library, Add. MSS 44927, pp.155–56).

40. John Henry Newman to David Moriarty, March 20, 1870, in *LD*, XXV, p. 58.

41. *John Henry Newman: Autobiographical Writings*, edited with an introduction by Henry Tristram (London: Sheed and Ward, 1956), pp. 154–59.
42. Friedrich von Hügel to Wilfrid Ward, October 2, 1911, St. Andrews University Library, MS VII, 143 (183).
43. Lord Acton, "Ultramontanism," *Essays in the Liberal Interpretation of History*, edited with an introduction by William H. McNeill (Chicago: University of Chicago Press, 1967), p. 166.

NOTES ON CONTRIBUTORS

SUBJECT INDEX

NAME AND PLACE INDEX

NOTES ON CONTRIBUTORS

LAWRENCE BARMANN is a professor of history at Saint Louis University, St. Louis, Missouri. He received his Ph.D. from Cambridge University, England, and he specializes in modernism and church authority issues (1850–1965). His publications include: *Newman at St. Mary's* (Westminster, Maryland: The Newman Press, 1962); *Baron Friedrich von Hügel and the Modernist Crisis in England* (Cambridge: Cambridge University Press, 1972); *The Letters of Baron Friedrich von Hügel and Professor Norman Kemp Smith* (New York: Fordham University Press, 1981).

ALAN J. CROWLEY is an assistant professor of English at Saint Anselm College, Manchester, New Hampshire. He received his Ph.D. from Boston College, and he specializes in nineteenth-century British literature, especially the literary theory of the English romantics. He has published essays on Newman.

M. JAMIE FERREIRA is a professor in the Departments of Religious Studies and Philosophy at the University of Virginia, Charlottesville, Virginia. She received her Ph.D. from Princeton University, and she specializes in the philosophy of religion, especially in the nineteenth and twentieth centuries, Newman studies, and Kierkegaard studies. Her publications include: *Doubt and Religious Commitment: The Role of the Will in Newman's Thought* (Oxford: Clarendon Press, 1980); *Scepticism and Reasonable Doubt: The British Naturalist Tradition* (Oxford: Clarendon Press, 1986); *Transforming Vision: Imagination and Will in Kierkegaardian Faith* (Oxford: Clarendon Press, 1991).

WALTER JOST is the chair and an associate professor in the Department of Rhetoric and Communication Studies at the University of Virginia, Charlottesville, Virginia. He received his Ph.D. from the University of Chicago, and he specializes in rhetorical theory and criticism and in the philosophy of rhetoric. His publications include *Rhetorical Thought in John Henry Newman* (Columbia: University of South Carolina Press, 1989).

EDWARD E. KELLY is a professor of English at Saint Louis University, St. Louis, Missouri. He received his Ph.D. from Fordham University, and he specializes in Newman studies and English literature in the nineteenth and twentieth centuries. His publications include *The Letters and Diaries of John Henry Newman*, volume XXI, coeditor (London: Nelson, 1971).

JAMES C. LIVINGSTON is the Walter G. Mason Professor of Religion at the College of William and Mary, Williamsburg, Virginia. He received his Ph.D. from Columbia University, and he specializes in modern European religious thought. His publications include: *Modern Christian Thought* (New York: MacMillan, 1971); *The Ethics of Belief* (Tallahassee, Fla.: Scholars Press, 1974); *Matthew Arnold and Christianity* (Columbia: University of South Carolina Press, 1986); *Anatomy of the Sacred* (New York: MacMillan, 1989); *Tradition and the Critical Spirit: Catholic Modernist Writings of George Tyrrell*, ed. (Minneapolis: Fortress Press, 1991).

GERARD MAGILL is an assistant professor in the Department of Theological Studies at Saint Louis University, St. Louis, Missouri. He received his Ph.D. from Edinburgh University, Scotland, and he specializes in Newman studies and fundamental moral theology. He has published essays on Newman and on moral theology.

EDWARD JEREMY MILLER is an associate professor of religious studies at Gwynedd-Mercy College, Gwynedd Valley, Pennsylvania. He received his S.T.D. and Ph.D. from the University of Louvain, Belgium, and he specializes in historical theology (especially Aquinas and Newman) and systematic theology (especially ecclesiology, christology, sacramentology). His publications include *John Henry Newman on the Idea of Church* (Patmos Press: Sheperdstown, W. Va., 1987).

KENNETH L. PARKER is an assistant professor in the Department of Theological Studies at Saint Louis University, St. Louis, Missouri. He received his Ph.D. from Cambridge University, England, and he specializes in English theology in the sixteenth and seventeenth centuries and the conversion of John Henry Newman. His publications include *The English Sabbath* (Cambridge: Cambridge University Press, 1988).

C. J. T. TALAR is an associate professor in the Department of Theology at Alvernia College, Reading, Pennsylvania. He received his S.T.D. from St. Mary's Seminary and University and his Ph.D. from the Catholic University of America. He specializes in European Catholicism in the nineteenth and twentieth centuries. His publications include *Metaphor and Modernist: The Polarization of Alfred Loisy and his Neo-Thomist Critics* (Lanham, Md.: University Press of America, 1987).

MARY KATHERINE TILLMAN is an associate professor in the Program of Liberal Studies at the University of Notre Dame, Notre Dame, Indiana. She received her Ph.D. from the New School for Social Research, New York, and she specializes in Newman studies, phenomenology, and the history of philosophy. She has published essays on Newman.

Subject Index

Analogy, Newman's use of, 68, 73, 114, 140–41, 171, 173–74, 178n.23, 190

Analysis: critical, 97; Heidegger's, 60, 62; Ricoeur's, 81–88, 91n.11

Anglicanism: Caroline Divines of, 33, 47; and the Church of England, 24, 30, 36–37, 40; Newman in, 27, 66, 144, 146, 155–57, 163n.43; theology in, 34–35, 38–40; Thirty-Nine Articles of, 30, 36, 155, 162n.41. *See also* Oxford Movement; Theology

Apprehension: real and notional, 16, 50, 66, 69–70, 73, 88, 132, 135, 140

Argument: and imagination, 49, 137, 141, 142n.2; Newman's style of, 23–26, 67–68, 89, 111, 148, 171, 187; warrant for, 55, 95, 133, 141

Arianism, 28, 36, 191

Art and aestheticism, 19, 61, 68, 71, 74

Assent: and certitude, 23, 132; as commitment, 83, 87, 89; and conscience, 147–49, 150; and dissent, 155–57; and imagination, 130, 132, 139; and inference, 66, 70, 139, 143n.29, 155; unconditional, 139, 145–46, 158n.7

Authority, ecclesial: the imposition of, 23, 104, 182, 188, 196–98; and intellectual inquiry, 49, 117, 121, 195; limits of, 145, 190; Newman's view of, 20, 152–55; submission to, 105, 150, 157, 168, 193,

197; and theology, 145, 150–51, 163nn. 48–49, 181. *See also* Magisterium; Modernism

Being: and Heidegger, 54, 67–68, 71, 74, 77nn. 16, 21; philosophy of, 45, 73, 83, 85, 134

Belief: community of, 148, 191–92; as context, 56–57, 66, 95; epistemology of, 83, 89, 106, 129, 131, 187

Biography, of Newman, 16–17, 155, 158n.2, 186–87, 198–99

Catholicism: and *Ex Corde Ecclesiae,* 123n.2, 124nn. 24, 26–29; and *Gaudium et Spes,* 120; and *Humanae Vitae,* 124n.30, 162n.42; and *Ineffabilis Deus,* 193, 204n.35; and *Lumen Gentium,* 125n.30; and *Pastor Aeternus,* 193, 204n.35; and the *Syllabus of Errors,* 149; and theology, 26, 103–6, 113, 149–51, 167, 181; and ultramontanism, 29, 50, 151, 157, 199, 201n.17; and Vatican Council I, 28, 30, 149, 161n.29, 163n.47, 191, 193–96, 201n.13; and Vatican Council II, 120, 125n.30, 151, 187, 196

Certitude: critical threshold of, 129–30, 139, 143n.29; and imagination, 133–38; and reorienting vision, 129–30, 139–41. *See also* Assent

Christianity: and culture, 71, 95–100, 104, 106, 120, 175

211

Name and Place Index

217